WITHDRAWN

THE DESIGN OF RENOVATIONS

THE DESIGN OF RENOVATIONS

Donald Friedman
and
Nathaniel Oppenheimer

W.W. Norton & Company
New York • London

Also by Donald Friedman
Historical Building Construction

A NORTON PROFESSIONAL BOOK

Copyright © 1997 by Donald Friedman and Nathaniel Oppenheimer

All rights reserved
Printed in the United States of America
First Edition

For information about permission to reproduce selections from this book, write to Permissions, W. W. Norton & Company, Inc., 500 Fifth Avenue, New York NY 10110

While precautions have been taken to ensure that all data and information furnished are as accurate as possible, the author and publisher cannot assume responsibility for errors or for the interpretation of the information. The data given here cannot replace the judgment of an experienced structural engineer familiar with the overall requirements involved during testing, design, and detailing.

The text of this book is composed in Berkeley Book, with the display set in Gill Sans
Book design and composition by Ken Gross
Manufacturing by Maple-Vail Book Manufacturing Group

Library of Congress Cataloging-in-Publication Data

Friedman, Donald.
   The design of renovations / Donald Friedman and Nathaniel Oppenheimer.
     p.   cm.
"A Norton professional book."
Includes index.
ISBN 0-393-73014-X
   1. Buildings—Repair and reconstruction—Case studies. 2. Buildings—Conservation and restoration—Case studies. 3. Structural engineering. I. Oppenheimer, Nathaniel. II. Title.
  TH3401.F75   1997   97-7558
  690'.24—dc21   CIP

Contents

1. Introduction — 7
2. Architectural Design Considerations — 12
   Case Study 2-1: Changing a Floor Elevation — 22
3. Material Considerations — 24
   Case Study 3-1: Beam Removals in Steel and Concrete — 30
4. Structural Design Considerations — 36
   Case Study 4-1: Analysis of a Building Frame — 48
   Case Study 4-2: Effect of Lateral-load Systems on Design — 50
   Case Study 4-3: Jacking During Column Transfer — 52
5. Research — 55
   Case Study 5-1: Misleading Documentation — 68
   Case Study 5-2: Unsafe Existing Construction — 72
   Case Study 5-3: Full-scale Load Testing — 73
6. Structural Steel Buildings — 75
   Case Study 6-1: Steel Beam Reinforcement Using Flange Addition — 83
   Case Study 6-2: Steel Beam Reinforcement Using Composite Action — 86
   Case Study 6-3: Steel Beam Web Reinforcement — 88
   Case Study 6-4: Column Reinforcement — 90
   Case Study 6-5: Column Reinforcement Through Encasement — 92
   Case Study 6-6: Steel Connection Reinforcement — 94

7. Reinforced Concrete Buildings — 96
- Case Study 7-1: Reinforcing Slabs by Adding Depth — 105
- Case Study 7-2: Reinforcing Slabs with External Reinforcing — 107
- Case Study 7-3: Concrete Column Reinforcement — 109
- Case Study 7-4: Creating Beam Splices — 111
- Case Study 7-5: Two-way Slab Modification — 113
- Case Study 7-6: Sistering Concrete Beams — 115

8. Wood Framing — 117
- Case Study 8-1: Sistering Joists I — 138
- Case Study 8-2: Sistering Joists II — 140
- Case Study 8-3: Barn Renovation — 141
- Case Study 8-4: Plywood Tee Floor Stiffening — 144
- Case Study 8-5: Attic Opening — 145
- Case Study 8-6: Roof Addition — 147

9. Masonry Buildings — 150
- Case Study 9-1: Chased-in Lintels in a Masonry Wall — 162
- Case Study 9-2: Rigid Frame in Shear Wall — 164
- Case Study 9-3: GFRC Substitution — 167
- Case Study 9-4: New Control Joints — 170

10. Other Materials — 172
- Case Study 10-1: Cast-iron Beam Analysis — 181
- Case Study 10-2: Wrought Iron — 183
- Case Study 10-3: Aluminum Ornament — 184
- Case Study 10-4: Glass Curtain Walls — 185

11. Foundations — 187
- Case Study 11-1: Footing Encapsulation — 195
- Case Study 11-2: Injection Grouting — 197
- Case Study 11-3: New Supported Slab — 199
- Case Study 11-4: Cantilever Grade Beams — 201

Index — 203

Chapter 1

Introduction

Effective renovation design relies on designers' understanding of materials, history, and function. The critical moment in renovation design comes when the research and exploration, the designer's knowledge of materials, and the array of possible repair and reinforcement techniques are brought together. The information from these sources combines to create a cohesive plan for a specific project. After the decision of how to alter the basic fabric of the building is made, renovation design is like any other building design, only more elaborate. The basic questions that architects and engineers face in the design process are complicated when an existing building's physical presence—its form, its materials, its peculiarities of age and construction—must be included. Considering these extra issues requires additional work, but careful research into the correct physical solution can suggest esthetic and space-planning solutions, an advantage of the renovation process over simple building replacement.

New building design is a design-heavy process, requiring little contact with the world outside the office. Once site information has been made available, the designers can safely remain at their desks until the beginning of construction. Renovation design, by contrast, is an exploration-heavy process, often requiring more time examining the actual building than in drafting and calculating. If the investigations are carried out effectively, the final design and construction stages of a renovation can progress quite simply.

"Renovation" is used here to mean construction that alters existing building structure. Adding a new wing onto a building through new construction on adjacent vacant land involves very little renovation work: the new wing is effectively a new building, and renovation is limited to the portions of the old building affected by the creation of a connecting link from new to old.

Advances in support technology, such as the use of personal computers for analysis and drafting or the ability to capture site photographs into construction documents, are important to all design. Renovation design, however, relies heavily on an understanding of basic principles of building design and construction. Basic principles are needed in the design of new buildings, but are often taken for granted or glossed over in the process of designing the structure at hand. In working on old buildings, basic principles are often the only information a designer can rely on. Basic principles have few assumptions that need to be field-verified.

Because this book is a discussion of applying these basic principles to renovation and the examples are picked to emphasize those applications, not every topic related to renovation is covered. Materials conservation, economic planning, and site safety are important and related to topics covered here, but not directly part of renovation design, and therefore are excluded.

Education

Architects have traditionally been the design leaders and, for all buildings but the most utilitarian sheds, will always remain in that role. Most architects learn a broad overview of structure that may not prepare them for the more intricate design problems of renovation. Most engineers are trained in the set rules and established guidelines used in the design of new structures. Renovation design requires that each project is approached with an open mind to nonstandard solutions. Most designers learn renovation design technique on the job and not in the school, and so may see the field as a collection of tricks rather than as a consistent set of basic ideas.

Most architects learn something about space planning in renovation and about historical changes in building layout, but their education does not deal with the reality of existing buildings. For example, architects are schooled in modern house design. Many architect-designed houses of the twentieth century have been designed with open plans, which requires that they be built with engineered wood, steel, or concrete framing. An architect familiar with these houses who wants to modernize a typical nineteenth-century or spec-built twentieth-century house may not realize the structural implications. The free plan is not only a twentieth-century invention in terms of architectural ideas about space; it requires modern materials to be properly built. Creating a freer plan within an existing house requires a knowledge of the structure of both existing houses and alteration technique.

Structural engineering education focuses almost entirely on the design, detailing, and construction of new buildings and facilities. When existing structure is used in examples, it is typically only to provide a slightly different set of constraints on the design of a single member. An example of this is the addition of a new mezzanine to an existing steel-frame building, where the columns' effective lengths are reduced as their axial load is increased. Examples like this, where all of the parameters are known, suggest that renovation is a noncreative field. In reality, a large part of renovation design is defining the problem so that it can be solved. The focus on new structure is obviously necessary for the introduction of students to design, as the principles involved are better taught when they can be isolated from extraneous information. For more advanced students, however, there is no reason that structural redesign and reanalysis cannot be taught. The de facto method of dealing with this issue is for engineers to learn the material during their first few years of practice, before they are licensed.

Real-world Influence on Design

Architects expect to have to adjust their design to the influence of an existing building. Engineers often need to be reminded that renovation design requires different techniques than new design. A basic principle of new design is that the forces go where the resistance is. That is, that the stiffer elements of a frame tend to carry more load than the more flexible ones. This does not necessarily work in analyzing forces in existing buildings, where the unknown pattern of structure can cause seemingly nonsensical loadings. When an existing building is analyzed, partitions meant to be solely room dividers often are found to be carrying floor loads. Engineers need to become familiar with the ways in which load travels in existing buildings, including in "nonstructural" structure, both to design alterations and to guide architects; architects need to be familiar with the concepts, to participate fully in discussion of structure.

Construction is generally divided along material lines. Engineering and architecture students first learn the basic rules of structural design without any mention of materials. They then spend the remainder of their educational lives and most of their careers interpreting these rules through practical problem solving involving specific materials. New building design reinforces the dependence on specific rules and rule-of-thumb tricks for each material, and a young professional can quickly lose track of the underlying principles that all the different materials share. These principles are not invisible, and in education are ordinarily repeated at the beginning of each course. It is imperative that the designer remember these underlying principles when designing for renovation, to be able to improvise using different materials and different combinations of materials throughout one design.

Renovation analysis and design includes not only the principles of any structural design (for example, reviewing total and relative deflections in addition to stress), but principles specific to dealing with existing structure. The physical properties of existing materials, such as the yield stress in a steel beam, cannot be changed, but geometric properties, such as area and moment of inertia, can be altered through reinforcement. The governing criteria in most members come from bending forces: bending in beams and slabs, and buckling in columns. All of the techniques given in cases studies here are based on selective strengthening through analysis of the member geometry; other techniques can be developed on this same basis, providing the physical means to make the geometric change can be found.

If renovation is examined building by building, it is too unwieldy to organize. The case studies in this book are meant as aids for designers to study the way materials can work together through these general principles to reinforce an existing structure. Architects who understand the basis of structural renovation can assess their renovation options at the beginning of a project, based on the existing building construction. Engineers who are familiar with the potential for reinforcing different materials can speed design and reduce conflicts during construction.

The process of renovation design is presented here in two sections. The first section concerns the process itself, including the effect of constraints from the different design professions and the process of examining an existing building. The second section is the application of the general ideas to the types of renovation possible for different construction materials. The case studies associated with the materials show basically similar engineering principles applied to wildly differing buildings and architectural programs. The case studies are all drawn from the authors' experiences in renovation design, and were picked because they represent real-world examples of the principles, including the sometimes vague or contradictory details.

An understanding of the basic principles shown in the case studies is more important than the details of the case studies because of the "mystery investigation" aspects of renovation work. The structure of existing buildings is often masked, making investigation difficult. An understanding of the basics of building design in general, the design techniques and intentions of past generations of structural engineers, and the concerns expressed in past building codes is crucial to good renovation design. Before a new transfer girder can be placed in an eighty-year-old steel frame building, the designer must grasp the original floor loading, wind frame design, live load reduction, and fire-prevention provisions of the building. Learning about a building's past is the first step in altering it for the future.

Chapter 2

Architectural Design Considerations

Many of the issues in architectural design of renovation also drive schematic design of new structures. Instead of starting with a site and a set of program requirements, the architect starts with an existing building and the program. Unlike new construction, where the budget and zoning laws are the only absolute restrictions on design, renovation is restricted by the practicality of changing the building structure. The concerns of historic preservation may further complicate many renovation projects. These restrictions are broken down in this and the next two chapters in the following manner: "Architectural Design Considerations" describes restrictions based on the interaction of structure with architectural design; "Material Considerations" describes restrictions based on the intrinsic properties of various construction materials and systems; and "Structural Design Considerations" describes restrictions based on the limits of engineering design and construction technique. Specific examples then follow in the chapters on specific materials. These divisions are somewhat artificial and are used for clarity of explanation; most real-life problems will involve more than one of the three types of restrictions.

The difficulty of a particular structural change can greatly influence the architectural design. If the installation of new masonry partitions requires reinforcing floor beams, metal stud partitions may be substituted. In a more extreme case, finishes such as marble floor tile may be unusable without intensive floor reconstruction, because of the 30 to 45 psf (1.0 to 1.4 kPa) weight of the stone and setting bed.

Gross changes in plan layout and use can be a great help or pose great problems, depending on the circumstances. New partitions can provide locations for the installation of new structural columns, greatly simplifying floor reinforcing. The addition of floor space or a change in use, such as the installation of a mezzanine within a large open space by building a floor at the level of the roof truss bottom chords, can add to structural loading without providing the means for reinforcing (figure 2-1).

In the case of an obvious change in load, such as replacing a glass curtain wall with masonry, the structural implications should be clear, but effects are often blurred by existing conditions. Past alterations may have created theoretically unsafe conditions, such as when a heavy tile floor is found in a wood-joist building. Analysis of the joists may find that they are, in theory, overloaded by the dead load alone, or the dead load in combination with a nominal live load.

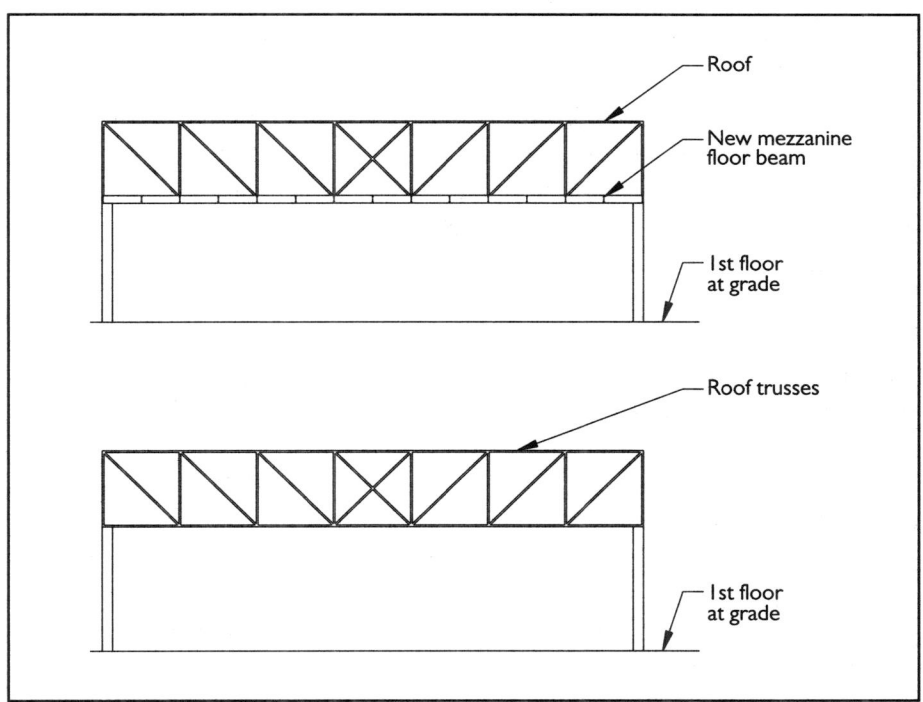

2-1. Adding a floor level at roof trusses

If the tile is not touched, it may be possible to justify its continued presence based on the condition of the structure, but there is no ready justification for removing it and replacing it with another tile floor that is known to be heavier than the theoretical floor load. Conditions that cannot be defended with calculations can sometimes be justified by a knowledge of the statistical nature of structural loading and strength. A structure that has survived for decades through varying loads and conditions of maintenance has "proven" its ability to withstand the actual loads to which it is exposed. However, even the existing

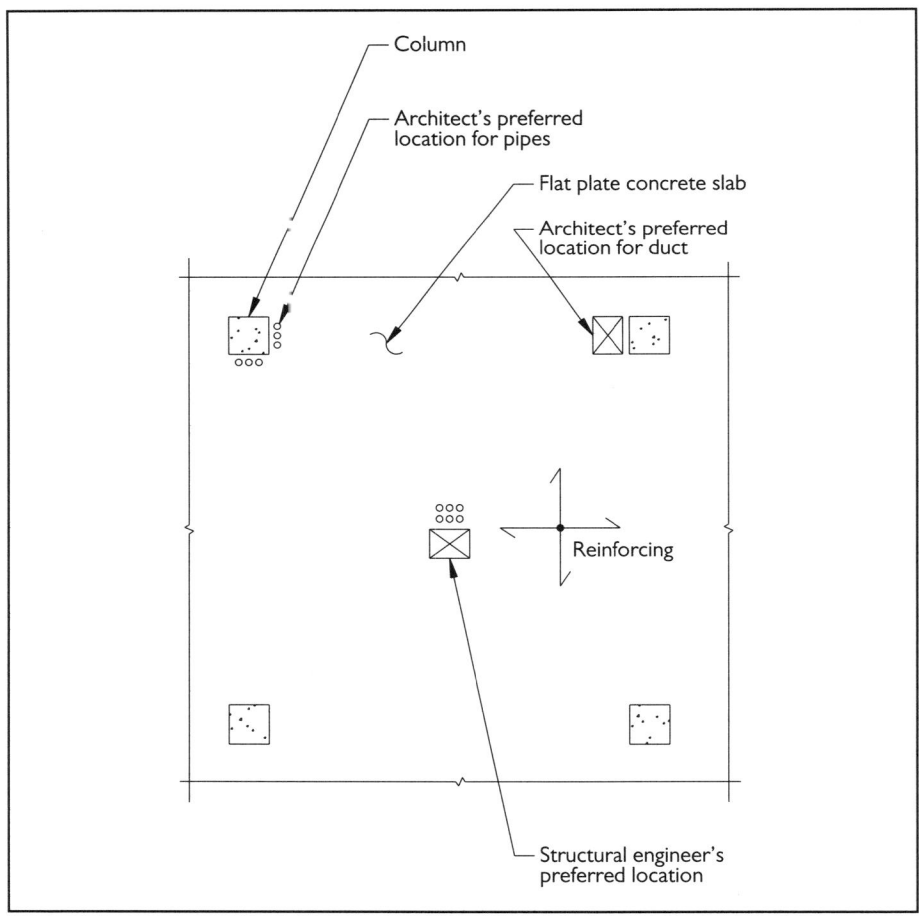

2-2. Flat-slab penetrations

condition may be a serious problem if the condition of the existing structure indicates damage from overstress. In this case, the de facto proof of adequacy does not exist.

New mechanical systems have more flexibility than certain types of existing structure, and can often be adapted to existing conditions to prevent excessive structural work. Schematic mechanical designs are often complete before the structural investigation takes place. Floor penetrations planned for the mechanical design may conflict with existing beam locations. A common conflict that involves architects, mechanical engineers, and structural engineers is the location of new plumbing or electric lines near columns in a concrete flat-slab building (figure 2-2). This particular problem also exists in new construction, but the renovating structural engineer has few methods of accommodating the other designers. The controlling factor in many flat-slab floor designs is the punching shear around the column—the tendency of the entire floor surrounding the column to break loose adjacent to the column shaft. Mechanical penetrations located next to the structural column to hide the pipes or conduits within the architectural column enclosure weaken the slab at its most vulnerable point. Unfortunately for space planning and esthetics, the portion of the slab most capable of accepting the holes is the middle of each bay, equally distant from the four corner columns. Unlike new construction, the area of high shear cannot be easily reinforced in renovation with a steel shearhead, a drop panel, or a column capital. All these methods of shear reinforcing are easy to install while the concrete is fluid, but difficult to make work with hardened concrete. The most common compromise is to spread the new mechanical systems among several column enclosures, reducing the severity of punching shear strength reduction at any one column.

Floor Plate Thickness

The decision in new construction to use concrete flat slabs instead of steel framing for structure is often based on the desired floor plate thickness. The floor plate, from the finish flooring on top to the ceiling on the bottom, is closely linked to the structure within (figure 2-3). Building occupancy largely determines the mechanical space required. Architectural space required is the minimal amount required for most finishes. The depth of the structural members and their fireproofing is therefore the factor most easily changed. By using a

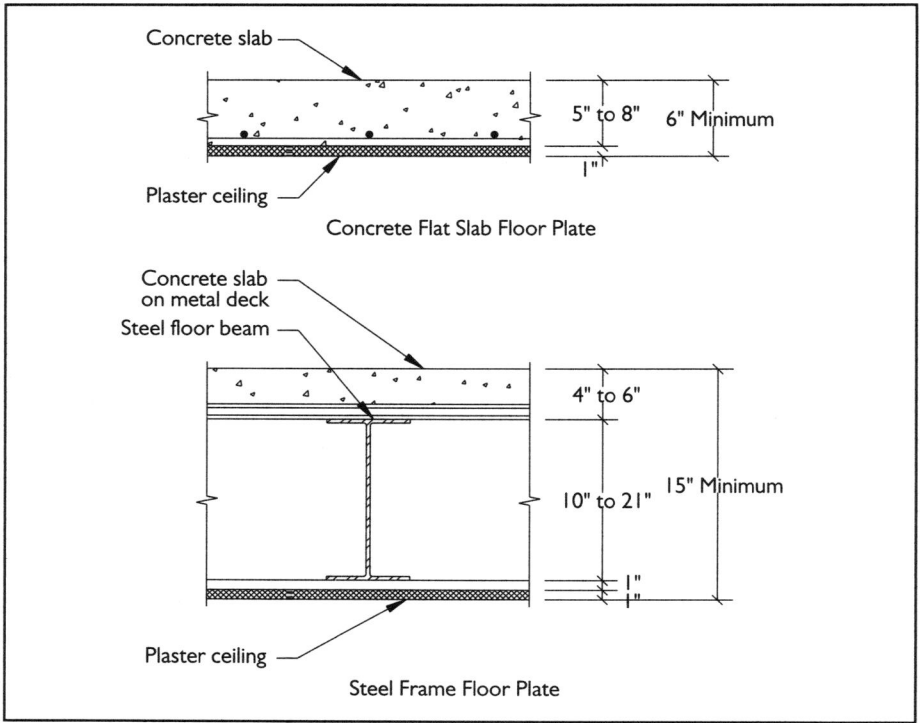

2-3. Steel and concrete floor plates compared

structurally thin system, more floors can be added within a given height, at the expense of future flexibility in alteration planning.

Steel buildings have more potential for alteration than concrete for several reasons, one of which is steel's typically thicker floor plate. There is usually room within the floor structure of a steel frame building (ordinarily with beams 10 inches [255 mm] or deeper) to add whatever new structure is required. A concrete flat-slab apartment house with a 5- or 6-inch (125 or 150 mm) total floor plate cannot have beams added within the floor if reinforcing is required for a mechanical penetration, tenant stair, or other alteration that reduces the slab continuity and strength.

Increasing the floor plate thickness during renovation can cause building code conflicts. The minimum floor-to-ceiling height is 8 feet (2440 mm) for most purposes. Lower areas are allowed as long as they are brief interruptions, such as that caused by a beam below the slab. In adding several beams in one room, the ceiling height requirement can become difficult to maintain. Adding beams within the existing thickness of a concrete floor is far more expensive, since it requires the demolition and reconstruction of entire panels or bays to hide the beams, rather than simple removal of only the portions of the floor scheduled for demolition.

Partition Thickness

Another dimension of great importance during renovation is the thickness of partitions used to enclose structure and building systems. Posts, columns, beams, and mechanical systems, both existing and new, are often hidden within partitions. The $3^{1}/_{2}$-inch (90 mm) standard thickness of the interior space in metal stud partitions is too small to contain any structure other than small pipe columns and small beams or any mechanical systems other than the smallest pipes and electrical conduits.

Trying to run significant amounts of structure through an existing partition will create bulges at most column and many beam locations. The best method of avoiding this esthetic peculiarity is to treat the partitions enclosing structural or mechanical systems in the same manner as a plumber's "wet wall": to increase its thickness by using two independent sets of studs or lines of block to support the two faces of the walls. If some floor space can be wasted in this manner, double partitions are an easy solution. In situations where every inch of floor space counts, this may not be possible. Tight geometric criteria are the hallmark of renovations where the controlling factors are code requirements, such as the Americans with Disabilities Act or the minimum allowable room sizes in housing codes.

Many older buildings contain partitions of fragile materials such as terra-cotta tile or gypsum block. These partitions cannot be altered economically, because of the tendency of the constituent blocks to crumble when worked. Rather than protecting essentially valueless finish materials, it is almost always cheaper and easier in these cases to remove entire sections of partition that were meant to be altered, and rebuild the areas in question in modern concrete block or metal stud.

Load Capacity

While engineers must deal with the results of changes in load or load capacity, architects' and planners' decisions often create these changes. Decreases in capacity from weathering or other damage are not, strictly speaking, load capacity problems, but rather maintenance and repair problems, and are discussed in chapter 3, "Material Considerations." The ordinary response to such decreases is to repair the structure back to its original state. The possibilities other than damage are changes in live load that reflect changes in use and changes in dead load that reflect the addition of fill, finishes, or mechanical systems to the floor structure. These changes are all architectural in nature, since the building structure is being changed solely to accommodate changes in function.

Changes in the intended use of spaces cause changes in the design live loads mandated by building codes. The changes can be either increases or reductions—for example, in the conversion of an office space to retail use or the conversion of commercial space to residential use. The most damaging change is the conversion of relatively lightly loaded spaces such as ordinary offices to open places of assembly. This change entails an increase in the live load from a minimum of 50 to 100 psf (2.4 to 4.8 kPa) at the same time that partitions that could have been used as locations to conceal structure are being removed.

Changes in use are the most common cause of live load changes but not the only cause. A use may require a different live load now than it did in the past, the most obvious example being the steady increase in truck wheel loads from 1900 to 1950. Most required live loads have decreased over time as extensive research has provided more accurate information, but examples of increases exist, such as the truck load on sidewalks and courtyards or the increased office loads where high-density storage will be used. There may also have been changes over time in allowable live load deflection. Especially when old masonry or stud partitions are removed, alterations have a tendency to "loosen up" buildings built before 1950, increasing deflections and increasing vibration intensity and longevity. In these cases, control of the altered live load deflection may be more critical than control of the altered stresses.

Live load requirements have been generally reduced over time as more research has gone into how load is applied to a given area. Particularly important in this trend has been the concept of probabilistic live load reduction. Live load reduction is a building code allowance in design that permits live loads less than those specified for an occupancy to be used for members supporting large areas of floor because of the low probability that the entire area will be loaded simultaneously. Live load reduction can be retroactively applied in the analysis of an old structure, finding capacity that by modern standards is unused.

In older buildings, live load reduction may not have been used, or may have followed standards more conservative than current codes. Load capacity can be "recovered" by reanalyzing portions of the structure under the appropriate modern code, taking full advantage of the allowable live load reduction. This form of "paper alteration" can save a large amount of actual, physical reinforcing without reducing a building's safety.

Drastic changes in dead load during renovation are rare, but can be more troubling than live load changes. Elevation changes requiring the introduction of fill onto floors, or the need to provide a slope to a flat roof, can easily increase the dead load by 30 percent or more, in extreme cases outweighing the original floor system weight. Finishes such as carpet and vinyl tile require reasonably flat surfaces below. Sloping or dished floors that are scheduled to receive fill to create flat surfaces may be signals that the existing floor is overstressed and cannot support the fill required to create a flat floor.

The standard method of creating a flat surface on a rough floor is to place a lightweight concrete fill such as vermiculite. Combining an elevation change with the floor topping can lead to large increases in dead load. Floor elevation changes of more than a few inches are best handled with a solution that provides a raised floor structure rather than solid fill. By building new structure rather than providing mass fill, the increase in dead load can be kept to a minimum (see case study 2-1).

Fireproofing

Materials were specifically installed for fire protection starting in the 1870s. Since then, many forms of fireproofing have been used. The original fireproofing material in iron-frame buildings was terra-cotta tile. Over the years, gypsum block, gypsum board, mineral wool, cinder concrete, stone concrete, loose cinder fill, cementitious spray-on, fibrous spray-on, and plasters and paints of various types have been used to protect the structure and inhabitants of buildings. None of these materials, except for stone concrete encasement, can support structural loads, either on purpose or by accident.

The modification of fireproofed structure requires removal of some of the protective material. The amount removed depends on both the extent of the renovation and the physical properties of the fireproofing. Tile blocks need to be removed only from the area where new steel is to be fastened to existing members, but the fragility and brittleness of the tile ensure that removal of any portion will cause damage to the adjacent tile. The property of the fireproofing that determines the possibility of alteration without removal is physical contact with the structure. Contact fireproofing, such as spray-on or concrete encasement, must be removed in its entirety in every work location. Fireproofing physically separated from the structure, such as gypsum board enclosures, can theoretically be retained except at access holes. More realistically, partitions and ceilings are often rebuilt in the course of renovation, so removal and replacement to provide access to the structure and then provide new fireproofing is usually economical.

There is rarely any historic importance attributed to fireproofing, and no esthetic or emotional barrier to its removal. Plaster that encloses steel columns that will be removed to reinforce the columns or add mechanical systems is not visible as an architectural entity in its own right. The columns have been seen as plaster-enclosed piers throughout their history, and if the enclosures are replaced by new plaster or gypsum board, it is unlikely that anyone will notice or care. Standard practice is to remove any enclosure-type fireproofing that is in the area of work and replace it with some combination of gypsum board, new plaster, and spray-on fireproofing. Construction is often the only time during renovation when existing conditions of structure can be properly surveyed. Removal and replacement of fireproofing can, incidental to the purpose of providing construction access, allow for a field survey of conditions that require repair, lengthening the building's life.

Material Retention

Depending on the circumstances, engineering solutions to renovations require the removal or retention of various amounts of the original material of the building. For various reasons, the solution decided upon may deliberately retain more material, or on rare occasions, deliberately remove more than a purely engineering solution would demand.

The simplest example is the retention of original material for the sake of preservation. This may be mandated by historic preservation laws, such as those that have been established by the state historic preservation offices, by the owner of the property, or by other organizations. The most structurally restrictive preservation is that requiring retention of finishes such as historic plaster, paint, stucco, siding, or shingles. Since structural alterations require access to the material behind the finishes, retaining finishes can force more complicated structural work.

Many jurisdictions use the percentage of original material present after work is completed to distinguish for tax and zoning purposes between renovations and reconstructions. Original floors and partitions that might otherwise have been removed are sometimes retained for this reason. In certain types of governmental work, such as low-income housing rehabilitation, retention of all viable structure may be mandated.

In many situations, it is easier to leave some nonessential material in place than to remove it. Since easier construction always translates to lower construction costs, obsolete material can be successfully kept. If a partition simply needs to be upgraded to obtain a fire rating, or moved forward a small amount, it may be easier to fasten new metal studs to the existing partition than to demolish it.

When removal of old material is potentially hazardous, removals are often curtailed. The two materials that require extreme delicacy are lead paint and asbestos. The abatement of the danger can force the removal of finish material otherwise kept or the retention of abandoned and encapsulated material, but is generally a self-contained topic that has little effect on the overall renovation project. In most projects, the abatement takes place before any other work is allowed to begin.

Project Scale

There is a certain scale of structural work expected for a given scale of architectural work. The simple renovation of a store in a large mall or mixed-use building, or an apartment in a high-rise apartment house, is not expected to require structural alterations of any significant degree. Projects small in size that require major structural work often have delays or other difficulties during construction because the overall scale of the project misled the contractors. In "large small projects," obtaining the desired quality in structural work can also be a problem, as quality-control procedures are more difficult to enforce on a handful of welds or a single concrete pour. The contractor with finish expertise retained to alter a store may not be comfortable installing a new transfer girder to remove a building column.

The other type of project with scale-related problems is the "small large project," where minor structural work is being performed throughout a large building. One example of this type of work would be the conversion of an office building to apartments where new mechanical chases must be provided throughout the floors. In projects of this type, coordination and organization of the repetitive alterations are more difficult and time-consuming than the actual structural design.

Case Study 2-1: Changing a Floor Elevation

Floor elevation changes of more than a few inches are best handled with a solution providing raised floor structure rather than solid fill. The details of providing a new floor surface vary with the existing floor material, from the traditional wood framing technique of using sleepers to the more obscure "concrete waffle fill." Sleepers are simply small wood joists of varying depth placed at right angles to the existing joists to fill the space between the existing floor surface and the desired floor surface. They need not be of high-quality wood or even well fastened, since they serve simply to transmit the floor loads down to the structural joists directly below (figure 2-1-1).

The concrete waffle on the other hand, is in part stressed: it reduces the thickness of fill by introducing a lightweight inert material, such as Styrofoam,

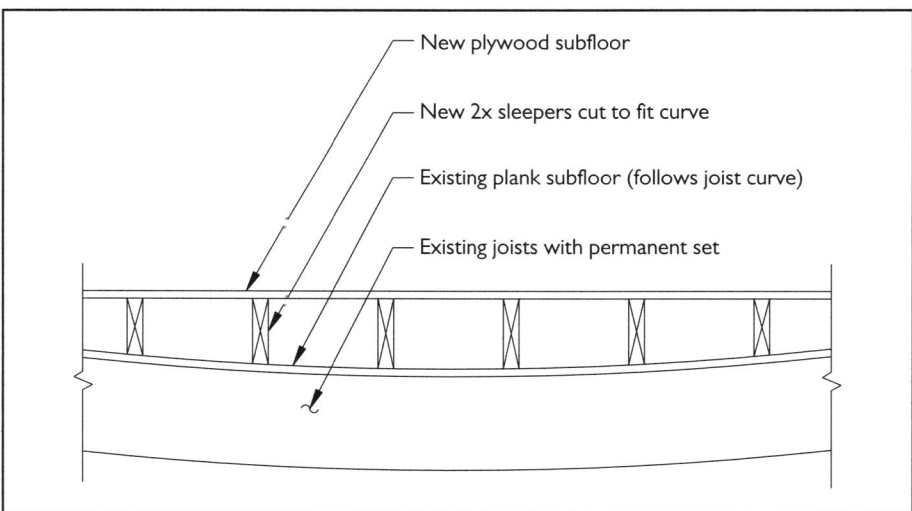

2-1-1. Sleepers over joist floor

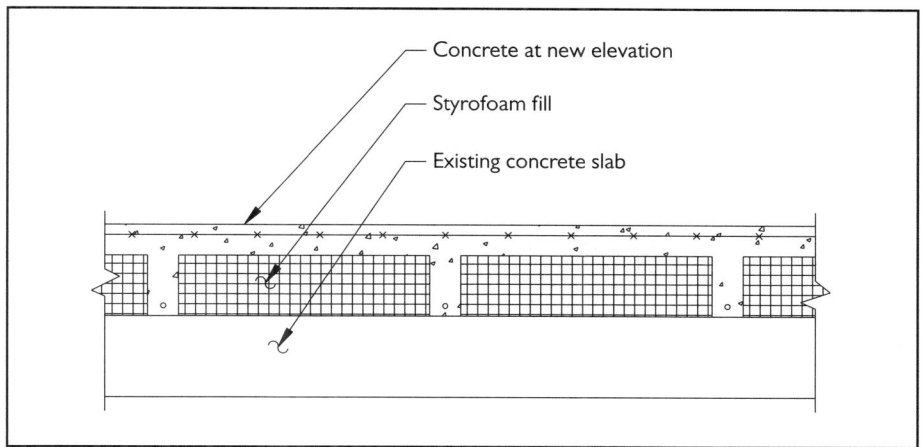

2-1-2. Concrete Styrofoam waffle fill

into the concrete. This changes the concrete to a series of supporting "walls" and a thin slab. The slab can be analyzed as resting on the Styrofoam or as spanning between the walls; spanning is preferred because it removes all function from the relatively uncontrolled fill material other than supporting the wet concrete. Slab and wall thicknesses of 3 inches (75 mm) are the smallest ordinarily used. Obviously, the thicker the fill layer, the greater the weight advantage for this system relative to solid fill (figure 2-1-2).

Chapter 3

Material Considerations

The amount of work required in the design and construction of any renovation is influenced by two independent factors: the scope of alteration to the existing building and the state of the existing structural elements. The state of the existing structure affects the scope of work through the material type, the element types being modified, and the relative importance of those elements to the building.

The same sort of architectural alteration in different buildings can have drastically different structural implications. Removal of a column is not uncommon in steel frame renovations, more difficult in concrete, and unthinkable in wood without major redesign of the building. The inherent ability to design reuse of a material and the ability to make on-site connections not foreseen in the original design vary tremendously. Steel beams can be easily analyzed for new forces in any direction and provided with new welded connections; concrete beams are difficult to analyze for forces in directions other than those for which they were originally reinforced, and need specialized mechanical fasteners and epoxies to join new members to old; the strength of wood varies in varying directions, and the material has severe limitations on connections other than simple shear.

Different members obviously differ in importance. Radical modification of the loading and design of a single beam is simple to deal with; the removal of columns to create open space at the base of a high-rise is never simple, regardless of the building's form. The difficulty of modifying a member varies directly with the tributary floor, roof, or wall area contributing load, and the dependencies of other portions of the building. The more complex the loading contributions are, the more difficult it is to adequately predict the full consequences of an alteration.

The structural effect of alterations depends closely on the framing type. The framing type, in turn, is directly related to the structural material so that a particular alteration can be spoken of as "easy in steel" or "difficult in masonry." Bearing walls provide both vertical support and lateral bracing; their removal requires analysis of the way in which the building will resist lateral loading as well as the floor structure resupport. Individual floor beams and small areas of slab are easily sacrificed in steel- or concrete-frame buildings. But since the floor structure serves as horizontal bracing for the entire structure in almost all frame types, known as "diaphragm action," the effect of removals on adjacent structure and the frame's overall stability must be examined when the extent of removal grows large. Again, this effect depends on the structural material, and what is considered a large floor removal in a concrete frame may have little effect on a steel frame.

Internal floors also act as bracing for exterior walls, either bearing walls or curtain walls, against wind load. If a section of floor is removed immediately adjacent to the exterior of a building, new beams may be required to brace the exterior wall.

The peculiarities of individual structural systems, such as concrete flat slab or flat plate floors requires analysis of the effects based on the inherent characteristics of that system. The locations where new floor openings can be safely created varies with the floor material and how it is used.

Hidden Structure

The methods of discovery described under the heading "Research" in chapter 5 are not complete or infallible. Physical and budgetary constraints coupled with the inevitable loss of documentation over time often place the designer in the position of working on structure that is hidden from view and not entirely understood.

The true condition of various portions of the building structure due to be modified may not be known until the work is actually in progress. Even the most extensive probing campaign will expose only a small percentage of the stressed material. For example, probing in a steel-frame building in which no existing member sizes are known typically will consist of exposing portions of the beams in the area of work to determine their size, and exposing enough of the floor structure to determine its means of support and weight. The vast amount of steel surface buried within the floor is ordinarily not seen, and can conceivably be in poor condition, requiring repair during the renovation.

Probing for information regarding a steel frame is made less difficult by the nature of the material. Steel- and wood-frame structures are comparatively "open," in that when the covering finishes or floor structure material is removed, the member surface exposed accurately represents the structure. Concrete, and to a lesser degree masonry, are "closed," in that the strength of the structure is dependent on reinforcing amounts and configurations that cannot be entirely determined by probing.

Probing is a statistical operation, drawing inferences from a small sample of the total. As will be discussed in chapter 5, a proper course of investigation provides a representative sample. When full investigation is not possible, or conditions are accidentally hidden from the investigation, unanticipated work is the normal result. This is not necessarily a disaster, and depending on the building occupancy and the condition of the owner's finances, may be the preferred method of operation. The amount of work that can be created by unknown conditions is obviously related to the material: the missing information about a concrete frame is likely to be more important than that missing for a steel frame. While it is always better to know all of the pertinent structural information before construction begins, cutting out concrete in an occupied space for probes is not realistic.

Another source of unanticipated work is accidental damage caused by the alteration work itself. No matter how carefully selective demolition is performed, some damage to the surrounding finishes and, on occasion, underlying structure is inevitable. The process of installing new structure is heavy work that will damage adjacent portions of the building. Finally, the difference in age between the new construction and old is often perceivable, requiring architectural work refurbishing the older structure to reduce the apparent differences. The decision to accentuate or hide the difference in age is the provenance of the architect and owner, but the consequences may affect the structural design or construction technique. For example, the decision to minimize the intrusion of demolition and rebuilding may require splices in new members to use the available access. Selective demolition specifications, which are either prepared or reviewed by the structural engineer of record, ordinarily contain references to the repair of incidental damage. The most commonly used language refers the contractor to the architectural finish portions of the technical specifications for the exact methods of repair to ensure continuity of appearance throughout the completed project.

Because of the possible variations described, contract documents for alterations are often intentionally more vague than their new-building counterparts. Allowances for extra work caused by unforeseen field conditions are an item that is independent of the ordinary allowance for extras caused by redesign or minor gaps in the contract drawings and specifications. Field conditions can easily account for a larger percentage of the final cost than ordinary extras. Typical details provided for a project often include repair details for routine damage that are to be applied as required. Designers thus assume responsibility not only for searching out these types of damage likely to occur and thus worthy of inclusion in the form of repair details, but also the design of simple repair details that can be applied on an unscheduled basis during the construction process without slowing all other work to a halt. Obviously, the extreme circumstance of finding previously unknown conditions that threaten incipient failure will require the suspension of less essential work, but ideally the provision of typical repair details and an estimate of the frequency of their use will give the contractor sufficient information to permit unimpeded progress towards the goal, the completion of the alteration.

Original Design Techniques

Structural materials have had very different historical development. Wood and masonry construction are both thousands of years old. While their analysis-based design is a relatively recent phenomenon, builders of past centuries determined, through trial and error, proportions for these materials close to those we now use. The history of these materials is one of rules of thumb and carryovers of ancient ideas.

Iron construction and its successor, steel construction, began as scientific analysis of structure was finally becoming well established, during the first half of the nineteenth century. While iron and steel design has been from the first based on technical rules, the rules themselves were originally based on empirical data, at first in imitation of wood and later based on iron-specific experimentation. Portions of the steel codes are based on experimentation and theory, rather than pure theory.

Concrete design is inherently more empirical than steel design. The material is not homogeneous and not isotropic, and is prepared in less controlled conditions. Despite the use of test mixes and batching inspectors, there will always be variations in the strength of concrete prepared at different times. The weather during a concrete pour plays a large role for which there is no counterpart during steel fabrication and erection. Finally, a completed concrete beam is subject to creep and strain cracking, both of which can produce unexpected patterns of deflection.

The original design of buildings can be incorrect for several reasons. Actual mistakes in design are rare, mistakes in construction somewhat more common, and mistakes due to incorrect design theory common in buildings built before 1880. As theory and technique advanced, the possibility for new errors would arrive and gradually fade as the new developments were absorbed into standard practice. The probability of finding an incorrectly designed clip-angle connection for a steel beam dating from 1925 is much lower than for one dating from 1890, but the difference in probability between 1925 and 1960 is negligible, because there were significant changes in the technology during the first thirty-five-year period, but not during the second.

Original Construction Techniques

The main issues concerning the original detailing techniques for the various materials are covered in the chapters on the materials. Differences in construction in various times range from differences that affect strength, such as the use of rivets in old steel framing, to differences that have no actual effect but can be used to date the structure, such as the use of board forms instead of plywood for concrete before the 1950s.

Materials have peculiarities that may provide unique ways of designing alterations. In modern steel construction, beams are often held loosely in place during erection by temporary bolts or the permanent bolts loosely placed. After the steel is plumbed and trued, usually two floors at one time, the final bolts are placed and torqued to place them in tension. During the eighty or so years when riveting was used for the majority of steel connections, this sequence was not possible, since there is no such thing as a temporary or loose, permanent rivet. Erection seats, consisting of steel seat angles held in place by only a few rivets, were often used for temporary beam-to-column connections. Since these seats were never removed, and are of the same steel as the structure around them, they can sometimes be adapted for reuse by increasing their carrying capacity with welds and stiffener plates. This type of "easy" connection reinforcing is based on the presence of the erection seats, which are artifacts specific to one material and one period of time.

Weathering

Different materials react in quite different fashions to the same outside influences. At one extreme is monolithic ashlar masonry construction, which is perfectly suited to weather exposure and can last indefinitely with little maintenance. It is difficult to imagine the monuments of antiquity built in any material but solid masonry. The most important upkeep is the removal of plants that find root in cracks in the masonry before they grow large enough to split the stones. The other extreme is ordinary steel, which cannot stand any substantial exposure to water or damp air without rusting. Protected steel, of course, can withstand extremely damaging conditions, which is how steel H sections can be used as submerged piles. In some cases, the actual agent of damage may be unclear, as with submerged wood piles. The water itself does not cause any damage, but microorganisms living in the water do, leading to some peculiar conditions. Wood piles last longer in polluted water because of the absence of damaging sealife, and damage to piles typically occurs only between the low-tide elevation and the top of the bottom mud.

The weathering characteristics of a specific material are determined by the exposure. This includes the location of the member within the building, the type and condition of the waterproofing, and the microclimate—any wind or water conditions specific to the building and, sometimes, the portion of the building. The most common use of exposed steel is in rooftop dunnage carrying mechanical equipment. Dunnage that carries compressors exists in a less damaging microclimate than dunnage that carries cooling towers, because the latter is exposed to a high relative humidity during all operating hours. This type of local condition can exist indoors, as wood joists below kitchens and bathrooms are susceptible to damage from water spilled on floors and from leaking pipes.

When a piece of a structure is being repaired for weathering damage, the extent of the repairs must take into account the type of damage inherent in the material. If rusted reinforcing and spalled concrete cover are observed on the bottom of a concrete slab that is regularly wet, such as a garage floor, the entire slab may be worthless. For the bottom reinforcing to have rusted, the water must have traveled through the entire thickness of the slab. In the process, the concrete at the top, used in design as the compression flange, may have lost material or cohesiveness. On occasion the top surface will be fairly intact, but the bottom rebar is seriously affected. Similarly, the presence of fungal or insect damage in one area in a wood frame building should serve as a warning flag that the surroundings must also be examined. Rust on a steel spandrel beam is not necessarily the same type of indicator of more extensive damage. While the surroundings should be checked to determine the extent of the damage, rust does not spread by itself the way that fungus does.

Architectural Finishes

Many of the steps described throughout this book, from probing to reinforcing, require the destruction of architectural finishes. Cases where this is not possible, most often because of historic value of a specific finish, such as a mural or historic stucco on a masonry wall, must be treated as described in chapter 2, "Architectural Design Considerations," for areas where work is restricted. On the other hand, old finishes that are not in themselves important can blur the distinction between the old architecture and the new structure.

Gypsum-based plaster is an excellent fireproofing material, still used in the form of gypsum board. During the beginning of iron-frame fireproofing, plaster was often applied directly to columns and beam soffits. The era when plaster was used as fireproofing overlaps with the era when bearing-wall buildings were being replaced with metal frames. Partition plaster removal, theoretically an architectural change, has no structural meaning in a building supported by masonry bearing walls. In a building with iron or steel columns, the presence of fireproofing other than plaster must be confirmed before plaster can be removed.

Case Study 3-1: Beam Removals in Steel and Concrete

The effect of similar alterations in different materials can be easily illustrated by the design of a new opening in an existing floor. One of the common alterations in large office buildings (and occasionally in apartment houses) is the construction of a private tenant stair to allow access between space on two floors without using the public stairs and elevators. This type of alteration may involve major architectural changes through partition and circulation changes, but structurally consists of two components: creating a hole in the floor and providing structure for the new stair.

As in any work, these components can range from very simple to extremely complex, depending on the degree to which the architectural design of the stair is related to the existing structure. The case described is at the simple end of the spectrum; the differences between various materials would grow more pronounced as the stair opening became more complicated.

The example assumes that the stair is in an office building with a sufficient floor-to-floor height to allow a straight run of stairs in one structural bay. Both the steel and concrete frames have identical layouts: 20- by 20-foot (6100 by 6100 mm) bays between columns, with one filler beam spanning in one direction, creating slab spans of 10 feet (3050 mm). The floor opening for the stair will be created by removing one panel of slab (figures 3-1-1 and 3-1-2).

In the steel frame, the beams and columns are all individual steel W sections, and the slab is $3^1/_2$ inches (90 mm) of lightweight concrete on 2-inch (50 mm) deep composite metal deck. This slab-on-deck system is common for ordinary spans. In the concrete frame, the 5-inch (125 mm) thick concrete slab was placed integrally with the beams.

Removing one panel of the slab in the steel frame requires literally no work other than demolition (figure 3-1-3). As long as the cut line of the demolition is located at the edge of the beam next to the panel being removed, leaving the concrete and deck over the top flange intact, the steel beams are still continually braced by the adjacent slab to remain. The slab is designed as a series of simply supported spans, with top reinforcing present to prevent cracks from developing, but not designed to provide continuity between adjacent panels of slab.

Analysis will be required only if the steel beams were designed to be composite with the slab. If shear connectors are provided between the beam top flange and the slab, the beams were designed as T-beams, using the concrete as an additional top flange. Removing the slab panel removes half of the concrete flange, but also removes roughly half of the load. If the steel beam is not composite, no analysis is required, as the beam does not lose any strength; if the beam is composite, the new L-beam must be compared to the old T-beam. Most of the time, this change requires no reinforcement because the reduction in load balances the reduction in strength.

32   MATERIAL CONSIDERATIONS

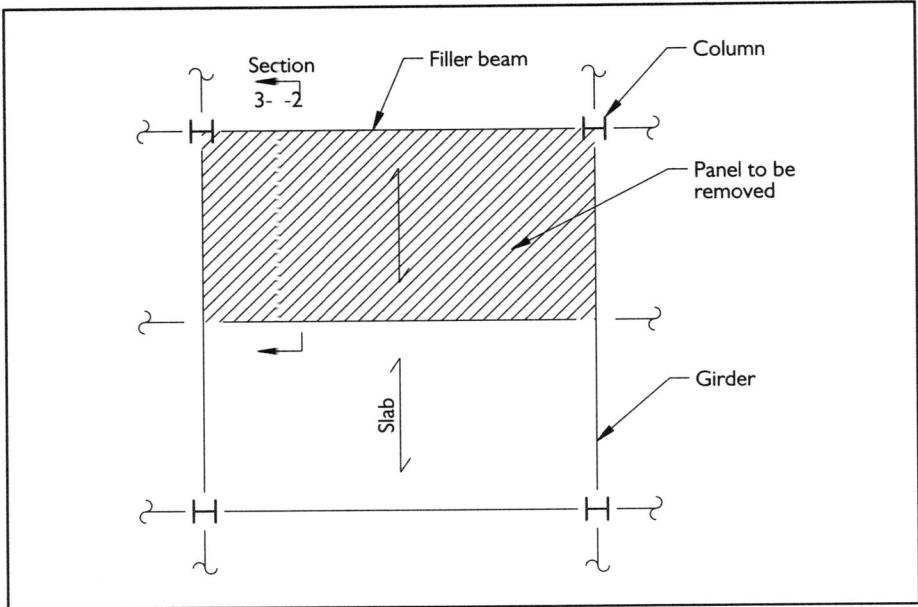

3-1-1. Steel framing floor plan

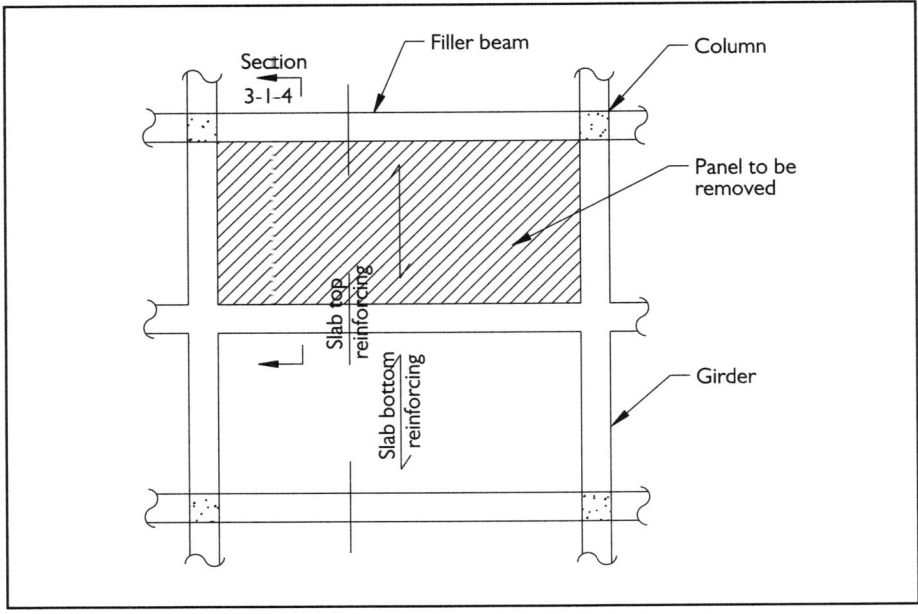

3-1-2. Concrete framing floor plan

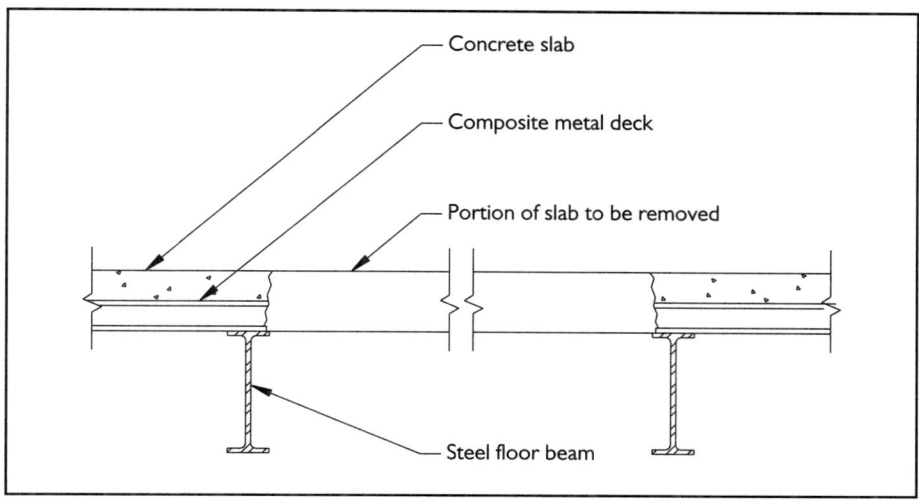

3-1-3. Steel edge detail

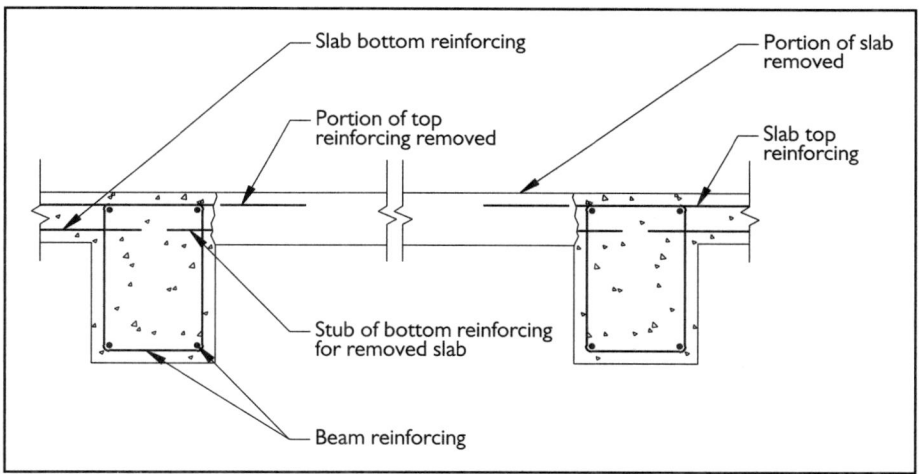

3-1-4. Concrete edge detail

Removing a panel in the concrete frame requires analysis of the remaining adjacent structure because of the nature of concrete design (figure 3-1-4). One of the primary goals of the structural engineer designing a concrete frame is to provide continuity between the different portions of the frame. This continuity does not necessarily affect the design but, realistically, engineers almost always take advantage of the efficiencies allowed in design by using it. The reinforcing required in the center of a slab span for the bending moment in a panel can be substantially reduced by taking into account the end moments developed by the top reinforcing placed for continuity. In removing a slab panel, the continuity on all four sides is disrupted, and the adjacent slabs and beams must be examined.

The layout described here is a "one-way" concrete floor, where the slabs span between parallel beams. The effect of the slab removal on the slab panels in the adjacent bays at right angles to the slab span should be minimal. While there would almost certainly be top reinforcing that runs from the demolished slab to these areas, the fact that the slab span is perpendicular to this reinforcing means that the reinforcing is not intended to carry load, but merely to restrict cracking from temperature changes and shrinkage.

The slabs on the other two sides of the demolished area, in the direction of the slab spans, must be assumed to be weakened by the alteration. Demolishing the slab to the edge of the beam does not allow for the top reinforcing steel to be stressed to carry the loads previously assumed. Even if the reinforcing were capable of carrying the load, these forces, which previously created a moment in the demolished slab, would now create torsion in the beam separating the two slab panels. Since this beam was not originally designed for torsion and in most cases cannot carry any torsional loads, the continuity at the end of the remaining slab must be assumed to be totally broken. Analysis of these now simple-ended spans is required to find if they can support their loads, and if reinforcement or another change to the proposed alterations is required. For example, if the slabs are found to be overstressed without the continuity at one end, but the beams are capable of carrying the torsion, the demolition can be detailed so as to expose the top rebar and attach it to the existing beam.

Concrete beams in one-way systems are often designed as T-beams, using the slab adjacent to the beam proper as a top flange. If a slab panel is removed from a floor designed in this manner, the beam strength is reduced, as is the load. Similar to the condition with steel T-beams, the simultaneous removal of roughly half of the strength and roughly half of the load usually does not result in overstress.

Top continuity steel is provided for the beams as well as the slabs. Ordinarily, it would be contained entirely within the beam cross sections, and so would be unaffected by the slab demolition. If the beams were designed as T-beams, the top steel may be spread through the slab, instead of being contained within the beam section. In this case, removal of the slab may reduce the strength of the two beams adjacent to the new opening and the four beams in the adjacent bays.

In more complex cases, the difference between working in the two different materials is more extreme. If the stair is L-shaped in plan, it is relatively simple to weld in new steel beams from below to create the desired floor opening. Concrete beams, however could not be readily added, forcing the use of steel beams in most cases. In concrete two-way slabs, destroying continuity steel may affect adjacent columns as well as slabs.

Chapter 4

Structural Design Considerations

Engineering design is usually a reactive process. An architect's program sets the broad design parameters within which the engineer's work must fit. The proposed schemes, including not only floor plans but such issues as the preservation of historic material or the maintenance of a desired floor-to-ceiling height, can severely restrict the engineering design. If the restrictions are too confining, the engineer and the architect must discuss the effect of the overall design on the structure, negotiating a compromise that respects the architectural design and structural constraints. The most effective mechanism for preventing conflict is the structural feasibility study, varying each parameter that has an important impact on the design.

    The structural restrictions imposed by physical properties of the materials of construction are not negotiable, and form a separate set of design parameters that may conflict with the architectural parameters. A third set of parameters is defined by the goals of engineering design. After all of the outside influences are taken into account, the various portions of the building must perform their roles as parts of an engineered structure, ensuring the safety and usability of the building. In short, the building must withstand gravity and lateral loading, provide usable floors and spaces for its inhabitants, and resist weather and fire. Meeting the balance of the requirements is meaningless if the result does not meet the criterion of functioning as a building.

    The relative importance of various engineering criteria depends in new buildings on characteristics such as the building's height, slenderness, or loading. In renovation, the extent of alteration and the location of the work must be added to this list. To use an extreme example, the removal of a loaded column by adding a transfer girder is never simple, but it is far simpler at the top floor of a building with only the roof loads to consider than it is at the base of a high-rise with forty floors of load above. Cutting a hole in a floor for a tenant stair can be easy if the opening is between two filler beams; it can be an enormous task if it involves removing a lateral system girder—a good example of a scheme that should be renegotiated, since the cost of such extensive renovations will be out of proportion to the benefits of the result. Moving the stairs slightly will cause minor changes to the architectural design, but will greatly reduce the cost and complexity of the structural work required.

Basic Principles of Engineering Design

Engineering statics and strength of materials are the foundation of structural analysis. Obviously, these considerations apply to all projects, although the emphasis changes with the type of member being analyzed. Certain topics that are usually ignored in new building design because their effects are negligible in new members are important parts of renovation design.

The internal stress most familiar to people dealing with building structure is bending moment. The case usually taught in introductory structures courses is that of a single-span beam with a uniform load along its length, and simply supported, that is supported against vertical moment only, so that the ends of the beam are free to rotate as the beam deflects. This is the model for most floor beams in wood and steel. The bending moment increases from zero at the beam ends to its maximum at the beam center. In steel and wood design, the maximum bending moment and the deflection associated with the maximum moment are the most important criteria for determining beam sizes. This means that increases in load or other changes that increase the moments are likely to require beam reinforcing. Moment design thus often controls renovation design the same way that it controls new design, but with an important difference: in renovations, the existing beam limits the possibilities.

A horizontal beam carrying vertical loads is subject to two main stresses: moment and shear. The bending moment usually controls both the design of new beams and the reinforcement of existing beams. Shear is usually examined across a vertical plane cutting through the beam (figure 4-1). At the end of a beam, the vertical shear is equal to the beam's reaction, so that a design for vertical shear ensures that the beam can carry its design load without failing by

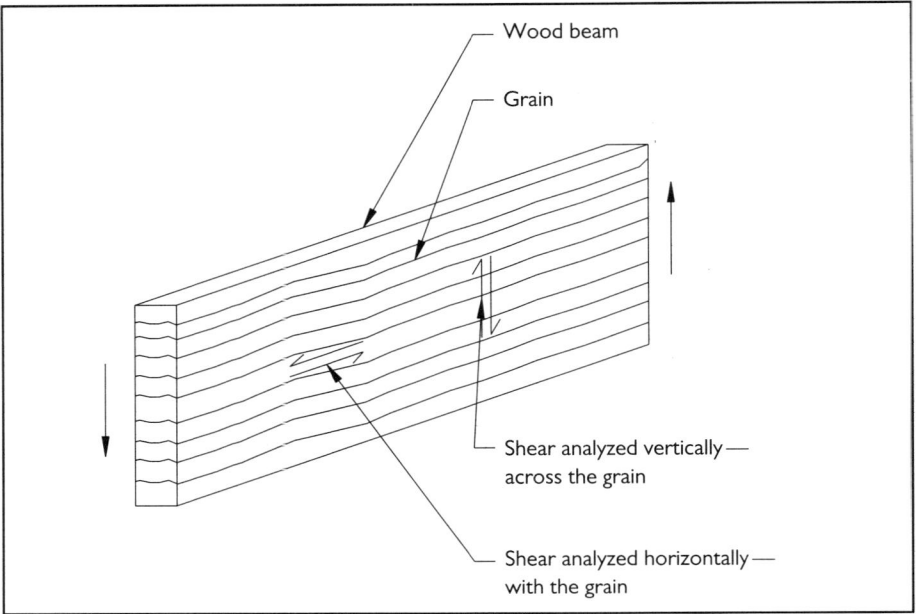

4-1. Vertical versus horizontal shear

"slicing" vertically. In designing changes to short, heavily loaded beams, the vertical shear may become critical. This is a special concern with concrete, where the shear is resisted by the vertical stirrups within the beam, which cannot be easily reinforced.

Shear can also be examined across a horizontal plane, but rarely is except in wood design. In a material that has equal shear strength in all directions, such as steel, or is stronger in resisting horizontal shear than vertical shear, such as conventionally reinforced concrete, there is no reason to review horizontal shear. Wood has drastically lower shear strengths parallel to the grain than across the grain, a fact well known to anyone who has tried using a handsaw in the two different directions. Heavily loaded wood beams may be constrained by the horizontal shear stresses at the beam ends. In beam reinforcing, horizontal shear suddenly becomes important, as different pieces of material are being combined to act as single beams. Horizontal shear can be pictured as the force transfer between the top and bottom of a beam. In a single-span, ordinarily loaded beam, the top of the beam is in compression that increases from zero at the beam ends to a maximum at the beam center; the bottom of the beam is in tension, also varying from end zero to a center maximum. Horizontal shear is the transfer of force from the point of loading to the far side of the beam. If the beam is made up of two or more pieces oriented horizontally, the shear forces must have some means of transferring from one piece to the next. If a force transfer mechanism does not exist, the separate pieces will act as individual beams whose total strength is significantly less than the strength of them all acting together. The welds that attach a plate to the bottom of an existing steel beam or the screws that attach a new plywood subfloor flange to existing joists must be designed for the horizontal shear forces.

Moments and shears are forces that must be resisted. Deflections are the visible effect of those forces acting within the beam. While resisting forces is more important than limiting deflections (having a plaster ceiling crack from movement is less distressing than having the floor structure supporting it collapse), deflections are usually considered in all types of design. In considering the effect of alterations, deflections of new and existing structure must be considered separately, as they may be substantially different.

The most noticeable effects of deflection occur when two members of different stiffnesses are located near one another, inadvertently showing their differences. For example, different sizes of wood floor joist can be used in many design situations. Differing sizes have roughly similar strengths but different stiffnesses. New joists should, if possible, match the size of existing joists to prevent sudden changes in floor stiffness from one side of a room to the other.

Differential stiffnesses are an issue at any scale. Weathering and maintenance problems of masonry curtain-wall buildings relate to the difference in stiffness (and therefore, the difference in relative motion) between the stiff, but weak, masonry and the more flexible, but stronger, steel or concrete. When alterations change a frame's stiffness (for example, when large portions of a floor are removed), the effects of changed movement under load must be examined.

Analysis

In general, there are few notable differences between the analysis of an existing structure and an unbuilt one. The analysis of an existing structure may be easier, since the physical existence of the various members reduces the number of unknown parameters that must be juggled. The level of specificity involved in a frame analysis does not depend on the actual details of construction so much as on the gross geometry and the form of connections. An interesting example of this is the common use of semirigid connections in low- and medium-rise steel-frame buildings built before computers promoted matrix analysis over the less accurate cantilever and portal analysis methods. The buildings designed in this manner do not have as even a distribution of forces as their more modern counterparts, but have been safe and serviceable for decades. They were built with analysis that did not accurately describe the details of their connections, but was capable of providing adequate girder and column sizes.

On rare occasions, a reanalysis of an old structure will reveal irregularities in the stress distribution that either inhibit alteration or require reinforcing of the structure to properly withstand the existing loads and conditions.

During the analysis of existing structure, the allowable stress that can be used must be determined. The allowable bending stress used for ordinary steel has risen from a range of 12 to 16 ksi (83 to 110 MPa) when the material first became common in the 1890s to 18 ksi (12.4 MPa) under the first AISC code, to 23.8 ksi (164 MPa) under the ninth edition (1990) of the AISC code. The allowable stress has risen in part because more thorough experimentation has clarified the material properties and in part because material quality improved greatly between 1880 and 1930.

The lower allowable stresses sometimes imposed on design by old material can sometimes be compensated for with design that concentrates stress within new material. In bending, the outermost portions of a section are the most highly stressed. Therefore, reinforcement techniques that increase the area or moment of inertia of a member by adding new material to its outer faces are doubly effective, increasing the geometric properties and putting new material at the locations of highest stress, "faking" an entire member of new material properties.

Different Eras of Construction

It is often said that buildings were better built in the past. Depending on the criteria used for comparison, there is a certain amount of truth to the statement. True plaster, solid masonry exterior walls, and masonry interior partitions all contributed to a solidity that is now extremely expensive and rare under any circumstances. At the same time, buildings are more thoroughly designed now, and therefore more consistently safe. The average quality of building has probably risen, since the minimum standards are far higher than in the past. Many of the less well built structures of the past have been taken down, or have fallen down by themselves, so the sample of old buildings is skewed toward quality. In terms of structural renovation, standing buildings erected before 1900 tend to have more reserve strength than those built later, but may be more difficult to modify; buildings built between 1920 and 1940 are similar enough to modern construction to permit straightforward design of alterations; those built after 1960 may contain advanced designs that are difficult to alter without prohibitively expensive changes.

Old buildings containing masonry nonstructural partitions, concrete slab floors placed integrally with beam encasement or tile arch floors filling the entire space between the beam flanges, two- or three-wythe brick or unit masonry exterior walls, columns spaced at less than 25 feet (7600 mm) on center, and beams designed for relatively low bending stresses tend to be far stiffer than modern buildings. Every change in design and construction technique made since the 1870s has made buildings more structurally efficient, using less material at a higher stress level, with more consistent safety factors. The payoff for efficiency, less material used at higher stresses, results in larger deflections under a given load and less redundancy of load distribution.

An example of the efficiency of modern design in reducing the number of roles one structural element plays is the use of concrete slabs on composite metal deck. Composite concrete slabs can span farther than tile arches and require far less labor during construction than tile or wood-formed concrete slabs. The use of prefabricated metal deck which serves both as form for the wet concrete and reinforcing for the final slab is inherently efficient, but somewhat inflexible. Like a tile arch floor, a composite slab on deck cannot be modified in any practical manner other than by providing new support beams at any proposed cut edges. Additional reinforcement cannot readily be added, and if the slab is used as a composite flange for the floor beams, even cutting small holes for ducts is problematic. Finally, the typical location of the slab-and-deck combination entirely above the floor beams reduces the lateral support provided to the beams. The beams are braced against lateral buckling of the top flange, but are unsupported by the slab at cantilevers or continuous beams that have the bottom flange in compression. Alterations that change the bracing requirements of beams in a composite slab-on-deck building often require the addition of individual brace beams.

Long-span beams and flat slabs in modern construction allow the uninterrupted space now required for office design, as well as great flexibility in changing the interior layout. Open-plan layouts have resulted in two major differences between older buildings and newer ones: the higher stress levels and greater deflections in beams and slabs, and wider spacing of columns. Long spans in interior floor construction are achieved through the use of high-strength steel, composite construction using the floor slab as the beam compression flange, and simply larger beam sections. The restrictions on floor plate thickness have meant that the beam depth cannot grow proportionally to the span, so the heavier beams used typically have wider flanges and are thicker, but are not very much deeper. Long-span cast-in-place concrete-frame buildings are more rare, and usually of post-tensioned construction. This method of using more of the compressive capacity of a concrete beam is the concrete equivalent to the steel frame composite efficiency, but has a similar drawback: modification of the resulting floors can be very difficult. Just as using steel beams composite with the slabs inhibits cutting holes in the slab and thereby loses a portion of the beam's strength, post-tensioning tendons cannot be cut, and regular spacing of them throughout a floor slab may require near reconstruction of the slab to cut an opening during an alteration.

All of the developments in curtain-wall structure since World War II, including the design of metal frames for glass curtain walls, the use of metal studs as backup for brick walls, and the provision of frequent expansion joints, have been aimed at making sure that curtain walls serve only the purpose of exterior enclosure. The use of expansion joints in the masonry and metal frames and the flexibility of the wall components are intended to prevent the walls from inadvertently carrying structural load. While it is never good practice to support structural components from curtain walls, the size and rigidity of older, all-masonry curtain walls allows for more leeway in design. Especially in renovations that entail changes to the walls or the floor structure immediately adjacent to the wall, the ability to brace minor beams to the walls, or resupport secondary structure such as existing stairs, while not recommended, adds flexibility to the design options. In each case, the actual stresses and physical condition of the wall determine whether using the wall in this manner is acceptable or not. Very often such changes have been made in older buildings, and the effect of such potentially incorrect work must be considered in planning new changes.

Lateral Loading

While lateral-load bracing systems resist forces other than wind load, most obviously earthquake forces, the bulk of the United States is designated seismic zone I or II, where the seismic accelerations are small enough that wind loads will control the design forces of tall buildings and any regularly shaped small buildings. Except in high-risk seismic zones, the lateral systems are commonly referred to as "wind bracing" or "wind systems." Gross changes to lateral load systems in areas where seismic design governs are different than those in areas where wind load governs in one major aspect. In seismic design the requirement that the various floors be of approximately equal stiffness is crucial, restricting the possibilities in removing members. Detailing also differs, because seismic design requires carefully designed continuity. This difference is roughly equivalent to the difference between seismic and nonseismic detailing in new design.

Unless a building is being completely renovated, with the large budget and zero occupancy that that implies, there is rarely a good justification for altering a lateral system. A small renovation, such as the installation of tenant stairs in a high-rise office building, should not entail the analysis of the entire structure, though that may become necessary if girders or bracing members that are an integral part of the lateral system are modified.

The danger in modifying lateral system members is that they are ordinarily subjected to several different forces, all of which must be taken into account. One example is removing the bottom flange of a steel lateral girder. An ordinary girder can be made shallower by welding new flange plates to the web and removing the material below, and only the girder's shear and moment capacity and stiffness need be considered. A typical steel girder supporting lateral forces may be carrying an axial load, and the change in depth will change the beam's centroid, potentially causing both local buckling problems and new eccentricity in connections to other members.

Similarly, cutting holes in the floors of a concrete flat slab building may affect the lateral system by reducing the moment capacity of slab-to-column connections. The effect will spread to the bays adjacent to the one where the slab opening is cut, as cutting reinforcing bars reduces the development length available for the reinforcing. If the slab-to-column connections are not part of the wind system—for example, in a building braced with shear walls—cutting a hole in the slab is relatively simple. The edges of the slab must be supported, and any top reinforcing needed for continuity, if cut, must be either replaced or tied back to be developed.

Building floors act as horizontal diaphragms within the lateral system. This crucial component transfers lateral loads from the bulk of the building to the frames or shear walls that carry the loads to the foundations. Removing large areas of floor within a building greatly reduces the stiffness in the horizontal plane at that level by reducing the diaphragm action.

Each column within a lateral system carries a portion of the lateral forces to the frame below, so any lateral column transfers must be accompanied by the appropriate bracing to other columns within the frame. Reinforcing of the columns to remain is often required by the increase in lateral loading. The schematic design of floor openings and beam removals near existing column transfers and building exterior setbacks may conflict with existing horizontal bracing. It is often easier to move a contemplated opening through architectural redesign than to move these pieces of the lateral system.

Deflection and Jacking

During any load transfer or changes, structural elements move. These movements can range from deflections of several inches at the midspan of long girders and transfer trusses to a few thousandths of an inch shortening in columns. Except in rare circumstances where movement in rigidly connected members causes significant secondary stresses, the deflections are a concern for their effect on finishes and attached mechanical systems, not for their effect on the structure itself. Secondary stresses are most often created when deflections in one member force deflections in supported members. Just as stress within a beam will always be accompanied by movement of that beam, movement is always accompanied by stress. Stresses created by forced movements are referred to as secondary stresses.

The deflections that naturally accompany load changes are not acceptable when they affect architectural finishes or appearances or when they cause unreasonably high movement or secondary stresses in supported structure. Masonry walls that are being transferred from a self-supporting condition to a beam-supported condition, such as occurs during window installation, are particularly vulnerable to cracking from secondary stress, as are plaster ceilings and wall finishes. Jacking, also known as "predeflection," is the imposition of load on the new members before the support of potentially damaged elements is transferred. This is often performed with hydraulic jacks, although dead weights of various types and various esoteric methods have been used. One example of an atypical jacking concept is cooling new transfer columns in dry ice to make them contract before placement. When the columns return to room temperature and consequently expand, they "self-jack," transferring load from the original structure without the deflection normally expected.

Jacking causes the new structure to assume the final deflected shape while it is physically isolated from the elements to be supported, protecting those elements from motion. This is an area where the design engineer's involvement with the details of construction is unavoidable: even if the contractor hires an engineer to design the shoring and jacking process, the design engineer must work with the contractor's engineer to coordinate the final and temporary configuration and loads.

Constructibility

Creating details that can be built as easily and as usefully as they can be drawn is a constant challenge for designers. In renovation, the challenge is increased by the probability that construction tolerances in the existing structure reduce the regularity of the existing portions of new details. Where renovations are detailed solely from existing drawings, and not from actual observation, it can be expected that the details will require some modification based on field conditions.

All small renovations in high-rise buildings suffer from an access problem. The size of materials that can be hauled in freight elevators is strictly limited by the dimensions of the elevator cabs, while the height of the building greatly reduces the possibility of hauling the material up a staircase or the outside of the building. When new steel beams are to be introduced on a high floor, the contractors inevitably ask for splices to allow delivery of the beams in pieces 8 to 12 feet (2440 to 3660 mm) long. The easiest course for the designer is to include provision for splices from the beginning, in order to provide them in a controlled manner and to have their cost included as part of the base project, not as a potentially more expensive extra.

Access can also determine the choice of material used. If work is conducted in or near an occupied space, the "wet" trades of masonry and concrete are anathema to many building owners. In reality these trades cause more mess than any work except large amounts of skim-coating plaster. In addition, fresh masonry and concrete must be protected during drying, and do not attain their full strength immediately, requiring the retention of any shoring for days or weeks after the work is finished. Steel, light-gage framing, and carpentry work, by contrast, can be performed very quickly and near occupied spaces without damage. Effects of the different construction trades on their surroundings are often an important factor in choosing materials.

The specifics of each structural material determine what is a constructible detail for that material. Concrete and masonry are not suited to being formed into thin members; wood is not easily connected in complicated geometry; and steel and aluminum are difficult to connect on site without shop fabrication. The details of the use of each material are covered in the following chapters. Only by comparing the built results with the design details can the art of constructible detailing be learned.

As described in chapter 2, "Architectural Design Considerations," the structural engineer often takes third place behind the architect and the mechanical engineer in deciding the overall scheme for spatial planning. At the same time, the ability of a contractor to build a planned alteration may require analysis of access to the site, temporary construction to secure that access, or modifications to the proposed new structure to reduce the access requirements. The first two items may be considered the responsibility of the contractor, but are still the concern of the structural engineer. The last item is entirely the engineer's, and consists of balancing against the site conditions the cost of additional work such as providing splices in long beams. Coordination with the architect is crucial, since additional access may be provided for work with which the engineer is unfamiliar, and reduce the need for additional details.

Unknown Structure

There comes a time in many renovations when minor information is still unknown and not enough time or money exists to continue predesign examination. In very small projects, this may be true from the beginning: there may not be any investigation budget. When this occurs, assumptions must be made about the unknown conditions. If a beam of indeterminate size can be observed not to suffer from overstress damage, it is ordinarily assumed to be adequate. In such cases, prudence dictates maintenance of existing stress levels in unknown members. An old building that has sustained known loads through its life and shows no signs of stress-related damage is usually assumed to be capable of resisting those loads. When these circumstances are taken to be present, the challenge is to determine that the new loads are equivalent to the old. Figuring the live loads on a given member is ordinarily an easy project; performing a similar takedown for dead load requires careful measurement and material composition assumptions.

Relative Costs

One of the reasons that buildings are altered is the cost savings over new construction. As environmentalists have recently begun to make clear, an existing building represents a huge investment in materials and energy. Every piece of a building cost money to fabricate and has a replacement cost; the more that can be saved, the less waste of existing and new effort. This is true at both the macro and micro levels: just as it is more efficient to save an old building and renovate the portions that do not meet the current requirements, it is usually more efficient to save an existing beam and reinforce it to carry the new loads than to remove it and replace it. During design, therefore, it is prudent to retain as much existing structure as is in usable condition and can be adopted to the new architectural program.

Professional estimators and contractors estimating costs for bidding have a more difficult job with renovations. There are more unknowns than in new construction, special techniques may be required to deal with obsolete materials, and logistics may play a larger role than in new construction. Some of these problems must be addressed in specifications, but as much as is possible should go on the construction drawings, where it is more certain of incorporation into the contractors' thoughts and estimates.

Replacement is usually the most expensive alteration option. The cost of demolition of large areas and reconstruction is more than new construction of a similar area, and markedly so if foundation or concrete work takes place within an occupied space. On the other hand, previous alterations may have disrupted any rational layout of structure, mechanical systems, and usable space. In that case, complete replacement is preferable, as providing at least simplified conditions, if not a clean slate.

Structural reinforcement, if not associated with large-scale architectural changes, can be fairly inexpensive, depending on structural material and layout. As described in the chapters on individual materials, the characteristics of each material determine the difficulty in operations that can be carried out in any material, such as reinforcing a beam.

Modification of the existing load path is the most expensive form of structural alteration, because it requires so many of the methods described. Load analysis, the design of new girders for relocating beams or new transfer girders for relocating columns, the access and installation clearance difficulties associated with new bay-wide construction, shoring, and jacking to prevent floor and partition movement all may be a part of moving a load path from its existing configuration.

Case Study 4-1: Analysis of a Building Frame

In this case study, a two-story roof addition is proposed for a nine-story steel-frame building. The building's original structural drawings are available, obviating the need for probes to perform a feasibility analysis (4-1-1). A few isolated probes are performed to observe the current condition of the steel as well as verify the information on the drawings. The steel is found to be in good condition and the drawing information accurate.

The structural drawings are very detailed and even note wind moments and reactions at each joint within the frame. The new addition will impose additional gravity loading on the building columns and will also affect the wind moments in the frames. The degree to which these moments are altered must be determined.

The first step in determining the feasibility of adding structure to this building is to determine where the moments and forces noted on the original drawings came from. It is imperative to understand the original intent of the designers before imposing new loads and design on the building. It is found that the distribution of forces noted on the drawings is consistent with standard frame design, and the feasibility study can continue with the assumption that the original design was standard. In other words, the frame can justifiably be analyzed as a new building as long as the older allowable stresses are taken into account.

The frame is now analyzed with two new stories added to its top. The gravity load is increased by the weight of the new structure and the wind load by the "sail area" of the addition. It is found that the existing columns can easily support the added loading of the new stories when live load reduction, not originally considered, is applied. However, it is also determined that the columns fail when the new gravity loads are combined with the new moments induced by the additional wind area and modern wind loading. The columns therefore will either have to be braced or reinforced, a costly and time-consuming endeavor.

In some jurisdictions, the designers may have the option of renovating the building under an older building code depending upon the cost of the renovation relative to the cost of the original building. Older codes usually contain less

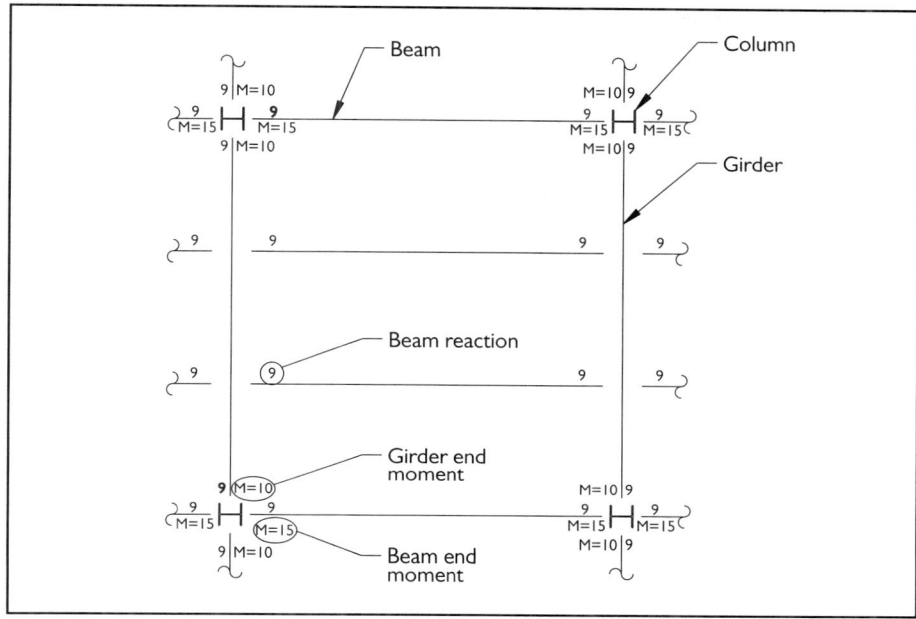

4-1-1. Sample floor plan with moments and beam reactions

stringent wind loading criteria, allowing the existing structure to prove adequate. The decision as to which code to use is often the most difficult portion of this type of work. Modern code requirements are based on technology now available and better information about the effects of load on structures and materials. To justify the adequacy of a building by using an old code's lower wind loading is not always the safest way to proceed, although it may be entirely legal. Similar problems are created by the ever-increasing seismic requirements in codes. Many engineers who might balk at using a reduced wind load to avoid lateral reinforcing may be inclined to "grandfather" their building to avoid a requirement to reinforce for seismic loading.

The factors noted in this case study very clearly underline the importance of proceeding with a feasibility study before undertaking a renovation like this. A properly prepared feasibility study will cover all of these issues and let the client, as well as the design team, determine the best course of action prior to full-scale design.

Case Study 4-2: Effect of Lateral-load Systems on Design

The danger in modifying portions of a building responsible for carrying lateral load is that they are ordinarily subjected to several different forces, all of which must be taken into account. Unlike ordinary floor beams, which are subjected to fairly constant load in one direction, girders designed to carry wind or earthquake forces have loads that can reverse direction and fluctuate rapidly in short periods of time—in earthquakes, changing direction repeatedly in seconds. Modification of these girders is therefore more difficult than modification of similar-size ordinary beams. The difficulty grows with the size of the girder, and can make a proposed alteration impractical.

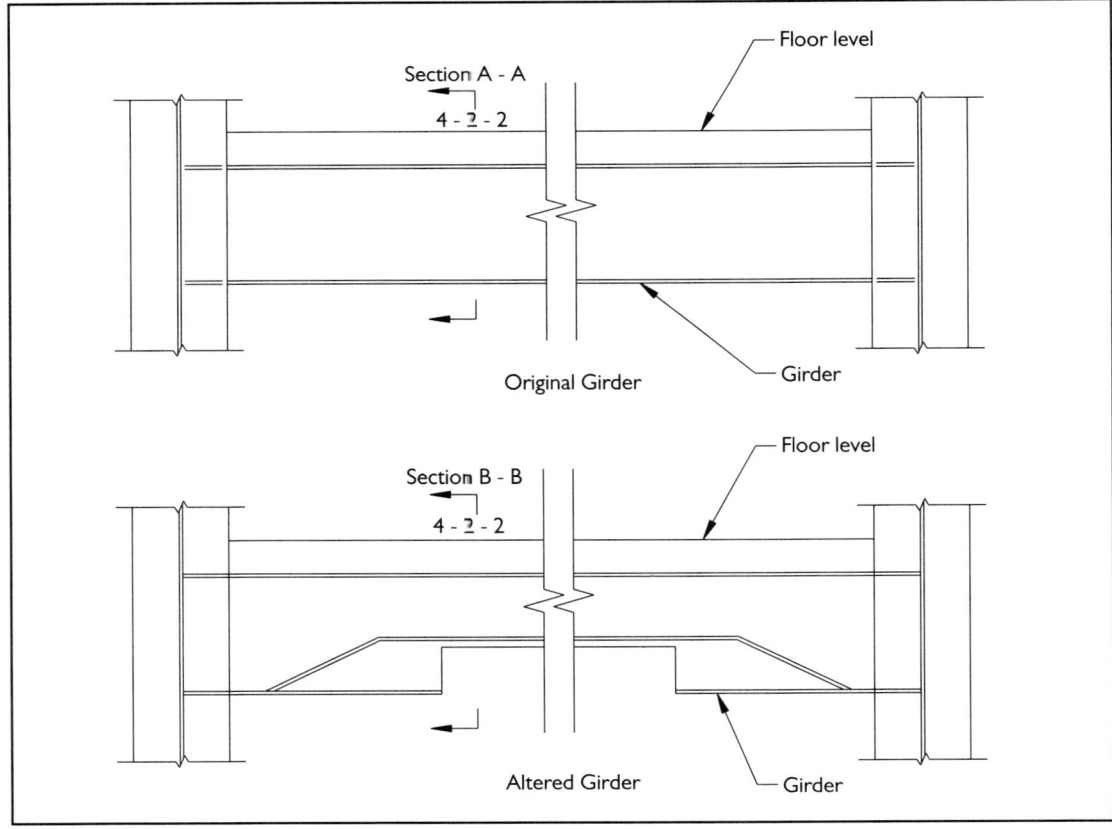

4-2-1. Alteration of a wind girder

Planning and layout changes occasionally require changes to structure because of simple spatial conflict. An example is the need to remove the bottom of a beam to create additional headroom adjacent to a new stair. In a steel-frame building, the difference between an ordinary floor beam and a lateral-load girder is critical to an engineer designing changes to the bottom flange of a steel wide-flange. An ordinary girder can be made shallower by welding new flange plates

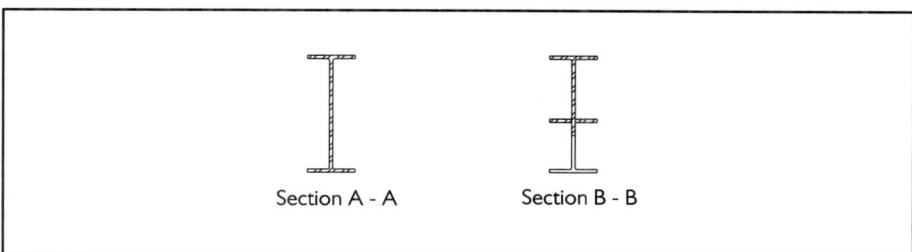

4-2-2. Section through original girder and altered girder

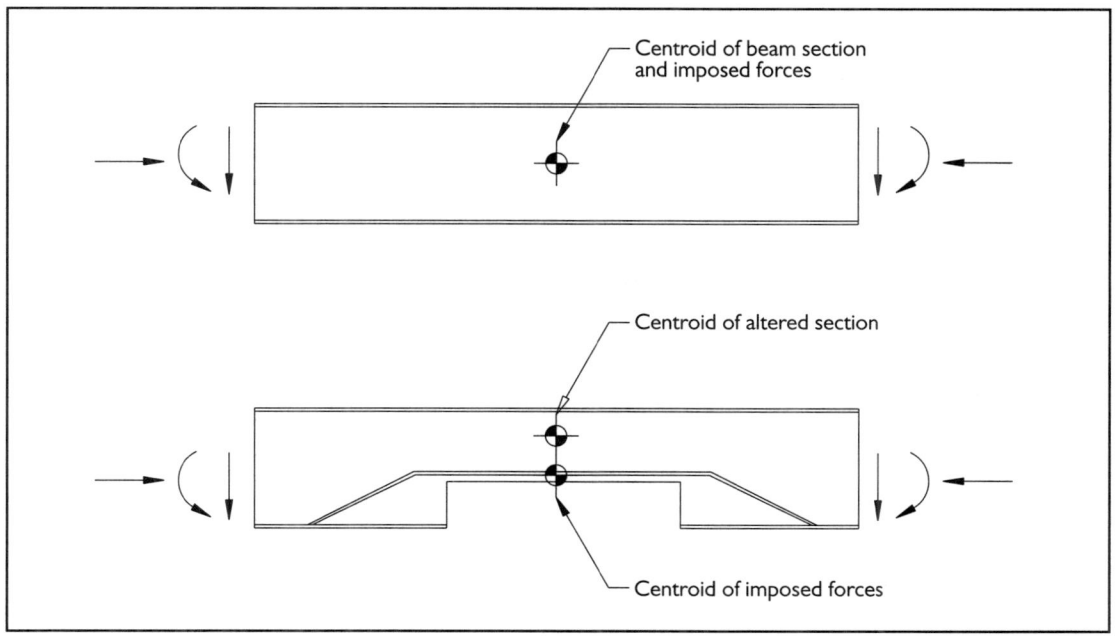

4-2-3. Original versus altered girder forces

to the web and removing the material below, as long as the girder's shear, moment capacity, and stiffness are preserved during the change (figures 4-2-1 and 4-2-2). A typical steel lateral-system girder of the same size will probably be carrying an axial load, and the change in depth will change the beam's centroid, potentially causing both local buckling problems and new eccentricity in connections to other members (figure 4-2-3). As the beam becomes shallower, the connections may have to be reinforced for new bending stresses caused by the change. These new stresses grow rapidly with the amount of change to the beam, and will quickly overwhelm the stresses from the original design.

Case Study 4-3: Jacking During Column Transfer

Many possible alterations require intense structural work to be feasible. Among the most difficult to achieve is the removal of an existing column within an occupied building. While the design of a transfer girder to carry the loads from the column shafts above to neighboring columns reinforced for the additional load or new columns provided specifically for the transfer is fairly simple, the actual implementation of the transfer is not.

All beams deflect under load. The amount of this deflection is calculated and compared to various criteria during design. Two commonly used criteria are that the total deflection under all load be kept to less than the length of the beam divided by 240 (L/240) and that the deflection caused by live load only be kept to less than L/360. These numbers are not based on objective criteria such as allowable stresses, but rather on human perception of flatness in floors and the range of deflection likely to cause cracking in plaster ceilings below the beams.

The standard deflection criteria may not provide adequate protection during the insertion of a new transfer girder. For example, if the column grid consists of regular 20- by 20-foot (6100 by 6100 mm) bays, and the new transfer girder entirely removes a column to transfer its load to two existing columns, the transfer girder will have a 40-foot (12200 mm) span, and using the standard criteria, twice the allowable deflection of all neighboring column-line girders. If, for example, the girder is actually designed using the higher live load criteria, the difference in "bounciness" of the floor may be perceptible to tenants, even though no difference in structure is visible and no plaster is seen to crack (figure 4-3-1).

When a transfer is inserted below occupied floors in a building, the potential for problems is very high. Most architectural finishes are brittle, and will

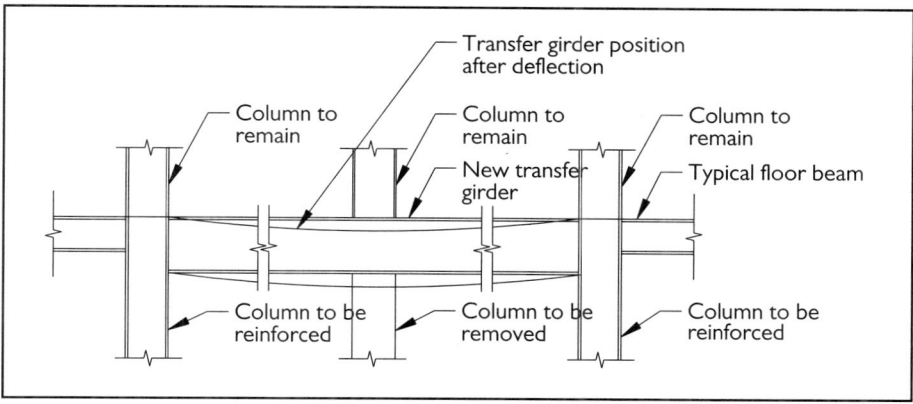

4-3-1. Column transfer diagram with deflection after girder installation

crack if the materials to which they are attached move appreciably. During construction of a new building, movements caused by the dead load deflection of transfer girders are not important, as they take place while the building is still a shell consisting of the structural frame and floor slabs. The design engineer has more freedom to control movements in new buildings through the use of deeper (and therefore stiffer) girders; all things being equal, beams installed during alterations tend to be shallower than those used in new design in order to avoid creating headroom problems.

If a new transfer girder is simply installed and the existing column shaft removed, the column shafts above the transfer will drop by the amount of the girder's deflection. While not ordinarily significant to the performance of the building's structure, such a drop will cause cracking in the finishes at every floor above the transfer. Rather than cause this type of disruption of the space above, new transfers are ordinarily installed with jacking.

The example described here is a five-story steel-frame office building with 20-foot (6100 mm) square bays. One column is to be removed between the first and second floors and the neighboring columns will be reinforced from the second floor to the foundation to carry the additional loads. The building was designed for a 50 psf (1.1 Pa) floor live load, a 30 psf (0.6 Pa) roof live load, and an 80 psf (1.7 Pa) dead load consisting of 20 psf (0.4 Pa) for partitions, 40 psf (0.8 Pa) for the floor slabs, and 20 psf (0.4 Pa) for the floor finishes and ceilings. The load in the column to be removed, measured directly below the second floor, is roughly 250 kips (57 kN).

The first-to-second-floor height is higher than the building average and can accept a new beam up to 36 inches (915 mm) deep, leading to a design of a high-strength steel transfer girder of W36x260. The dead load deflection of this beam is approximately 0.7 inches (18 mm); the live load deflection is 0.4 inches (10 mm). Through the use of jacking, the dead load deflection is minimized to prevent disruption of the second through fifth floor spaces.

The new transfer is put in place, but not attached, before any alterations other than the reinforcement of the existing columns at its ends are made. The girder is attached to the column, and hydraulic jacks are used to push up on the ends of the transfer. The jacks can be connected to the columns that will carry the transfer girder: the upward jacking force is equal to the dead load reaction of a typical column, and therefore will be less than the neighboring columns' combination of dead and live load. By the time the jacks have reached the reaction that the transfer girder would have if loaded only by the dead load above, the girder has deflected its full dead load amount. No movement has taken place above, since the column is still in place. While the jacks are in place, the transfer girder is given its final connections to the columns on either side. The column to be removed is then cut, with a section removed so that the remnant is incapable of carrying load. At this time the jacking force can be removed.

Once the column is cut, the transfer girder is carrying the load above. By predeflecting the girder with the jacks, it is already stressed by the amount the dead load would cause, and has already moved through the associated deflection. The only deflection that will accompany the transfer of load from the column to the girder is that associated with the live load, which is usually much less. Depending on conditions, the jacking force may include some portion of the live load deflection.

Chapter 5

Research

The most important aspect of renovation not explicitly taught in school is the "detective work." An important part of the success of a renovation project is establishing the history of the building, its structural systems, and the causes of any known damage. Without this information, the final design documents will almost certainly be incomplete, a common cause of delays and extra costs. If it is possible to obtain information without excessive delay or cost to the client, it should be completed during the schematic design phase of the project. Persuading others of the importance of research can be difficult, especially when it requires time, money, or annoying tenants. When a client raises the first or second arguments, the best answer is usually to compare the time and cost of research—probing, for example, with the time and cost of a delay during construction for redesign. The success of this argument is contingent on the client's trust for the design team. The third issue requires careful diplomacy to minimize friction that can cause problems later on.

There are two useful sources of information, corresponding to primary and secondary sources in basic research. The primary source of information is always the building itself. The most complete set of construction documents imaginable from conscientious engineers and architects does not necessarily reflect the exact built conditions; the built conditions themselves do. In addition, examination of the actual building may uncover deterioration or damage. Secondary sources of information, even the hypothetical complete set of construction documents with partial drawings of previous renovations, show someone's idea, or model, of existing conditions. That model is subject to testing by examination of the primary source, by selective examination of the actual conditions represented on the drawings. The equivalent of tertiary sources, interviewing someone familiar with the building's documentation or history, should be used sparingly, if at all. Memory is too unreliable when people's lives are at stake. Talking to building superintendents, contractors, or even the building's designers can be useful as a starting point for an investigation, but every fact, without exception, that comes from interviews must be checked.

Documentation must always accompany investigation. It is foolish to go to the effort necessary to determine unknown basic information about the structure of building and not carefully record every fact learned. Not all information belongs on the construction drawings eventually produced: excess information can confuse the contractors and, on occasion, even lead to higher bids when the scope of work is overestimated. This does not mean that all information does not belong on an organized drawing. Field notebooks are often the personal property of the individual engineer or architect, and the information in them is rarely reproduced and properly filed. A good compromise solution when information exists that will not be present on the construction drawings is to take a set of sepias or other reproducible of those drawings and add all of the information from the field notes. Those drawings can then be filed as existing condition drawings for that date.

Sometimes investigation uncovers problems that have no connection with the project. If, for example, an unsafe facade condition caused by deteriorated masonry to spandrel beam ties is discovered during the investigation preceding an interior renovation, the designer has a responsibility to call attention to the situation. On the other hand, just because a condition is discovered does not mean that the designer has to assume responsibility for repairing it. If the condition is not an immediate danger to anyone, the proper course of action is to notify the building owner or any others responsible, such as a managing agent. The nature and seriousness of the condition should be stated, and the need for further investigation or remedial action noted as required. The same report should be made if the condition appears to be immediately life-threatening, but with emphasis on the seriousness and the suggestion of an immediate course of action to ameliorate the danger. This can include shoring, the construction of protection such as sidewalk bridges, or evacuation of a portion or all of the building.

Original Documents

The most obvious sources of information not readily visible, original design or construction documents, are also the easiest to use. While the level of detail on old drawings varies widely and is rarely extensive enough to answer all potential questions, the drawings are the result of essentially the same design process that we use today. Often, ninety-year-old design drawings are no more difficult for a designer to read than those produced today. In some cases, it is even possible that old drawings will contain more information on a given topic than their modern counterparts. Loose lintels, for example, were regularly shown on floor plans as late as the 1930s, while on modern drawings lintel sizes are usually buried in a general note or, worse, in a specification thrown away after construction.

There are more similarities than differences between old and new drawings. A floor plan almost always shows dimensions to any grid or column lines used, beam sizes in a steel frame, the location of floor openings, and the perimeter building lines. Old drawings tend to show all masonry walls, even curtain walls, at equal weight as steel or concrete structure. This is probably a historically intriguing carryover from the days of masonry bearing-wall buildings, but it is an enormous nuisance in reading the drawings. A single heavy line is usually a beam, but a pair of heavy lines can stand for a masonry wall, a concrete beam, or, in the era before large rolled-steel beams, a pair of beams acting in tandem as a girder. Since all three of these possibilities are realistic floor supports, and since buildings often had mixed structural systems before 1920, the possibility for true confusion arises.

One of the serious problems in reading old drawings is very simple: actually reading the information provided. The standard drafting alphabet taught before World War I was more ornate than what is taught today, and usually written in italics. The combination of small, ornate, and slanted lettering and slightly different terminology can easily cause confusion. When dealing with dimension strings, the assumed reading can be verified by scaling the drawing, but for notes and beam sizes there is no solution other than to check the readings several times.

Another destructive aspect of time is the physical aging of the drawings. Ink-on-cloth originals hold up well when stored out of sunlight, but even a confirmed optimist would not ordinarily expect to find original reproducibles of a building more than twenty years old. Old paper prints, like new paper prints, are fragile, subject to fading, cracking, tearing, and the scribbling of careless people. Anyone who uses original prints has the responsibility to protect them as well as possible from damage. If the project budget allows, the safest course of action is to have new reproducibles photographically made from the prints, so that new prints can be used for the work while the old ones are archived. A less expensive course that creates a reasonably permanent record is to microfilm the drawings.

Material designations have changed several times just in the twentieth century. In reading a drawing for a steel frame building, sources such as "AISC Iron and Steel Beams, 1873–1952" should be used, and exact matches for beam names located. Concrete data are more complicated, since real standardization of information was not established until the 1920s. Beam and column sizes may be shown on plan, in sections, or in schedules; reinforcing rod sizes may be shown in the same places, and patented reinforcing systems or odd-sized bars may have been used. The various methods were often thrown together on a single set of drawings. The use of schedules for beam and slab data is a relatively recent development; before World War II many projects had beam widths dimensioned in plan, depths and longitudinal bars in section, and stirrups in beam side elevations, which were often combined with floor-slab sections showing the depth and reinforcing of the floor. The possible combinations of data location are endless, leading to the conclusion that all existing drawings, however unlikely, should be examined for any missing structural information.

Another flaw in old drawings is their limited range in time. Most drawings available are either original design drawings that do not reflect changes made later, or alteration drawings with incomplete information about the original design. No matter how complete a drawing may seem, the information to be used should be verified on site as completely as possible.

Subcontractor shop drawings may be found during research. In many cases, steel erection plans were saved by owners and contractors as as-built drawings. With the exception of possibly confusing notation, the erection plans are often clearer than the contract documents that they represent. Since erection drawings are meant to be read on construction sites and show actual member dimensions in addition to column line dimensions, they are generally less schematic than design drawings. Depending on when a given set of erection plans was produced and the type of members represented, the actual sizes may not be shown. The types of designations vary from the member sizes to a series of consecutive numbers to obscure codes representing the detail-sheet number and information. If the designations are anything other than the member sizes, the drawings may need to be supplemented by probing to determine sizes, since key and index drawings are the least likely drawings to be saved.

Drawings produced years after the construction of a building often contain meaningful information. Another set of design professionals may have hacked away at the same problems in investigation twenty years earlier for a different alteration, and had the foresight to include their findings on their drawings. The owners of many older buildings, for which the original drawings have been lost, keep records of repairs and alterations, creating a library that grows in completeness over time. The drawings found in such a collection, or in building department files, are likely to be modern in layout and scope, and have only one serious failing: they cannot be trusted entirely. Information gathered in investigations may not be accurate, and if the investigation was performed by someone not under the direction of the designer, it cannot be assumed dependable. Just as the information in original drawings requires confirmation, any data used for design that originates with previous alteration drawings should be checked in some fashion.

Field Investigation

The simplest field investigation of a building is a walk-through to observe the finished surfaces and any exposed structure. Based on the investigator's familiarity with construction of different types and eras, previous field experience, and the amount of information about the building available from document search, this simple technique may provide all the information required for design. The degree of thoroughness used in field investigation is determined by the overall condition of the building, the extent of the renovation to be performed, the amount of information available from other sources, and the time and budget allocated to preliminary studies. The most straightforward case is a minor renovation to a modern building for which the original drawings are available—for example, the installation of tenant stairs in a steel-frame office tower. In a case like this, with the floor slab and framing known, and a very small probability of unknown exceptional conditions, it is possible to design the entire renovation without seeing the site and to arrange for a site investigation during the finish demolition to permit verification of the assumed conditions.

An example of a more complex case is a major renovation in an old building with a mixed structural system in poor condition. In a hundred-year-old building, with a mix of masonry bearing walls, steel beams, tile arch floors, cast-iron columns, and steel beams and concrete slabs from previous renovations, it may be necessary to start from scratch with architectural floor plans and locate each structural member to create a framing plan. If the condition of the members is suspect because of possible weathering damage or overstress, there is no substitute for actual observation of the condition of every single member. If damage is expected, and provisions have been made for repairs, it may be necessary only to expose and examine enough members to confirm the damage. Obviously, it is simpler to identify poor conditions requiring removal than to confirm fair conditions requiring only repair or no action at all.

Field investigation must be performed in a systematic manner to curtail errors. There are sources that provide a framework within which investigations can be held, such as the ASCE's "Guidelines for Structural Assessment of Existing Buildings." All the sources emphasize the repetitive collection of data to lessen the possibility of drawing conclusions from exceptional facts. When a reasonable number of conditions are examined, the typical cases can be distinguished from the exceptions. The number of conditions required for a good sample depend on the same factors listed at the beginning of this section: the overall state, the scope of the proposed work, the amount of available information, and the time and budget available during investigation. A crucial aspect of this work is separating incidental or isolated failure from overall failure. This is most readily achieved by looking for patterns of damage rather than concentrating on the exact location of each crack. Patterns usually tell the most comprehensive story.

Visual examination can sometimes reveal all the required information. In many older wood-frame buildings, the joist size and spacing are visible at some locations. Unlike concrete and steel, which can have hidden defects, most wood deterioration is easily visible. Insects leave entry holes on the surface of the wood, and fungus is readily apparent. A dull pocket-knife blade, the screwdriver found on many combination knives, or a dull ice pick or awl makes a perfect tool for testing the effect of fungal growth. If the fungus is simply growing on the outside of the wood, the point of the tool will not penetrate the surface under hand pressure more than it would if the wood were fresh. Most forms of decay reduce the wood density to the point where the tool can easily be pushed in. Using an awl allows the tester to determine the depth of the damage, and is the first step from simple examination to probing.

Structural investigation does not stop with identifying the members in the area of interest. Any changes in load intensity or path caused by alterations are of concern, and may mean investigating the columns or transfer girders several floors below the area where an interior alteration is planned.

While on site, the investigator may approach anyone who is familiar with the history of the building for a brief interview. Building managers or superintendents often are knowledgeable about the basic building construction and previous alterations. While memory and opinions cannot be used as the basis for design, they can provide leads toward completing the preliminary investigation.

Probing

A wide range of activities called probing all are meant to expose structural members for observation of their condition. The success of probing depends on the experience of the designer in locating the probes so that they fairly represent the structure and reviewing the conditions found. Probing is the simplest form of destructive testing and provides only visual information. The least destructive probe is the removal of finished surfaces in a small area to expose one condition—for example, cutting a hole in a dropped gypsum-board ceiling to expose a beam-to-column connection not entirely detailed on existing drawings. Probing can be extended to making a series of small openings—for example, to measure several column sizes—and finally to uncovering large areas, such as removal of an entire ceiling to expose the condition of wood floor joists above (figures 5-1 and 5-2).

Probing through finishes is as safe as any construction operation can be, so long as ordinary safety precautions are observed for such dangers as live electrical lines hidden within walls. Often, simply exposing the surface of the hidden structure provides inadequate information, although it may provide such basic data as concrete column sizes or filler beam spacing. The next step is the removal of materials that are not stressed or are lightly stressed, but are part of the basic building structure, such as masonry fireproofing around a steel column, concrete encasement on a steel beam, the bottom rebar cover in a concrete slab, or

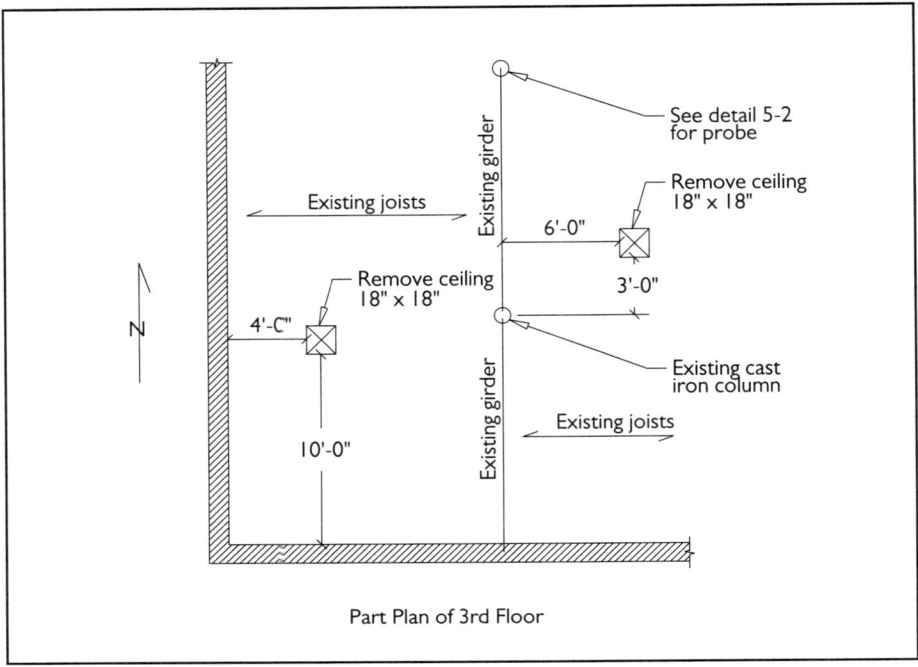

5-1. Typical probing diagram

a few bricks in a bearing wall. This type of probe is useful for obtaining access to interior structure, such as rebar, for measurement.

The line between easily removable structure and vital structure is not always clear during the probing process. Unusual rebar configurations in flat-slab buildings with irregular layouts can result in bars ending in unexpected locations. If the bottom cover is removed to expose the bars to allow determination of the slab capacity, the bars' tensile capacity may be reduced accidentally. A floor slab protected by cement finish on top and a plaster ceiling below may turn out to be a flat tile arch rather than the expected concrete, and the probe that exposes this fact can destroy the arch bearing at one end. Finally, even the safest probe can be disastrous if the original structure was built incorrectly. A preliminary determination of the type of structure to be removed should be made before probing begins to limit accidental damage.

The potential for damage to the structure under examination is the dominant reason for the engineer to be present during probing. The probes should be

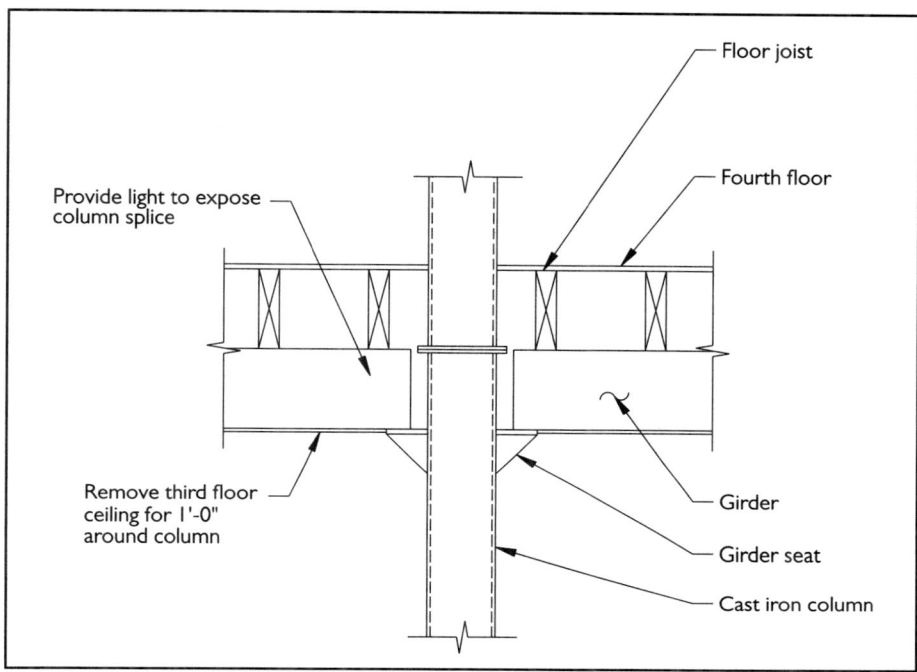

5-2. Probing section

carried out in a careful and deliberate manner, and the condition of the structure checked at all times, to ensure that the process of examining the structure does not lead to any failure. An improperly placed probe can destroy a steel connection or the continuity of a concrete joint. The logic of locating probes is exactly the same as the logic of designing new structure; the critical locations are the same and familiar to any designer.

The most potentially informative probe commonly performed is the removal of small pieces of the actual structure for observation and testing. This form of probing is necessary when the actual materials used must be defined. A small piece of a wood joist can be removed to determine the wood species and moisture content, and therefore its allowable flexural and shear stresses. A small piece of old steel or wrought iron can be tested for chemical composition, including impurities such as sulfur or silicon that would interfere with welding, and for mechanical properties such as yield and ultimate stress. Cores can be drilled from existing concrete and tested for their ultimate compressive stress in much the same manner as the testing of cylinders created during a concrete pour. Chemical tests can also be performed for chloride ion content and electrolytic potential.

The engineer of record has little to do with the tests beyond ordering them performed, and locating the material to be removed for testing so as not to interfere with the stability and safety of the building. A lab employed by the owner or general contractor performs the actual testing. The difficulty is in finding accessible locations of low stress, where the removal of material is possible. The most common location of coupon removal from steel beams is the lower flange at a simple connection; for concrete floor slabs, cores are usually taken near a span end. Removal of samples from all members is not equally safe. The investigation should not interfere with heavily loaded columns for the sake of samples when other members of the same age are available. Similarly, the samples should come from filler beams, not girders, from the middle-middle strip of flat-plate floors, and from joists and not their supporting beams.

Probing that includes removal of actual pieces of structure can be considered the least disruptive form of destructive testing. The damage caused by most probes can be easily repaired, or at least the finishes patched to prevent danger to the building occupants. Full-scale destructive testing may leave nothing worth saving. Often, the probe patches can be done cheaply, in all senses of the word, since the area in question will be thoroughly ravaged by construction shortly afterward. Even when temporary architectural repairs are required, as in interior renovations of occupied space, the repairs need not comply with ordinary standards of care, so long as they are not actively unsafe.

The most disruptive common type of probing might best be described as selective demolition probing. Material that was scheduled for demolition is removed in the presence of the engineer responsible for the design of new structure, who can use the opportunity to investigate the existing conditions, and if necessary shore and stabilize the existing structure. This technique is a critical tool in cases where the known information about the building is insufficient to allow for the production of detailed demolition instructions.

Progress in selective demolition is extremely slow when the work must be halted regularly to allow for an engineer's inspections and the insertion of shoring. The extra cost associated with the delay is justified when the extent of damage or the capacity of framing are unknown. Ordinary investigation, including probing, can usually determine enough information to obviate the need for this technique, leaving its use to the less typical parts of buildings. Areas where the manner of construction is not readily visible, and may differ substantially from the surroundings, include mechanical and elevator shafts, stairwells, alterations such as the filling in of an internal court, rooftop additions, and filled-in openings of any type in floors, walls, or roofs. In these settings, frame buildings may contain bearing walls; bearing-wall buildings, posts; concrete buildings, steel beams; fireproof buildings, wood-joist floors. Once the construction type is identified, the details that are to be expected can be identified, although nothing is sure until actually seen.

The logic of selective demolition probing is the same as any other probing or demolition work. The object is to avoid undermining any remaining structure as each piece of the building is removed, even if those pieces are as small as individual bricks. When, for example, a steel beam is found supporting a brick wall, it is not always clear whether the beam is wall-bearing or frames into a post. The portion of the wall that might be supporting the beam must remain undisturbed until the end condition is determined. This kind of uncertainty is overcome piecemeal, by removing material known to be unloaded, and re-observing the structure with the greater clarity now possible.

Destructive Testing

Two types of structural testing are properly described as destructive testing. The first is testing to failure, to find the ultimate strength of the material or assembly tested. The second is testing to a specified stress or load level, regardless of the consequences. The first type, even if performed in situ, allows for preparation for failure and replacement. The second is often more ambiguous.

The sample tests used in probing are destructive on a small scale. The cores removed from existing concrete are usually crushed to determine the ultimate strength of the concrete. Concrete samples are also tested for porosity and for destructive constituents such as chloride ions. In any case, there is nothing left of the core after the tests are complete. Steel coupons can be tested to failure to determine the ultimate yield strength of the material, sliced apart for microscopic structure examination, or chemically tested for the percentage of carbon and trace elements. The structure as a whole is not affected, and since the material removed is selected for its unimportance, this type of testing is considered a part of probing.

Destructive testing of wood structures is difficult if no members can be sacrificed entirely. Unlike steel or concrete construction, a wood floor literally may contain no areas that are understressed enough to permit their removal. This anomaly is due to the status of wood as the only nonisotropic structural material. A typical wood beam has to be designed not only for the bending stress in the outermost flexural fibers, but also for horizontal shear stress at the supports, because the allowable stress value parallel to the grain is so much lower than the value perpendicular to the grain. By orienting wood beams with the grain parallel to the beam axis, we strengthen them in bending, but weaken them at their point of highest shear stress. A coupon cannot be safely taken from the end, as with a steel beam. While the wood code allows for notching and round holes in beams, it sets very specific requirements as to size and placement. These requirements must be followed as closely during investigation as in new construction. Often, a small piece of joist will be found loose from the natural checking of the wood. Since a 3- by 1-inch (75 by 25 mm) piece is generally sufficient, these naturally occurring fragments can be used as coupons. Actual stress testing generally requires a full joist.

The best solution to the problem of finding adequate pieces of wood to test is to sacrifice an entire member. If planned alterations entail removing joists or pieces of joists—for example, the cutting of a stair opening that requires the shortening of a half-dozen joists—those pieces are adequate for testing. Their removal will have to be performed out of sequence—that is, long before they would be removed in the normal course of construction—in order that the information may be available for design. To actually test the bending or shear stress that a piece can withstand requires several large samples because of the variable nature of the material. A better solution is to send pieces to a lab that specializes in wood analysis, such as the National Forest Products Association (NFPA) lab, which is largely responsible for the testing that has gone into the creation of the National Design Specification (NFPA NDS 1991). The lab can identify the wood species and thus provide indirectly the design information required.

Beyond the destructive testing of materials and individual members is the full-scale load testing of floor and frame assemblies, which involves loading the entire floor area far beyond the load expected in normal service. For example, the BOCA code allows for testing of preexisting assemblies provided that the loads used in testing are 200 percent of the superimposed dead load and the code-mandated live load. This means the floor will be exposed to stress levels that reduce the theoretical safety factor to approximately one. Such extreme testing is necessary to justify the acceptance of unknown conditions, but can easily lead to failure of structures not capable of accepting such overloads. Part of arranging such tests is a prior analysis of the effect of collapse on adjacent structure: if the failure of the tested element or assembly can cause failure of other structure—for example, a floor slab falling onto and overloading a floor slab below—then the other structure must be protected or shored to prevent its failure, or the test redesigned.

In a controlled full-scale test, the structure must be examined afterward to determine whether damage has taken place that calls into question the soundness of the structure both for the sake of the test and, even if the test is considered successful, for the future use of the structure after its intentional overload. The tested material is often monitored with strain gauges to develop a detailed picture of the structure's performance.

Nondestructive Testing

While nondestructive testing might seem logically to follow field investigation as a nonintrusive research technique, its expense makes it the least common research method. The concept of testing without endangering the tested material is bound up with a high-technology outlook. The easiest benchmark to find in any sort of testing is complete failure of the test sample. That is why the earliest organized research into material properties was based on the ultimate strength of the material. Even when people recognized that a beam or column became useless long before ultimate failure, it took time before allowable loads and stresses based on working stresses were able to displace those based on ultimate failure. Ironically, the use of load and resistance factor design in concrete design, and its introduction into steel and wood design, is a return to allowable stresses based on ultimate failure. Nondestructive testing is a step in the opposite direction, finding, if only indirectly, the allowable stresses without any possibility of failure.

Nondestructive testing of buildings often requires advanced equipment to be effective. Even the measurement of building movement is more dependable when performed with advanced (although not necessarily high-tech) surveying equipment than with steel tapes. True surveyors' equipment is rarely needed within a building, since a difference of a few inches per hundred feet should not affect a structural analysis, but the high-tech approach can eliminate probing.

Geometric information generally sought after in probing, such as rebar size and spacing, concrete voids structural steel location, or steel beam depth, does not require physical sighting to be useful. Condition assessment, such as the thickness of rust on a steel spandrel beam, may not require visual observation to be useful, while some of the more complicated geometric information, such as bracket configuration, may be beyond the capacity of affordable technology.

Gross geometric data can be collected by physical means. An ad hoc, low-technology test for steel beams that are exposed and may be rusted is to tap them with a steel hammer or length of pipe. Solid steel rings a high note, while delaminated rust sounds dead. Similarly, good wood sounds out when struck sharply with a hammer or other implement, while wood that has lost material to insect or fungal attack sounds dead.

The more advanced methods, such as the various forms of X-ray and ultrasonic equipment, can elicit more complicated information than the simple presence of steel. The condition of existing structure, including the presence of delaminated rust, voids from freezing during curing in concrete, and voids from weathering in masonry piers, can be found. Unfortunately, these techniques require more time and expense than can ordinarily be expended on a renovation project. Their only extensive use to date has been in the preservation and restoration of monuments, where saving the original material has overridden other considerations.

A more common form of nondestructive testing is the removal of nonstructural earth to observe foundation conditions. The removals can be limited to small holes in test boring, or be larger and easier through hand-digging of test pits. These methods can provide extensive subsurface data that may not have been available to the original designers of a building or that may have changed since the building was erected. Because the material being removed is not stressed, this can be considered nondestructive investigation. Because the investigation is more than a simple examination for surface conditions, but discovers the presence of ground water and the type of bearing material, it should be considered testing, rather than observation.

Case Study 5-1: Misleading Documentation

Collections of drawings saved by building owners are rarely organized. The research described here took place during a minor alteration in a high-rise apartment house. The building was built with a chute down to a garbage incinerator.

Case Study 5-1: Misleading Documentation

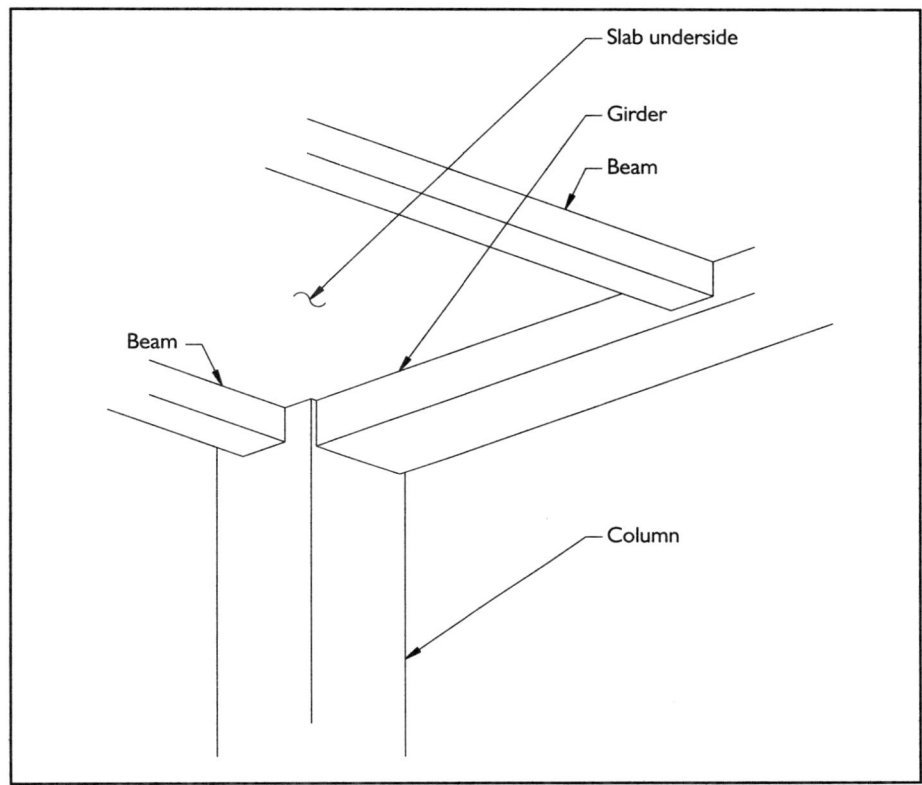

5-1-1. Diagram of compactor-shaft visible conditions

The incinerator was to be replaced with a compactor, which was somewhat larger than the furnace to be removed. Two masonry walls near the base of the shaft had to be removed, but it was not clear if the shaft walls were bearing on these walls, or if there were supports at the base of the shaft (figure 5-1-1).

During preparation for the work, the manager's storage room was searched for drawings. The first roll of drawings examined proved to be a complete structural set, signed and sealed by the design engineer in 1959, and filed with the city Building Department. The drawings showed a concrete frame building, which did not entirely match the site conditions observed (figure 5-1-2). The beams, girders, and columns seen in the basement during an initial walk-through were apparently concrete, but with proportions not commonly used for concrete. The filler beams, for example, were only 8 inches (200 mm) wide.

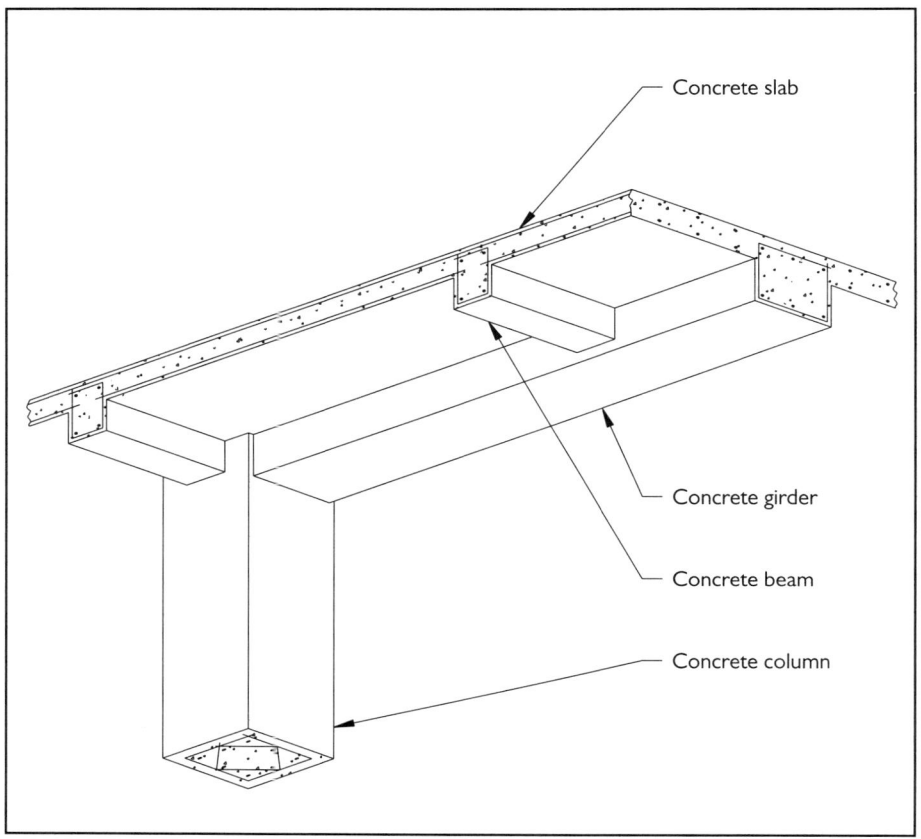

5-1-2. Diagram of possible concrete framing

After further examination of numerous drawings and discussion with the owner, it became clear that the building had been redesigned before construction. A complete set of structural drawings dated 1962 was found, showing a steel frame encased in concrete, with a note in the title box: "These drawings supersede the drawings filed [in 1959]." The proportions of the members previously noted were easy to understand as the width of steel members plus 2 inches (50 mm) cover on each side (figure 5-1-3). While the nature of the frame could have been determined through probing, there was a limited budget for such a small project.

Unfortunately, establishing that the building was a steel frame did not answer the original question concerning the support of the shaft above the walls

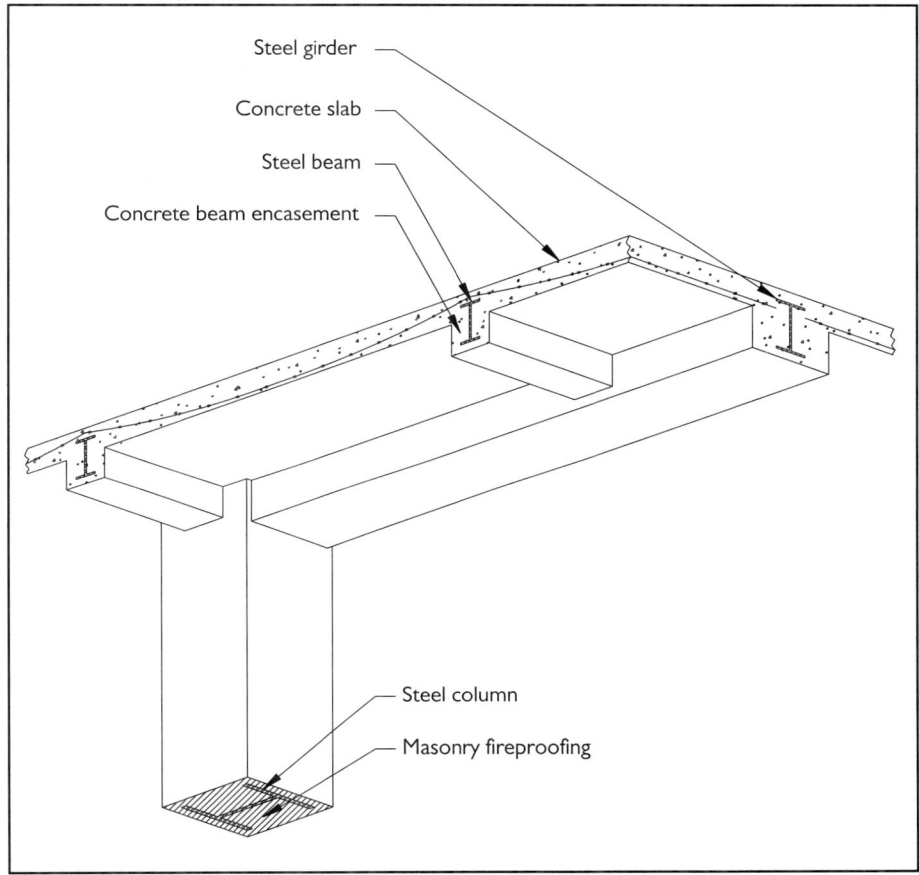

5-1-3. Diagram of possible steel encased in concrete

to be demolished. It was not possible to probe within the shaft because it measured only 2 by 2 feet (610 by 610 mm) in plan, not leaving enough room for a laborer to work. Demolition proceeded, with the engineer present to investigate while work was under way. As brick was removed from the top of the offset walls near the shaft, more of the bottom of the shaft walls was exposed to view. After roughly two hours of demolition and investigation, secondary steel beams supporting the shaft became visible. After two more cycles of demolition and investigation, connections between the secondary framing and the main building beams were exposed to view, meaning that the demolition could proceed as originally planned.

Case Study 5-2: Unsafe Existing Construction

The distinction between removable finish and vital structure is not always clear, even during examination. In this case, probes meant to expose floor structure could have caused a collapse if they had been cut. A tenant stair had been added between the first and second floors in a masonry bearing-wall building (figure 5-2-1). The existing wood floor joists had been cut and a new wood header installed. Gage-steel joist hangers were used to fasten the existing joists to the new header, but had never been nailed to the header, with the result that the joist ends were resting on the ceiling below. The ceiling supports had been acting as de facto structure, carrying joist reactions to the header (figure 5-2-2).

While extreme, this case shows why an engineer should be present during probing. It is important that probes be cut carefully, and the condition of the structure monitored, to ensure that the process of examination does not cause failure. An improperly placed probe can destroy a connection or the continuity of a beam. The logic of locating probes is the same as that of design; the critical locations are identical and familiar to any designer.

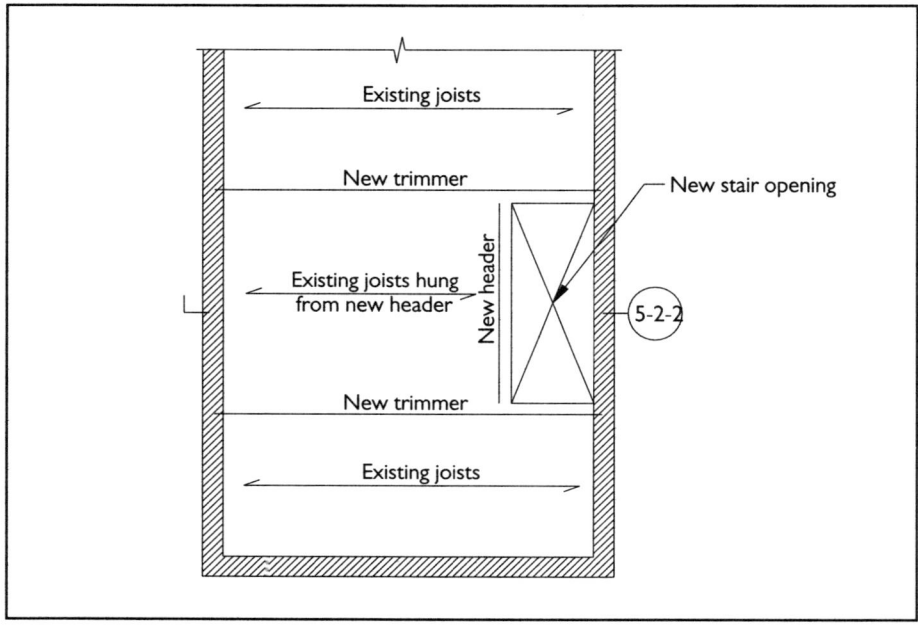

5-2-1. Plan showing joist hanger locations

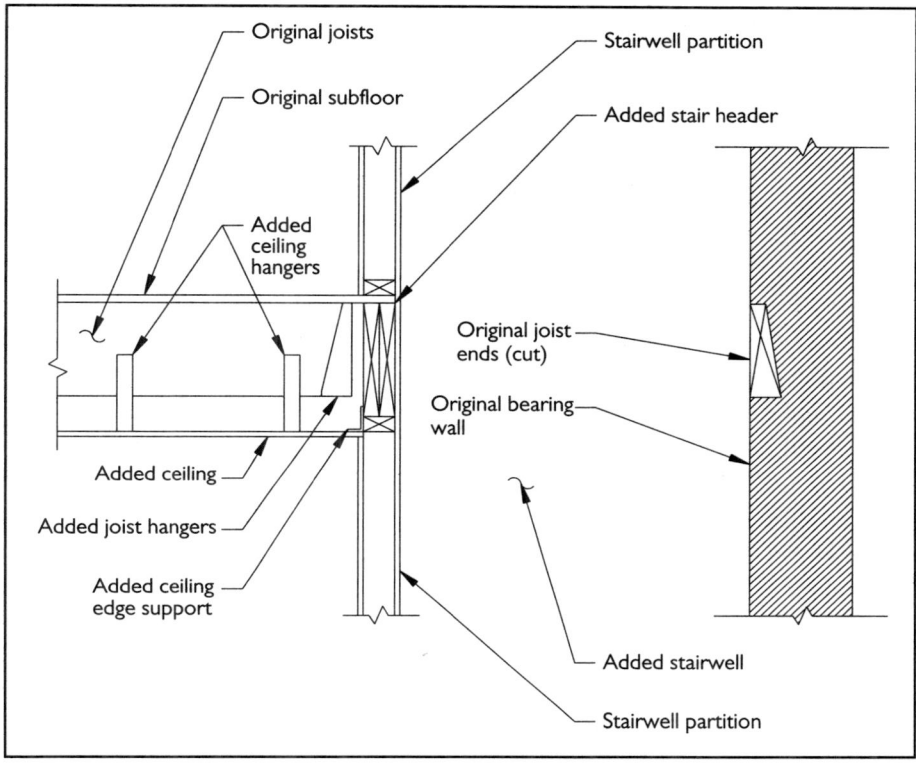

5-2-2. Detail of unattached joist hangers

Case Study 5-3: Full-scale Load Testing

Analysis may not be possible with obsolete construction. If a portion of a building has a history of successful use, logic says that it is capable of sustaining some load, but modern knowledge of structural design may suggest that the capacity is not what was intended by the original designers. This conflict usually arises during alteration or changes in use, when the load capacity of, for example, a floor slab may be in question. The most straightforward method of resolving the conflict is full-scale load testing.

The testing in this case involves loading a large floor area in a firehouse in excess of the loads expected in normal service. In this example, the local building code provisions for testing of preexisting assemblies were followed, including, in part, loads used in testing equal to 150 percent of the true dead load and 180 percent of the code-mandated live load.

A section of concrete slab designed and built as the apparatus floor of a firehouse in 1898 was tested for capacity in 1991. The details of the original construction were clearly shown on the original drawings, and were typical for concrete of the late nineteenth century. By modern standards, the embedment lengths of the reinforcing bars were too short, the bars themselves not properly deformed, and the concrete full of small voids. These flaws all tend to reduce the capacity of the bars to develop their tension, as is required for reinforced concrete design to work. During the renovation and upgrade of the firehouse to ensure that it would be safe for modern, heavier firetrucks, the floor was tested. A section of the floor was rebuilt using the same methods planned for the entire floor, and then loaded with concrete weights to the overloads described above. The deflection of the floor was measured during the test and compared to the deflection predicted by modern concrete design.

Chapter 6

Structural Steel Buildings

Alterations using new steel beams and columns and those performed in buildings with existing steel framing are generally agreed to be the easiest to design and construct. The use of welding for new connections and flame-cutting of existing members allow framing configurations to be changed with little more effort than that required for new construction. This is in sharp contrast to the difficulty of creating continuity in renovations of concrete structures and the difficulty in creating any form of new connection other than simple bearing in wood structures. The inherent properties of steel, including its high strength-to-weight ratio, ease of connection in tension as well as compression, and ductility, allow for great flexibility in the layout of framing.

Methods of Connection

There are some practical restrictions on welding new to existing steel. The most obvious is the suitability of the existing base metal. Older steels may contain unacceptably high levels of sulfur, silicon, or carbon, each of which interferes with the fusion of the metal. Even in cases where the average composition of the steel meets acceptable standards, the amount of variation in chemical composition was greater in the past than is now acceptable. A general rule of thumb regarding weldability is that steel that conforms to the ASTM A9 and A7 standards, even in their earliest forms, is almost certainly weldable, while steel produced earlier, before 1900, may not be. The earlier the date, the less likely the steel can be safely welded. If the steel is known to conform to a usable ASTM standard, coupon testing is not necessarily required. If the building is of an age where the steel should be acceptable but may not be, and it is unknown—for example, dating from the 1910s—some coupon testing is called for. If the building was built before 1900, extensive testing is called for, since the quality of the steel may vary widely. In one case known to the authors, a set of box columns erected in the 1880s were built up of channels and plates. The channel steel almost matched A7 steel in chemical composition, but the plate steel was noticeably weaker, with a carbon content closer to wrought iron.

Any time that welding to loaded, existing members is considered, the state of stress in the existing metal must be considered. At the time of welding, the steel is fluid and obviously incapable of resisting any load. To use a common example detailed in Case Study 6-1, when a WT section is welded to the bottom of an existing beam to act as a new bottom flange, the connection is typically a weld placed where each side of the T web meets the existing beam bottom-flange bottom surface. This weld temporarily reduces the ability of the bottom flange to carry load by removing the possibility for stress to travel between the web and the bottom flange. If the beam is loaded, it may collapse from this temporary incapacity. Similar conditions exist when welding reinforcing plates to a column. In either case, the member should be shored for the full load present at the time, either the dead load and construction live load if the building is unoccupied during renovation or full design load if the building is occupied. If shoring is not possible—for example, when the alterations are being made on a single floor of a building by one tenant and shoring would interfere with other tenants' spaces—welding must be scheduled to maintain the integrity of the members in question. This usually means alternating placement of short lengths of weld in different locations to preserve the capacity of the member. If only a few inches of weld are placed at one time, the strength of the beam is not significantly affected, but waiting for welds to cool can increase the cost of a weld by several hundred percent.

In some cases it may appear desirable to bolt new steel members to existing ones. There are several reasons why it is not advisable to simply burn a hole in the old piece to serve as a bolt hole. Holes may be drilled under any conditions, provided that quality-control procedures can ensure holes that meet the geometric standards required for bolting. Burned holes, by contrast, will have irregularities that serve as stress concentrators, reducing the allowable shear and bearing stresses that can be safely imposed. The metal at the edges of the hole will have been exposed to extreme heat, changing the chemical substructure of the metal to the point of decreasing its strength and toughness. Finally, burning is a less controlled process than either drilling or the bolting that will follow. However, drilling requires more access than burning, and may not be feasible with hand-held drills and thick elements of existing members. In tight quarters, burning may be the only practical method. The safest way of burning holes to avoid the problems noted above is to burn a hole smaller than the hole desired, and ream out the rough opening. The reaming operation removes the metal damaged by the heat of burning. With new or reused holes, a perfect fit is not required if slip-critical connections with high-strength bolts are used. To create the conditions required for slip-critical connections by the governing specifications, the existing paint may have to be removed below the bolt head, nut, or washers.

Existing rivet holes have clean edges, since they were made in the same manner as modern bolt holes: drilling or punching and reaming. High-strength bolts can carry greater loads in tension than rivets of equal size, and under certain conditions, greater loads in shear as well. Connection capacities therefore can be upgraded by simply replacing rivets with high-strength bolts. If existing holes are present in the correct locations, it is a fairly simple matter to remove rivets by chiseling off a head and knocking or burning out the shaft remnant. In old designs, as in current bolted details, individual connection pieces are almost never held in place by only one connector. While the individual conditions must be studied, removal and replacement of rivets one or two at a time is usually safe. Local unbraced lengths for members or elements in compression must also be studied.

Because of the difficulty of driving large rivets in the field, riveted designs tended to use more and smaller connectors than bolted designs. If rivet holes are to be reused, it is unlikely that many holes will be larger than $7/8$ inch (22 mm) in diameter, limiting new bolts to $3/4$ inch (19 mm) diameter. Common high-strength bolts, ASTM A325, are comparable in strength to the old rivet standards; heat-treated high-strength bolts, ASTM A490, are nearly twice as strong. If the change in connections does not indicate drastic changes in framing layout, it is not likely that the restriction on bolt size will interfere with design. If rivet holes are being reused for major alterations, they can be enlarged in the same manner described above for the creation of new holes.

Column Reinforcement

There are two methods of strengthening steel columns without changing the framing configuration. The actual compressive stress can be reduced by adding area to the column, or the allowable compressive stress can be increased by making the column less slender. The design of columns in any material is largely governed by buckling concerns, but because of the high strength of steel for a given weight, steel columns are often far more slender than concrete or wood columns. The area of the column can be increased simply by fastening new material to the existing column shaft, although the amount of load actually transferred to the new steel depends strongly on the presence of load during the fastening operation. The slenderness can be reduced by increasing the radius of gyration relative to the column length. The first method is, in theory, linear: doubling the area will halve the stress. The second method is much more complicated to design, but easier to build. If the existing column is relatively slender, a small increase in radius of gyration or a small reduction in length may provide a large percentage change in allowable stress. If the existing column is stocky, its allowable stress may be nearly equal to the maximum value. If, as is most common, the column is of moderate slenderness, the work involved to reduce KL/r is similar to that involved in increasing the area. The choice between the two methods often turns on the difference between the theory and the reality.

There is no accepted method of equalizing the stress between the material of an existing loaded column and reinforcement applied to it other than the onerous process of removing the load from the column through shoring and jacking. For this reason, as much live load as possible should be removed from a column before connecting the reinforcement. On the other hand, if the intent of reinforcing is to increase the radius of gyration, the presence of load in the column is far less serious. Shoring and jacking a column is so time-consuming and difficult when compared to the straightforward steel work that adding area is often eliminated as a possibility.

A totally different approach to column reinforcement, which combines some of the theories of adding area and increasing the stockiness of the column, is to encase the steel in a concrete shell. The concrete can be used in two different ways. The first is to increase the steel strength through composite action with the steel column and through bracing the steel column, with the concrete sharing loads with the steel. The second is straightforward: the concrete shell is specifically reinforced in the same manner as a concrete column, and provided with dedicated connections to some portion of the floor structure, carrying only the loads specifically designated for it. If the existing footing is capable of sustaining the increased load, the concrete can simply end in bearing on the footing top surface. This type of solution is attractive when space is limited, since the concrete shell can occupy the same location that fireproofing would, and serve as fireproofing.

The existing steel and the concrete encasement can also be analyzed as a unified column. Without jacking, true composite action cannot be achieved for the same reason that steel reinforcing is incapable of carrying load that exists during the reinforcing. Only if the existing load can be entirely removed from the column can the column be analyzed as a "new" composite column. In all other cases, if the concrete is reinforced with ties and provided with some form of shear connection to the steel shaft, the effect of the encasement is to carry a portion of the live load applied after hardening. The amount of load carried will be in proportion to the ratio of dead load and construction live load to loads incurred later. The other effect of the encasement, regardless of whether composite action is relied upon, is the increase in the steel column strength caused by the concrete's restraint of the steel web and flanges against local buckling.

One drawback in column encasement is that the beam-to-column connections are buried. Under most circumstances this is a nuisance, but not necessarily detrimental. The existing connections should be reviewed for adequacy before the encasement is put in place. Assuming that they are found to be adequate, the difficulty in future access created by the concrete is not a problem except during major renovations, which require their own analysis. Depending on the dimensions of the encasement, the beam-connection type, and the relative flexibility of the beam, the concrete surrounding the beam may be prone to crushing as the beam flexes under load. It is not possible to leave a gap around each beam if the concrete is meant to be carrying load; if the encasement is present as fire protection and to reduce local buckling, then gaps can be provided by packing the beam in Styrofoam before the concrete is poured. The resulting holes must be fireproofed.

Beam Reinforcement

Almost all forms of steel-framed construction leave the beam bottom flanges exposed or covered only by fireproofing materials (figure 6-1). Most forms of beam reinforcement take advantage of this fact by reinforcing the beam from below. Physically, this is the path of easiest access, but since the work disrupts

80 STRUCTURAL STEEL BUILDINGS

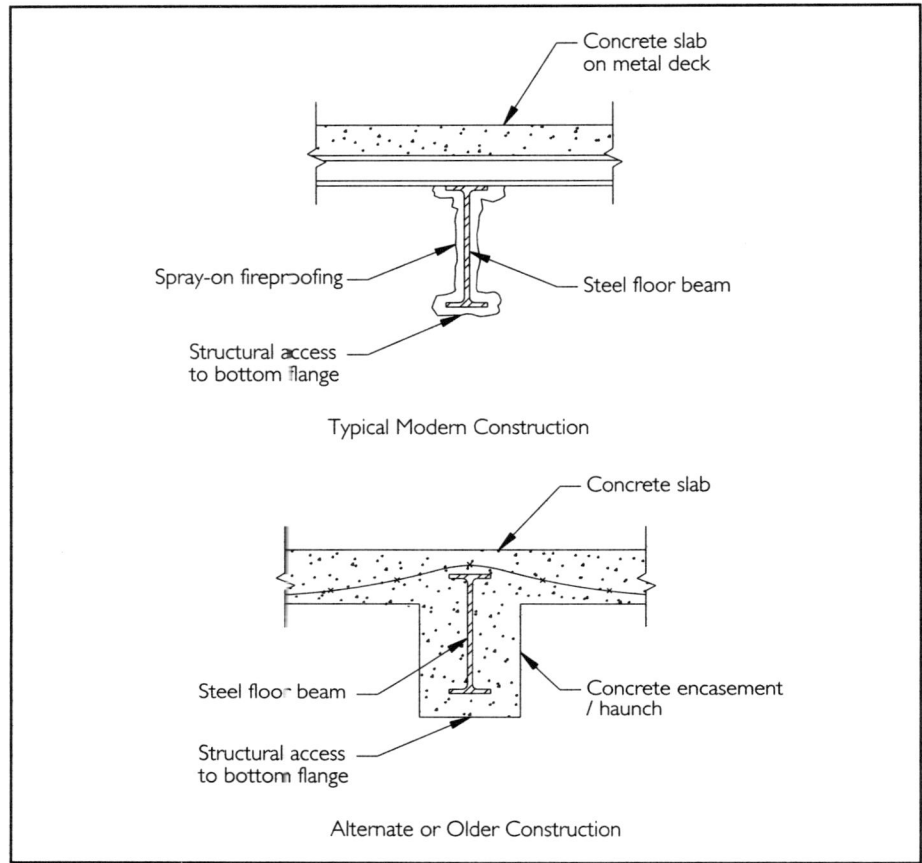

6-1. Section showing access from below to steel beams

the floor below, this solution may not be practical in a multitenant building. In circumstances where access from below is not allowed, far more work may be required to reinforce a beam. Access from above requires, at least, removal of several inches of fill material without damaging the adjacent supporting structure. If there are top rebars for concrete slabs, access from above requires either the removal and replacement of these bars or the removal of sections of the bars and splicing in replacement sections.

All members, regardless of their loading, have internal stresses. Creation of steel sections by hot-rolling leaves fairly high internal stresses, locked in as the

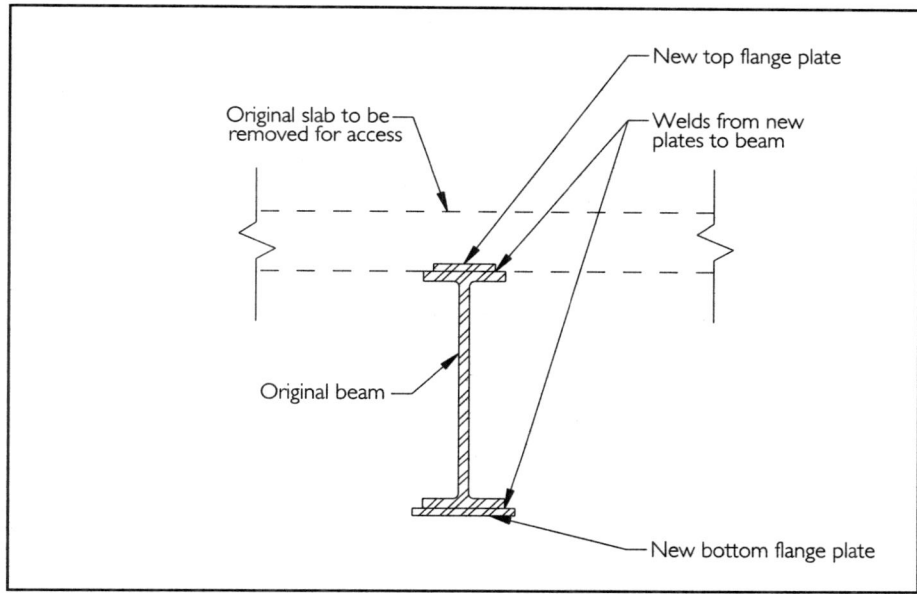

6-2. Section showing beam reinforced top and bottom

sections cool. Residual stresses are ignored during design calculations, because their effects cancel out, although they affect code provisions based on experimentation, such as column load formulas. The process of welding to a rolled section, especially long linear welds such as those used for section reinforcing, creates new residual stresses as the welds cool.

Any section installed in a building will carry some load, if only its weight, creating additional internal stresses. Except in extreme renovations where the building is stripped down to its skeleton, the dead load during renovation is fairly close to the final dead load. Since dead load is ordinarily between 30 and 50 percent of the total load, internal stresses from loading, unlike residual stresses, cannot be ignored.

A design that analyzes a reinforced section by taking the total loads over the combined sections is an oversimplification. The original beam or column, before welding, has internal stresses from load, but the reinforcing material does not. Under the proper circumstances, some or all of the stress in the original section may be transferred to the new material. When new material is located at the points of highest stress, typically the extreme top and bottom flanges of a beam, stresses higher than the ordinary maximums may be allowed in the older material. So long as the stresses in the new, most highly stressed material remain below the maximums, there is no danger to the stability of the beam from higher stress in the older steel. Even the condition of the old flanges reaching the yield stress is not, by itself, dangerous. The engineer can control the degree to which existing load is transferred by specifying jacking, loading sequences, and weld sizes and sequencing.

The simplest method of reinforcing a beam is when the floor material is entirely removed, or can be removed to a degree that allows the symmetrical reinforcement of both top and bottom flanges (figure 6-2). In addition to simplifying design, the resulting configuration is the most efficient in its use of the steel. Assuming that the new top flange will be braced by the new floor slab, the analysis of the steel can proceed in the manner described in general terms above. If the new flange is braced, buckling of the old top flange is not considered. In the case where the reinforcement consists of plates, the reinforcement is usually considered as a thicker flange, not as two distinct ones.

If the existing floor system consists of a set of steel beams supporting a concrete floor, there may be easier ways of reinforcing the beams than adding plates or tees. New steel beams are often designed using concrete floor slabs as composite top flanges. An existing floor slab can be made to act compositely with existing beams through new connections.

Connection Reinforcement

The types of load increases described in the beam reinforcing case studies do not always require connection reinforcement. Connections for steel beams often have been built by simply providing the maximum number of rivets or bolts that fit, at ordinary spacing, in the beam web. This form of empiric design is often faster and easier for the steel fabricator and erector than actually designing each connection separately. The result is a large number of connections that are oversized for their original load, and thus have reserve capacity for new loads.

Existing connections may need to be reinforced by themselves or as part of an overall upgrade of the steel structure. Given the usual condition that there is reserve strength in the beams that allows an increase in load without reinforcement, it is possible for the existing connections to become the bottleneck in strength.

The use of welding allows for the easy addition of connection pieces and better attachment of existing pieces. Assuming that the existing steel has been tested for weldability, few methods of increasing load capacity are simpler than welding existing clip angles to the main members, or adding a stiffener plate and extra welds to increase the capacity of a seated connection.

Beams in small buildings with short spans and lightly loaded beams in any building are often connected in ways that are not easily upgraded. Single clip angles, unstiffened seat angles, and cantilevered four-angle connections are details that are inherently more flexible than ordinary double-angle and shear-plate connections. Changes that increase the loads on floor beams increase the connection reactions at the same time as they increase the moments in the beams. All of the beam reinforcing details discussed in this chapter increase the strength and stiffness of the beams, but do not increase the strength of the connections at all. Since the smaller type connections are more difficult to upgrade than ordinary connections, they may need to be replaced.

Case Study 6-1: Steel Beam Reinforcement Using Flange Addition

Increasing the load-carrying capacity of existing beams that will be overstressed by changes in the building geometry or changes in the occupancy loading is very common. In this example, a space that has been part of a large office is being converted to a storage area; the individual office-defining partitions are being removed and high filing cabinets are being added. More extreme load changes are possible, including the installation of compact file storage systems (see Case Study 6-2).

Specifically, a filler beam supporting an area of floor 20 feet (6100 mm) long and 7 feet (2130 mm) wide was originally designed for the minimum office live load of 50 psf (1.1 Pa), an allowance of 20 psf (0.4 Pa) for partitions, and the 78 psf (1.6 Pa) dead load of permanent construction (figure 6-1-1). The change in use causes the partition load to disappear and the live load to increase to 150 psf (3.2 Pa). All forces and stress associated with this beam increase 35 percent from the change.

In almost all forms of steel construction, there is access to the bottom flanges of the existing beams for the renovating engineer. In modern concrete-slab-on-metal-deck construction and tile arch construction the beam bottoms are bare except for fireproofing. In board-formed concrete slabs, the beams are

84 STRUCTURAL STEEL BUILDINGS

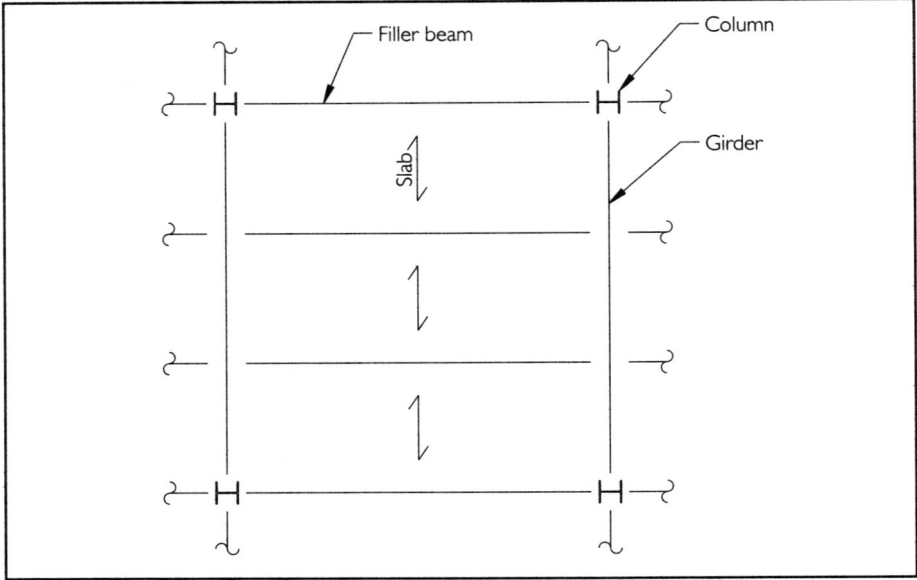

6-1-1. Plan at reinforced beam

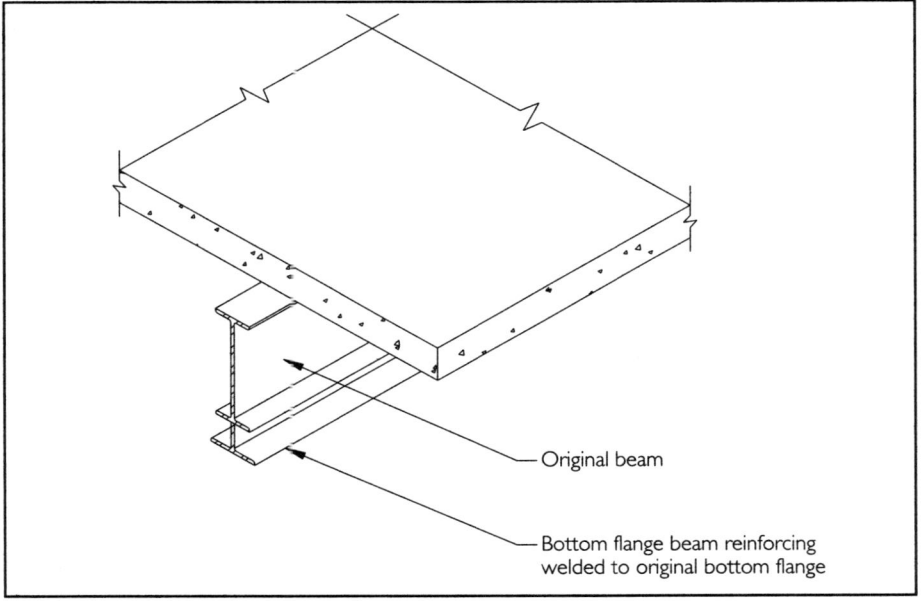

6-1-2. Steel beam reinforced with T

typically encased in concrete, but in most of such construction, the encasement is simply fireproofing that can be removed. Once the material covering the bottom flanges is proven nonstructural, it can be removed for access. In contrast, the top flanges of the floor beams are ordinarily inaccessible unless a section of floor is demolished. For this reason, the most popular method of reinforcing steel beams is to weld plates or inverted T shapes to the bottom flanges (figure 6-1-2). This is less efficient than the symmetrical welding of identical shapes to both the top and bottom flanges, but is far easier to construct.

When a beam is reinforced by the addition of material intended to act as a new or enlarged flange, the transfer of stress from the existing beam to the new material must be addressed. Reinforcing should take place under circumstances of reduced load. Shoring may be necessary to prevent failure during the alteration, as the weld heat reduces the steel strength locally, but shoring will not remove the construction load stress. Typical shoring prevents downward motion of the beam, but does not remove stress caused by the existing load. In order to get a beam to an unstressed state, the shoring would have to jack the beam upward, a more difficult task than simple load support. The result is that the existing beam usually contains some flexural stress not present in the new steel. Conservative analysis says that load equalization between the existing and new structure cannot be assumed because it will not occur in a controlled fashion. This leads either to jacking the existing beam before reinforcing to remove dead load stresses from the metal (the example shown in this case study) or to a two-stage analysis where the original section (the unreinforced beam) carries the dead load and the new section (the reinforced beam) carries the live load. The other possibility in steel design is to take advantage of the clear-cut yield point in steel, which allows relatively large deformations without damage to the metal. In a design of this type, the reinforced beam is assumed to carry all of the loads, and any overstress in the existing bottom flange is neglected so long as the existing steel stress stays below the allowable ultimate stress.

There are several methods of analyzing such a beam when it is loaded beyond the capacity of the original beam. The top (compression) flange of the beam is free from local buckling effects, and so may be loaded to the same stress as a tension flange. When new reinforcing is welded to the bottom flange, it is basically unstressed while the existing beam has some flexural stress. If the existing beam is old enough, it was designed with a lower allowable stress than is now used. The new steel bottom flange is farther from the neutral axis than the old steel, and the new, asymmetric section will have a neutral axis closer to the bottom than to the top, so its stress will rise much more rapidly as the load increases. A design that brings the new bottom flange up to the maximum stress allowed by the current codes often results in the old beam bottom flange being technically overstressed. As long as the new bottom flange steel is not overstressed and the original steel is not stressed past its ultimate stress, this situation is not dangerous. Overstress is defined as the bending tension or compression exceeding a certain percentage of the yield stress or ultimate stress; since the original bottom flange is not the primary load-carrying element after the addition of the tee, stresses between the code-defined maximum stress and the actual maximum are allowable.

Adding a WT 3 or 4 inches (75 or 100 mm) deep to the bottom of the existing 12- or 14-inch (305 or 355 mm) beam can easily obtain the desired increase in both section modulus and moment of inertia, that is, both strength and stiffness.

Case Study 6-2: Steel Beam Reinforcement Using Composite Action

The increase in beam strength from adding plates and Ts may not be sufficient. The use of T sections for beam reinforcing can be limited by headroom concerns in the space below, and the section modulus increase obtainable through bottom-only reinforcing may not be adequate for the conditions. In this example, a space in a large office is being converted to a compact file-storage area, with the individual office-defining partitions removed and a premanufactured rolling file system added.

This example has the same floor as the previous case. The tributary area of floor is 20 feet (6100 mm) long and 7 feet (2130 mm) wide, with an original live load of 50 psf (1.1 Pa), a partition load of 20 psf (0.4 Pa), and a 78 psf (1.6 Pa) dead load. The change in use eliminates the partition load and increases the live load to 250 psf (5.3 Pa).

With such a large change in loading, an extreme change in beam section is needed. This case could be handled with a gross change, such as replacing the beams or adding new beams to cut down the tributary area of each existing beam, but these types of solutions can be more disruptive than upgrading the existing beams. In order to reinforce beams for this type of load change, the efficiency of reinforcing both flanges of the beam is required. In new buildings, composite construction is a common method of using the reserve strength of the concrete floor slab to strengthen the floor beams. When a beam to be reinforced

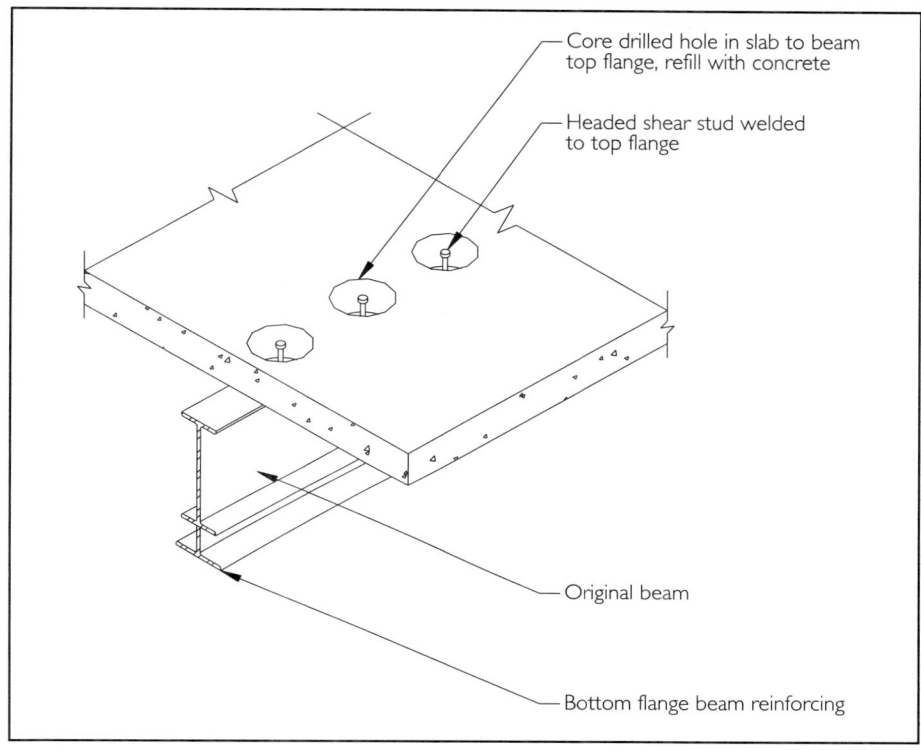

6-2-1. Steel beam reinforced with new studs

supports a concrete slab floor, the composite action can be retroactively created. This can be combined with bottom flange reinforcing with plates as previously described.

Depending on the type of existing slab, the change to composite construction from noncomposite can sometimes be achieved without any physical work, through reanalysis. The concrete-encased steel beams of the 1920s were designed as bare steel, the encasement existing to support the slab from the beam lower flanges and to fireproof the body of the beams. Not until the third edition of the AISC manual (1937) did composite design by encasement appear. Therefore, a set of beams that qualify for composite construction by the ninth edition of the AISC code (1990), by being fully encased in reinforced stone concrete where the encasement is integral with the surrounding slab, qualifies for an automatic increase in its capacity if it was designed noncomposite. This increase can be substantial, since the beams were designed for a bending stress of 18 or 20 ksi (2.6 or 2.9 MPa), and will now qualify, as composite sections, for an allowable bending stress of roughly 25 ksi (3.6 MPa). Many slabs and encasements of the twenties are cinder concrete, not stone concrete, so the opportunity to take advantage of this code change does not occur frequently.

In most cases, the slab can resist the compressive stress of composite action, but there is no existing mechanism for transferring load between the slab and the beam. When a mechanism is created, the beam and slab act compositely, reinforcing the beam from the top (figure 6-2-1). To keep a section with balanced strength, the newly composite section can be balanced by adding a plate to the bottom flange. A balanced section gives the largest increase of section modulus and moment of inertia for the effort.

Composite beam analysis of the existing beam using and slab leads to the use of standard ¾-inch diameter shear studs at 12-inch (305 mm) spacing.

Case Study 6-3: Steel Beam Web Reinforcement

In some cases access to the flanges of a beam is limited. If the increase in section modulus required by an alteration is small or, as in this example, the reinforcement is a repair of moderate weathering damage, it may be possible to reinforce a beam at its web. Since the efficacy of added material decreases the closer it is to the neutral axis of bending, web reinforcing is always less efficient than reinforcing the flanges. This lack of efficiency must be balanced against the access conditions.

This example is a spandrel beam in a masonry curtain-wall building. Many older curtain walls were built with inadequate expansion joints and with the backup masonry in direct contact with the spandrel beams and columns. During facade repairs, the steel is often found to be damaged by water seepage through cracks and through the masonry itself. In order to minimize inconvenience for tenants and the cost of the repairs, repairs to these beams are typically performed from outside, from the same hanging scaffolds that are used to repair the masonry. Since the top flange will ordinarily be inaccessible because of the floor slab and the bottom flange will be impossible to expose without creating a hole clear through to the interior space, any repairs must be confined to the outside web face. Finally, damage to these beams is typically limited to the half-flanges outboard of the web and, less frequently, to the outside face of the web.

Case Study 6-3: Steel Beam Web Reinforcement

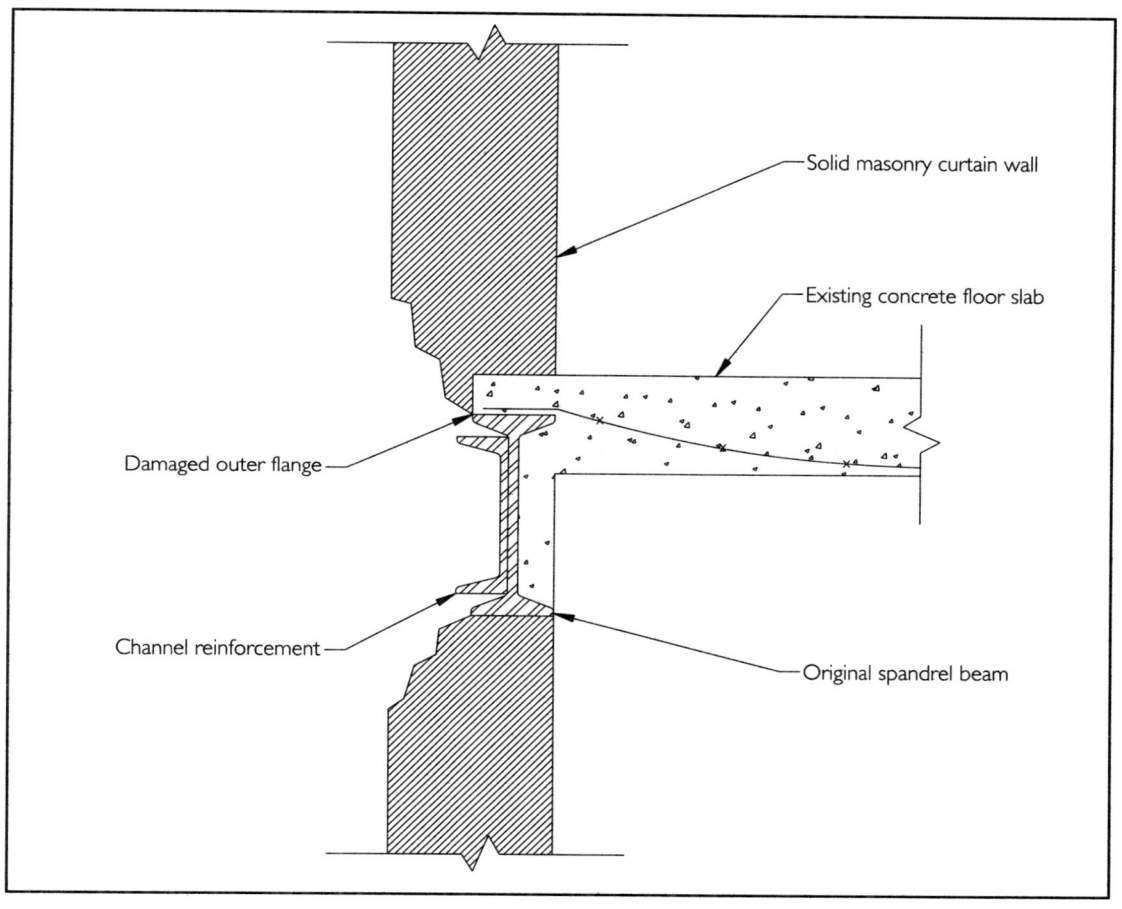

6-3-1. Steel beam with web-channel reinforcing

The spandrel beam here is an old 10B21, equivalent to a modern W10x22, which has lost 50 percent of the material in its outboard flanges to corrosion. This does not necessarily mean that half of each flange is missing for its entire length, or even at any one spot. It means that enough material is damaged so that only half of the outboard flanges can be considered capable of carrying load near the beam midspan, the point of maximum moment.

The repair required for this condition is in effect to replace the damaged flange portions. With the interior flanges and web in good condition, the loss of half of the outboard flanges results in a 20 percent decrease of the beam's section modulus and a 20 percent decrease of the moment of inertia. The solution is to weld a channel of sufficient section modulus to make up the missing strength to the outboard face of the beam. The channel must be small enough to fit between the fillets where the flanges and webs of the beam meet, suggesting the use of a channel section 8 inches (200 mm) or less deep (figure 6-3-1).

A C7x9.8 has a section modulus and moment of inertia greater than was lost by the damage, and is therefore adequate for the reinforcing. A more sophisticated analysis would check the allowable stress that the beam was designed for, based on the building erection date. If the beam is ASTM A9 steel and the building was built in 1924, then the first edition of the AISC code was used in design. That code limited bending stress in ordinary beams to 18 ksi (2.6 MPa). Later editions of the code, using the same specification for steel composition, upgraded the allowable bending stress to 20 ksi (2.9), based on further research into the behavior of beams under load. Using the higher allowable stress specified in the more modern code provisions implies that the reinforcement-supplied additional section modulus can be reduced by 10 percent, suggesting a C6x8.2 as an acceptable choice.

Case Study 6-4: Column Reinforcement

There is no realistic method for transferring existing load in a column to new material added during a renovation. If the load can be removed from the existing column through shoring and jacking, it can be reapplied to both new and old, but this is rarely feasible. In a one- or two-story building it is often possible to shore and jack columns for their full height, but doing so in a low floor of a multiple-story frame would require such monstrous shoring as to be impractical unless required at all costs.

An additional constructibility concern makes transferring load to the new steel difficult: if the column area is truly to be increased, it must be increased everywhere. The presence of existing floor-beam connections and column splices makes adding material continuously to the full height of a column even more difficult by requiring that the beams be shored, disconnected, and reconnected, and splices reconfigured so as not to interfere with the additional material.

In this example, plates are added to a column to decrease its effective slenderness, thereby increasing its allowable compressive stress. With the addition of plates to the exterior of a wide-flange column, the column's moment of inertia increases more rapidly than its area, increasing its radius of gyration. Basic column slenderness is measured in terms of length divided by radius of gyration.

Most building columns are of moderate slenderness. This example assumes that the building frame resists lateral load through the use of cross-bracing attached to columns other than the column of interest. The column being examined is effectively pinned on both ends at splices and is not subject to lateral loading, including applied moments. The column must be examined for minor moments created by unbalanced gravity loads, but given the circumstances of the case study, there are no moments.

The column section in question runs from the third to the fourth floor of a ten-story building built in 1935. The column is surrounded by four bays similar to that described in the beam reinforcing cases, each 20 feet (6100 mm) long and 21 feet (6400 mm) wide and originally designed for the minimum office live load of 50 psf (1.1 Pa), an allowance of 20 psf (0.4 Pa) for partitions, and the 78 psf (1.6 Pa) dead load of permanent construction.

The fourth and fifth floors in these bays have been changed over to storage, causing the partition load to disappear and the live load to increase to 150 psf (3.2 Pa). The original design used 15 percent live load reduction at the ninth floor, increasing 5 percent per floor to 40 percent at the fourth floor. The new design live load keeps the reduced loads at the upper floors and uses the new live load at the fourth and fifth floors.

The original column is a W14x74. The compressive stress in the column under full design load is approximately 17 ksi (2.5 MPa). The column was designed under the second edition of the AISC specification (1934), which gave an allowable stress of 18 ksi (2.6) for a column of this description.

Two factors affect the allowable load: the area of the column and the allowable stress. Since these two are related nonlinearly, the usual design of reinforcement will require several iterations to reach an appropriate solution. If two plates 14 inches (355 mm) wide by ½ inch (13 mm) thick are welded across the toes of the flanges, turning the H-shaped column into a box, the most dramatic effect is the increase in the weak axis moment of inertia and radius of gyration (figure 6-4-1). Since the overall allowable stress is based on the maximum L/r ratio, increasing the lower r value—that of the weak axis—is most helpful.

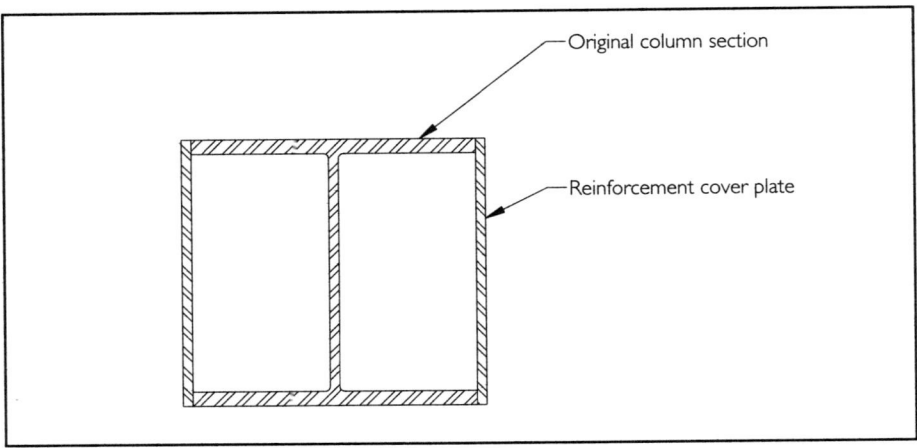

6-4-1. Section of plate-reinforced column

There will be a small section of column at the beam connections at each floor that is not reinforced. This can be accepted so long as the stress in this area, which is obviously braced by the surrounding beams and is between column shafts above and below that have acceptable actual stresses compared with their allowable stresses, remains below the crushing stress for steel.

Case Study 6-5: Column Reinforcement Through Encasement

A different approach to column reinforcement, which combines adding area and increasing the stockiness of the columns, is to encase the steel in a concrete shell. The concrete can be used in two different ways—to share the load in the steel, or to carry its own load. The second is straightforward: the concrete shell is specifically reinforced in the same manner as a concrete column, and provided with dedicated connections to some portion of the floor structure. If the existing footing is capable of sustaining the increased load, the concrete can simply end in bearing on the footing top surface. This type of solution is attractive when space is limited, since the concrete shell can occupy the same location that fireproofing would, and serve the role of fireproofing (figure 6-5-1).

The steel and the concrete encasement can also be analyzed as a unified column. Without jacking, true composite action cannot be achieved for the same

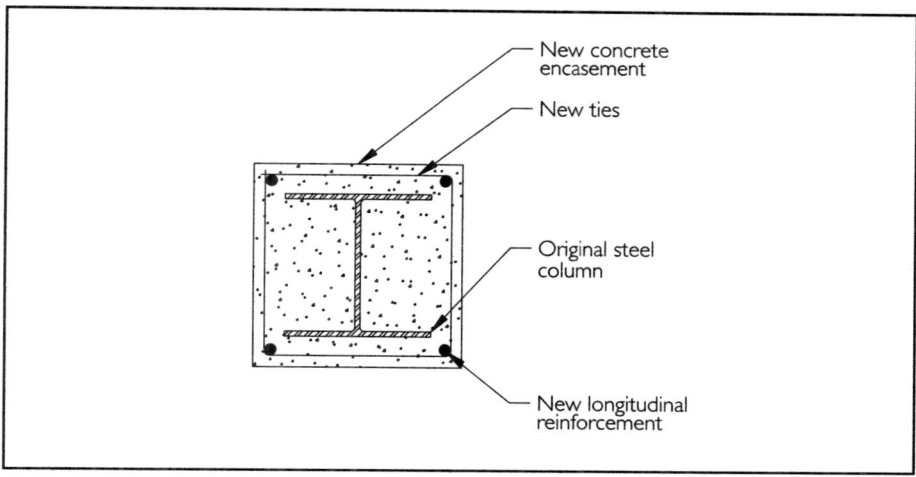

6-5-1. Section of encased column

reason that steel reinforcing plates are incapable of carrying load that exists during the reinforcing work. Only if the existing load can be entirely removed from the column can it be analyzed as a "new" composite column. In all other cases, if the concrete is reinforced with ties and provided with some form of shear connection to the steel shaft, the effect of the encasement is to carry a portion of the loads applied after hardening. The amount of load carried will be in proportion to the ratio of construction loads to permanent loads. The encasement, regardless of the presence of composite action, increases the steel column strength by preventing local flange or web buckling.

One drawback of column encasement is that the beam-to-column connections are buried. Ordinarily, this is a nuisance but not necessarily a problem. If the existing connections are reviewed for adequacy before the encasement is in place, the difficulty in accessing them matters only during major renovations, which are relatively rare. Depending on the encasement dimensions, the beam connection type, and the relative flexibility of the beam, the concrete above and especially below the beam may crush as the beam flexes. It is not possible to leave gaps around each beam if the concrete is meant to be carrying load; if the encasement is present as fire protection and to reduce local buckling, then gaps may be provided by packing the beam in Styrofoam before the concrete is poured. The resulting holes must be fireproofed.

Case Study 6-6: Steel Connection Reinforcement

A connection sometimes used for lightly loaded or difficult to reach beams is the single-angle clip. This consists of a clip angle welded or bolted to the supported beam and bolted to the carrying girder (figure 6-6-1). Bolts are preferred for the clip-to-girder connection for the same reason that this connection has a fairly low capacity: the asymmetrical load path from beam to girder creates secondary bending stresses within the clip angle. (Bolts are also used for ease of erection.) Because the beam is being supported to one side of its web, it has a tendency to rotate which the angle is not rigid enough to resist. The angle will warp under load, allowing the beam to rotate and pulling the angle away from the girder. A double-angle connection using the same-size angle is more than twice as strong, since the symmetric load path eliminates any tendency toward rotation of the beam, reducing the warping of the angles and prying of the connectors.

Single-angle connections are associated with riveting and bolting because welding has popularized the single-plate connection at the expense of the single angle. The single plate, also called a strike plate or shear tab, is simply a plate welded perpendicular to the carrying girder and field-bolted to the carried beam.

When the load is increased on a beam, reinforcing of existing connections is often not required, because most double-angle and single-plate connections have a fairly large reserve capacity. Smaller beams that have single-angle connections are likely to have smaller reserve capacities, with actual reactions near the capacity of the connections. Single-angle connections, while not common, therefore make up a disproportionately large number of connections that need to be reinforced under increased load.

The obvious method of reinforcing a single-angle connection is to turn it into a double-angle connection (figure 6-6-2). There is usually no conflict in adding another angle to the girder, but if the angle is bolted to the beam, the bolt heads on the beam web will interfere with the new angle. In order to eliminate this problem with the least extra work, the existing angle is first welded to the supported girder, allowing the removal of the now-redundant bolts. At that time, the new angle can be welded in place with a minimum of difficulty. During this process the beam is never entirely disconnected, but as the web capacity may decrease temporarily during welding, it is prudent to shore the beam.

Case Study 6-6: Steel Connection Reinforcement 95

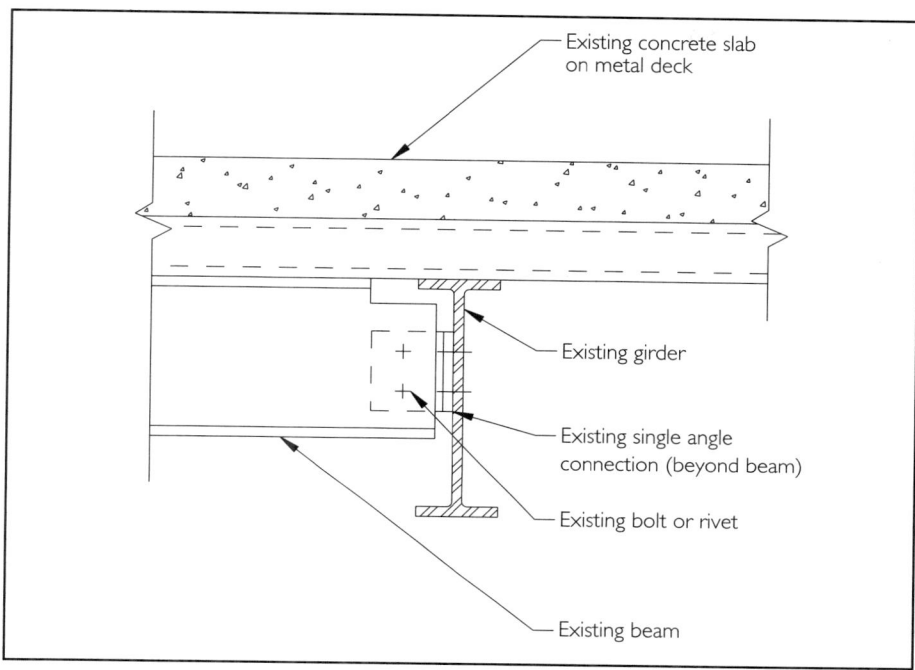

6-6-1. Section of single-angle connection before addition

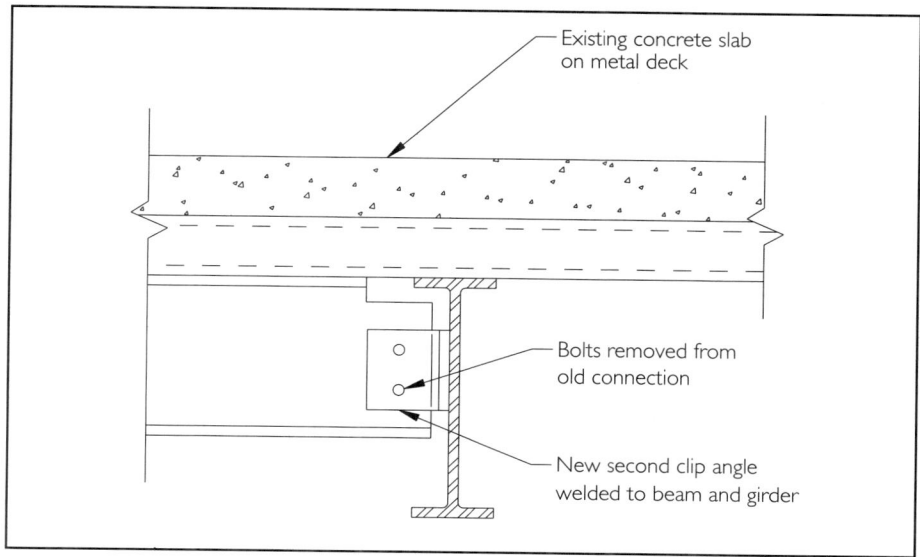

6-6-2. Section of single angle with second angle added

Chapter 7

Reinforced Concrete Buildings

The greatest advantage of concrete as a construction material is the structural continuity of all monolithically placed slabs, beams, and columns. This advantage also poses the greatest difficulty in renovation. All modern cast-in-place reinforced concrete design uses continuity to spread the effect of any load through several members. Many familiar concrete designs, such as T-beams that use the slab as a top flange, unbraced frames that use all beams and columns to resist lateral load, and girders continuous over multiple spans, are less common in other materials, where the elements of buildings tend to be more discrete. Continuity must be maintained during alteration to provide resistance against wind and seismic loading and protection against progressive collapse.

Establishing continuity between new and existing members can be extremely difficult, but is necessary if ordinary concrete design procedures are to be used. For this reason, small modifications to concrete-frame buildings, such as cutting HVAC duct openings through one-way slab floors, are often framed out in steel, which is easily designed and built without continuity.

Archaic Systems and Detailing

Reinforced concrete is the only structural material to use an entirely different design paradigm than that used when the material first became popular. Older materials, such as wood and masonry, have undergone changes in the process of

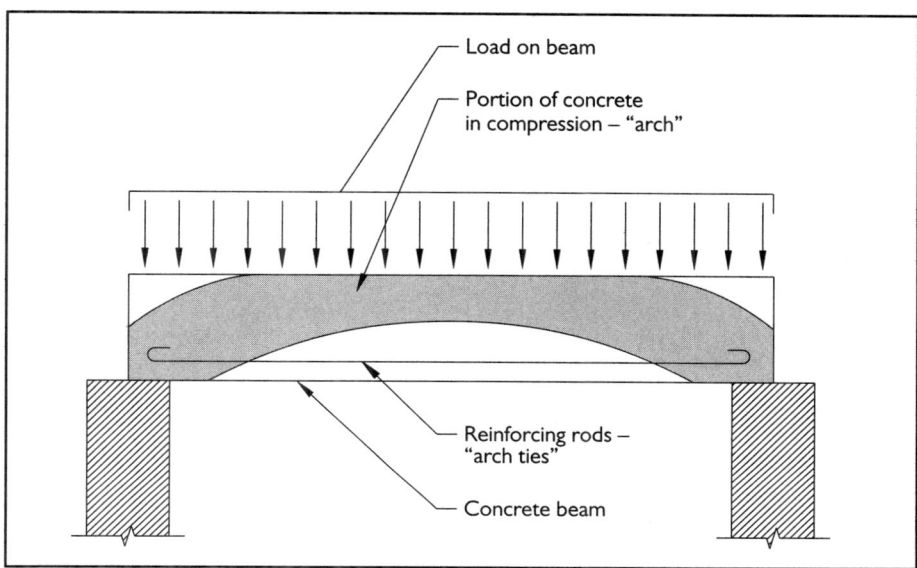

7-1. "Arch" within concrete beam

going from rule-of-thumb design to scientific design, but few changes in actual practice resulted. Iron and steel design has been a fairly consistent technique from its beginnings to the present day, although the exact formulas used have changed. Reinforced concrete beams, on the other hand, were originally seen as relatives of masonry arches, with the bottom layer of reinforcing steel providing a tie for a pure-compression "arch." This arch was not actually visible, but consisted of a load path within the concrete portion of the member (figure 7-1).

Details from before 1920 used in concrete construction may differ dramatically from modern practice. The majority of details used after this date are similar to those used by a current-day engineer. However, rebar layout in unusually configured details is further complicated by designers' personal styles as much as by expressions of engineering principles. When complicated concrete details are being reexamined by an engineer other than the original designer, the process is fairly slow because of the difficulty in understanding someone else's intentions.

Changes over time in concrete detailing fall into two broad categories: changes based on differences in the reinforcing types used and changes based on differences in design theory. The first group is relatively easy to identify, since the unique details for certain types of proprietary reinforcing are always associated with the presence of that reinforcing, which is readily identifiable and fairly rare. Most obsolete reinforcing types were patented before 1910 and were used primarily by the construction companies owning or controlling the patents. Two examples of this are the Kahn and the Cummings systems. These similar systems, popular during the 1910s, used prefabricated assemblies of longitudinal bars bent up, in part, to form diagonal shear reinforcing. The Hennebique system, imported from France, used a similar set of prefabricated units, but with thin steel straps welded to the longitudinal reinforcing to serve as shear reinforcing.

Differences in reinforcing detailing based on changes in design theory are sometimes difficult to define. There is not always a direct link between the theory used in design of a particular member and that member's appearance. A good example is the use of hooks at the ends of longitudinal rebar in concrete beams. At the beginning of the twentieth century, these hooks were present because the prevailing theory of concrete design, that a simply supported beam acted as a tied arch, required that the ends of the reinforcing (the juncture of the reinforcing "ties" and the portion of the concrete considered to be the "arch spring points") be capable of full load transfer to the surrounding concrete. The same beam designed today might have hooks at the ends to ensure that the bars were capable of developing their full tension capacity without pulling free of the surrounding concrete. The physical movement that the hooks are meant to prevent—sliding of the reinforcing relative to the concrete—is the same in both cases, but the designer's explanation of the cause of the sliding is entirely different. An examination of nothing but a rebar layout diagram would not give any clues as to the theory used to design the concrete.

There is an advantage to ambiguity. If an existing design is similar enough to modern designs that current rules can be used, the theory originally used does not matter to the renovator. Thus, if the rebar layout is known, the structure is analyzed by modern methods, without regard to the original theory. The ability to reanalyze old structures without knowledge of the original design is crucial to concrete because of the relative lack, when compared to steel, of historical design information commonly available.

Even when conditions are noticeably different from modern concrete, modern theory may be applicable. In addition to the many patented reinforcing systems, there were dozens of patented reinforcing rod styles and unpatented but nonstandard styles used in the ordinary manner. In examining a concrete building built before 1920, it is not unusual to discover that the slab reinforcing is laid out as usual, but that the bars themselves are small T or channel section instead of the more familiar circular rods. Some form of anchorage is required for these bars, since most of them are undeformed. Ordinary rebar has been fabricated with greater deformations through the years, as design theory has come to rely more on bar tensile development through mechanical interlock with the concrete than through chemical bonding. If hooks or other gross mechanical anchorage is provided, there is no reason that the geometric properties of nonstandard reinforcing cannot be calculated and used for a modern slab analysis.

The archaic designs discussed so far were used mostly in concrete frame buildings. One-way slabs of this type can be found in steel frame buildings, along with another obsolete system, the draped mesh slab. This system, made obsolete by the introduction of composite metal deck, was extremely popular in steel frame buildings of the 1920s, '30s, and '40s. It was originally introduced as yet another patented system, but was in use long enough, in enough different variations, that it became nonproprietary.

The basis of the draped-mesh system is catenary action. The reinforcing is continuous mesh placed so that it is near the top of the slabs at the filler beams (the slab supports), and near the bottom at the slab midspan. All vertical loads applied to the floor slab are carried by the mesh tension to the supports (figure 7-2).

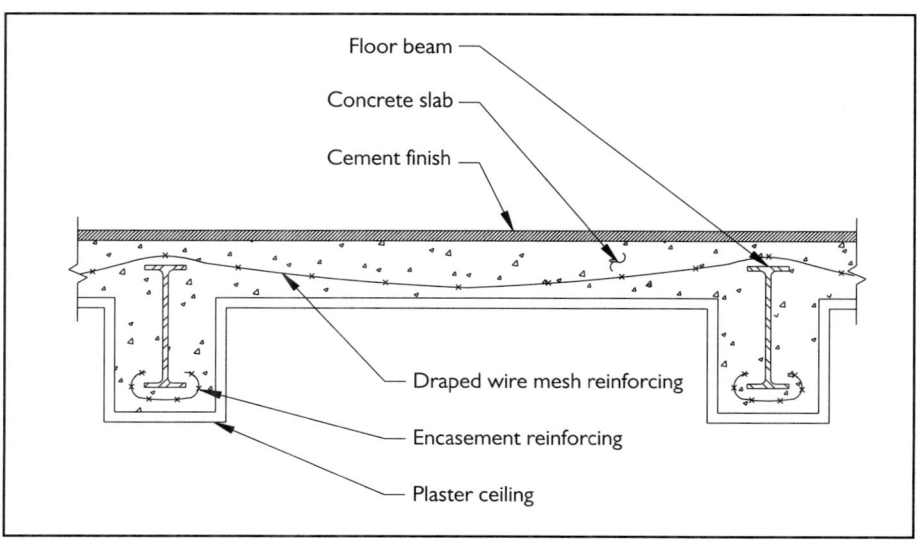

7-2. Draped-mesh slab

100 REINFORCED CONCRETE BUILDINGS

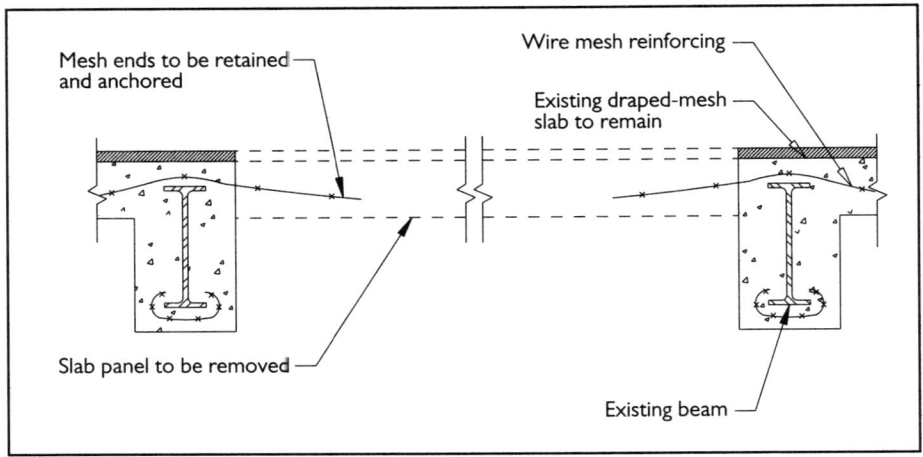

7-3. Cutting draped mesh

Removing a portion of a draped-mesh slab is difficult. Without true flexural reinforcement, there is no way that a small piece of slab can be analyzed as a cantilever. This type of construction presents two entirely different sets of conditions depending on the direction examined. Since the slab depends solely on the beam-to-beam catenaries, cutting the slab parallel to those spans has no real structural effect.

On the other hand, draped-mesh slabs are extremely sensitive to alterations that interrupt the catenaries. If steel beams cannot be introduced below the slab to support a cut edge, it is easier to remove an entire span of slab than a piece. Cutting a catenary near a support beam also weakens the adjacent slab span unless the wire mesh is mechanically fastened so that it can develop its full strength. While the original construction of draped-mesh slabs often dealt with this situation by hooking the wires over the beam flange at slab edges, welding the wires in place is a detail less subject to slip and construction error (figure 7-3).

New Connections in Concrete

The renovation of concrete is different from the renovation of steel in several ways, but the most important is the difficulty in changing the properties of an existing member. Unlike the relative simplicity of welding additional pieces to an existing steel member to increase its area, section modulus, or radius of gyration, the vast majority of concrete renovations require either extensive detailing to create connections between new and old material or a design that avoids the problem entirely through the use of other materials. Except in rare circumstances, steel frames are not modified or reinforced through the use of concrete members; concrete frames are as often modified or reinforced through the addition of steel beams and posts than through the use of equivalent concrete members.

Concrete beams and columns are often altered through the addition of steel sections using expansion bolts to change the section properties or by the addition of new concrete material through the use of both mechanical fasteners and epoxies. The mechanical properties of the connectors may determine what types of section changes are feasible. Expansion or epoxy bolts have minimum spacings to maintain their capacity, and the bolt allowable loads are proportional to the bolt embedment in concrete.

New connections in steel use welding to fasten new steel to old with little difficulty because simple welds are usually stronger than the connection forces require. In concrete, the ability to structurally connect new material to old so that they work together as one beam is questionable. This limitation may not be overly restrictive in simply adding gross area to a column; it prevents many schemes for reinforcing beams, where horizontal shear transfer across the joint is crucial to the desired reinforcing action. Epoxy bonding agents, while capable of greater shear strength than the concrete base material, are not often used alone for structural connections. Chemical bond is used, in part, to transfer load between rebar and the mass of concrete, but the sheer quantity and mechanical interlocking of concrete surrounding the rebar on every side creates redundancy for this load mechanism. The general design trend runs against using only a plane of epoxy to transfer load between new concrete and rebar and an existing beam or column.

While it may be an attractive idea to temporarily remove enough concrete to slide in new rebar as a way of changing the reinforcing pattern of an existing member, it is not usually practical. Demolishing 2 to 3 inches (50 to 75 mm) at the top or bottom of a slab without damaging the existing rebar ¾ inch (19 mm) down is slow and difficult, and therefore expensive. The process is difficult because there is no readily available method of removal other than the use of compressed air or electric hammers. Even electric hammers are not the tool of choice, since they are too weak for serious concrete removal. At the same time, the type of selective demolition required for rebar introduction requires delicate tolerances, as the concrete between and around each existing bar must be chipped out without inadvertently cutting into the body of the bars. The process of introducing new bars once the concrete has been removed presents greater difficulty. New reinforcing capable of introducing significant increases in continuity and strength will almost certainly be bars in the range of 5 to 10 feet (1520 to 3050 mm) long. Most slabs have reinforcing in both directions at spacings of less than 18 inches (460 mm), making placement of new reinforcing from outside the slab plane effectively impossible. If an opening is being cut into the slab, it is sometimes possible to slide new bars in from the new cut edge of the slab. In general, this approach is not cost effective and often not physically realistic.

Column Reinforcement

Any strengthening of concrete columns must go outside the normal theory of reinforced concrete design. The strength of the column concrete and the reinforcing percentage within the column volume are fixed. Concrete columns are almost always designed continuous with the columns and floor structures at their tops and bottoms, and most concrete frames are designed unbraced, and therefore subject to sidesway. Columns of this type have effective lengths longer than their actual lengths. The low allowable strengths for slender columns make increasing the radius of gyration or adding bracing along the column shaft much more effective methods of increasing strength than attempting to increase the strength of the column cross section.

When increasing the radius of gyration is not enough, the column area can be increased through the addition of new rebar and new concrete outside the existing perimeter of the column. Given the relative difficulty in jacking concrete structures and the independent difficulties in jacking columns, it is difficult to get loads into the additional material other than live loads imposed after the reinforcing has taken place.

When concrete was first used, the relative importance of the different types of reinforcing was not well understood. Columns from before 1910 may have no reinforcing ties, no longitudinal reinforcing, or limited amounts of both. Mature concrete column theory has focused on confinement of the longitudinal reinforcement and core concrete as the keys to column strength. This focus is responsible for the increase in allowable strength in the ACI code when spiral ties are used in the place of hoops for lateral reinforcement. The spirals do a better job of confining the column interior. Taken to an extreme, this theory results in concrete-filled steel tube columns, which have allowable loads closer to steel columns than to concrete columns. It is theoretically possible to modify a concrete column into a concrete-filled steel column, although such a modification does not directly address the existing stress in the concrete.

Beam Reinforcement

The easiest method of reinforcing a concrete beam is to provide a parallel steel beam. "Sistering" provides a new beam of precisely the strength required, without concern for the condition of the existing beam or any possible original design flaws.

In the case of a filler beam spanning between two girders and responsible only for supporting slab, sistering the beam with two channels placed flat against its sides and dry-packed tight to the slab underside is simple and effective. The fact that this type of upgrade is more popular than an all-concrete solution to the problem proves the relative ease of working with steel during alterations compared to installing new concrete. It is theoretically possible to increase the strength of a concrete beam in a manner similar to that used for steel beams, by adding new material to the underside to produce a deeper, more heavily reinforced section, but work of this type is always more expensive than upgrades using steel shapes (see Case Study 7-4).

Slab Reinforcement and Modification

Beams and one-way slabs are designed in a similar fashion. Both are altered and reinforced in similar ways. There is one difference, based on the nature of the dominant stresses. Shear stresses are of significantly reduced importance in slab analysis and design. Given the relative shallowness of slabs compared to beams, moment and deflection design dominates slabs. Even under the highest point loads that slabs are ordinarily subjected to, the wheel loads of a truck, the governing code (AASHTO) neglects the effects of direct shear.

Slabs can be reinforced for increased loads in one of two ways: increasing the depth to the reinforcing by adding material to the top surface of the slab and increasing the amount of reinforcing present (see Case Studies 7-1 and 7-2). The second option is not readily available for beam reinforcing because the amount of reinforcing in slabs tends to be far below the maximum allowed, while beams are usually heavily reinforced.

Two-way slabs are unique structures, without counterpart in other materials or other building elements. The theory of two-way slabs says that load flows to the stiffest part of a continuous structure. Since the short spans directly between columns are stiffer than any other portion of a flat slab, these column strips become the primary supports, carrying the more flexible middle strips that do not intersect columns (figure 7-4). Technically, flat slabs may have drop

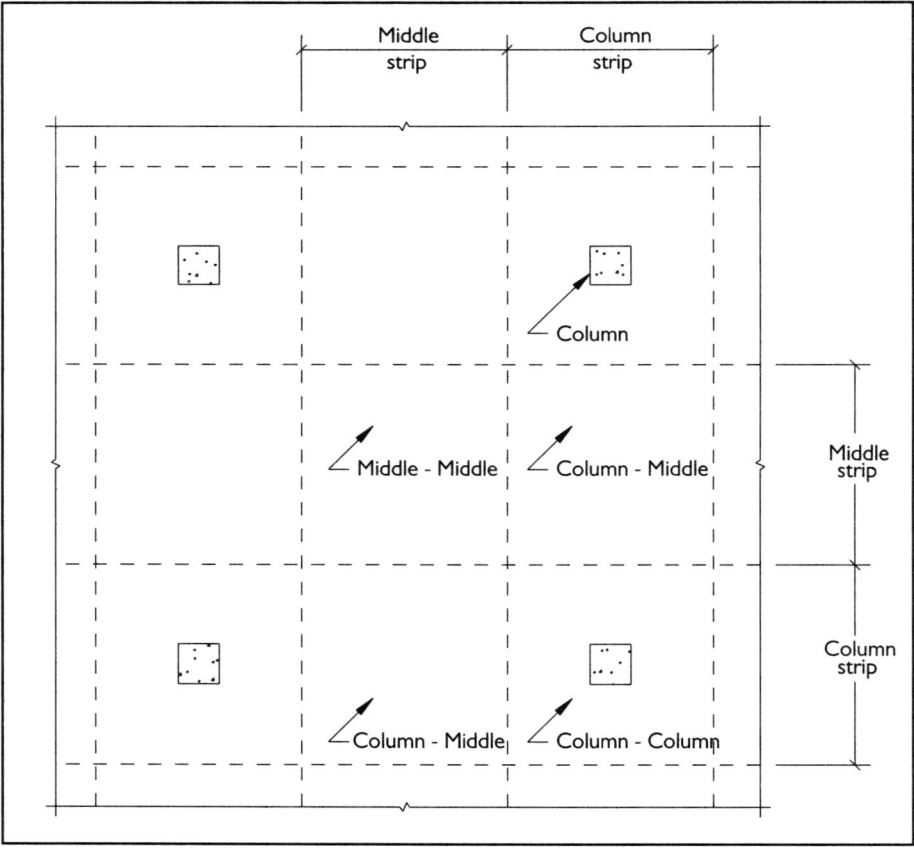

7-4. Definition of middle and column strips

panels and column capitals, while flat plates are uninterrupted concrete slab of equal thickness.

Since the intersection of two middle strips of a flat slab or flat plate is considered to be dead weight carried by the column strips surrounding it, it can be removed without affecting the overall structure. As codified by the ACI, openings of any size are allowed in the middle-middle strip without reanalysis of the slab action. If such holes are acceptable in new construction, they are obviously acceptable in renovations. Reinforcing is only required at the actual cut edge, which will not be aligned with existing rebar except by chance. Alterations to any other part of a two-way slab system requires careful analysis of the effect on the surrounding structure, including adjacent bays.

Case Study 7-1: Reinforcing Slabs by Adding Depth

Several physical properties determine the strength of a concrete slab design. The strength of the slab is strongly related to the amount of slab reinforcing, the slab depth, and the strength of the steel used for reinforcing. The slab strength is related to the strength of the concrete, but not directly; increasing the concrete compressive strength is the least effective method of increasing the overall slab strength. The width of the slab does not enter into the calculations at all, as slabs are designed on a "per foot of width" basis.

The amount and strength of reinforcing is difficult to change (but not impossible—see Case Study 7-2), but the slab depth is relatively easily modified. More concrete can easily be placed on top of an existing slab, so that the issues in reinforcing a slab by increasing its depth become issues of detail and effect on surrounding structure. Increasing the slab depth decreases the reinforcing percentage, since the quantity of rebar remains constant as the volume of concrete increases (in contrast to Case Study 7-2, where the reinforcing percentage is increased).

Placing wet concrete in contact with existing concrete does not create a bond between the two. The cold joints between separate pours must be specifically avoided where continuity is required: additional reinforcing is specified crossing cold joints during new concrete construction. Any dirt, oil, or other coating on the old concrete also prevents the bond between new and old. To avoid this problem, the top surface of the old concrete is removed (mechanical roughening), and a bonding agent, usually an epoxy, is placed before the new

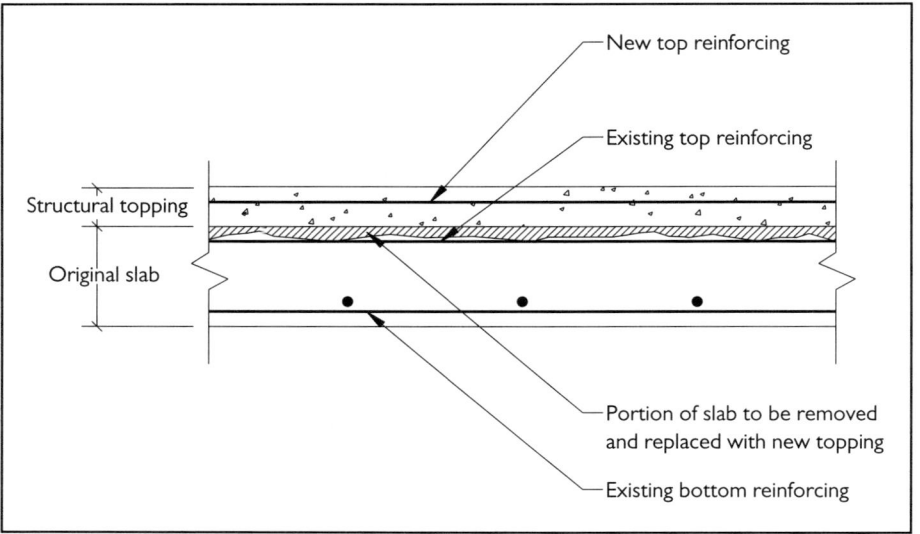

7-1-1. Adding depth to a slab

concrete (figure 7-1-1). While the overall compressive force in the top of a concrete slab is large, the stress that must be transmitted across the cold joint is low. The stress in question is shear in the plane of the cold joint, and is usually an order of magnitude lower than the allowable values for the concrete and the epoxy.

The reason concrete is not added to slab tops more often is that the weight of the additional concrete affects the beams supporting the slab, the columns supporting the beams and the foundation supporting the columns. Unless the floor has a large reserve capacity (which is unlikely if slab strengthening is required), the added dead load of the concrete must be taken from the live load capacity of the floor. There are situations when adding the dead load is feasible, but they rarely occur in ordinary buildings.

The final design issue with this repair concerns engineering design criteria. A minimum percentage of reinforcing is permitted in concrete slabs, specifically to ensure ductile behavior. By increasing the slab volume without changing the amount of reinforcing, the reinforcing percentage decreases. In most slabs, adding an inch or two to the depth will not force the percentage below the minimum, because the original percentage is not usually right at the minimum.

The efficacy of this type of change depends on the original form of reinforcing. Most concrete slabs built before 1920 and a large percentage built between 1920 and 1940 were reinforced in ways that are distinctly different from modern construction. The method described here depends on the slab being a typical flexural slab that grows in strength as the slab gets deeper. Draped-mesh slabs would not benefit from this style of reinforcing, as the strength of the slab depends on the amount of reinforcing and the depth of the reinforcing drape, neither of which would be increased by adding slab depth.

Case Study 7-2: Reinforcing Slabs with External Reinforcing

In most types of steel and concrete buildings, the floor slabs are less highly stressed than the beams and columns. Analysis of an existing floor system for increased loads will often find that one-way concrete slabs have excess capacity while the supporting beams are overloaded. This common occurrence is one reason for the emphasis on reinforcing beams in the case studies. Two-way slab systems are an exception to this generalization, and are discussed in Case Study 7-5.

The building described here is one of the rare cases where there was a simple solution to the overstress of the beams, but the concrete slabs could not be upgraded as described in Case Study 7-1.

The building in question is a firehouse in continuous use for roughly a hundred years at the time of renovation. The above-grade portion of the three-story building consists of wood-joist floors supported on brick bearing walls. The first-floor structure consists of two spans of concrete slab, from one side wall to a center girder to the other side wall. The girder was concrete placed integrally with the stabs, and supported on brick piers in the cellar. As this structure had been designed for the load of fire trucks used before 1900, it could not support the weight of modern trucks. The building currently houses a rescue truck, which is somewhat smaller and lighter than a pump or ladder truck, but the floor had been reinforced for the load of the heaviest fire truck with the use of screw-jacks from the cellar slab to the underside of the first floor.

Because the cellar was unused, except for a small area where the boiler and other mechanical services were located, reinforcing the girders for the new loads of a modern truck was simple, requiring only a reduction in headroom. There was relatively very little rebar in the slabs. Reviewing the possibility of increasing the strength through increasing the slab depth showed that the depth would have to be increased by nearly 10 inches (250 mm), architecturally unacceptable even if it were structurally acceptable, which it was not. The solution finally used

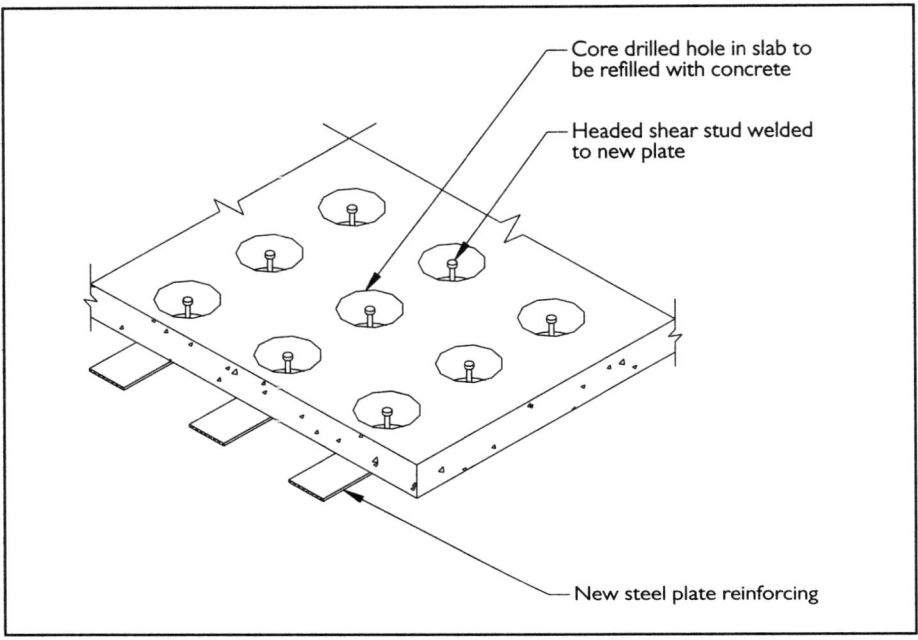

7-2-1. External reinforcing detail

was the introduction of new slab reinforcing from below.

Anyone familiar with construction pictures concrete reinforcing as ordinary rebar entirely embedded within concrete. This is a good description of almost all concrete construction, but it is not necessarily the only way to reinforce concrete. Reinforced concrete design theory only requires shear transfer between the concrete material and the steel material. The steel needs to be protected against water and fire. This protection is ordinarily provided by the concrete encasing the rebar.

New reinforcing was added to the slab in the form of flat steel plates fastened to the slab underside (figure 7-2-1). The plates were connected to the concrete for shear transfer through the use of shear studs identical to those used in composite steel-beam design. Core holes were drilled through the slab to allow for placement of the plate with the preattached studs. The plate was fastened into place through the use of temporary shelf angles at each end (the bearing wall and the center girder), and the core holes were filled with concrete bonded to the surrounding existing concrete. The steel was then protected with cementitious fireproofing.

The amount of new steel was based on the required moment capacity of the slab and checked against the maximum allowable reinforcing percentage for safe concrete design.

Case Study 7-3: Concrete Column Reinforcement

Any strengthening of concrete columns must go outside the normal theory of reinforced concrete design. The strength of an existing concrete column and the amount of reinforcing within the column volume are fixed. Concrete columns are designed fixed to the beams or slabs at their tops and bottoms, and most concrete frames require continuity between the columns and adjacent structure for

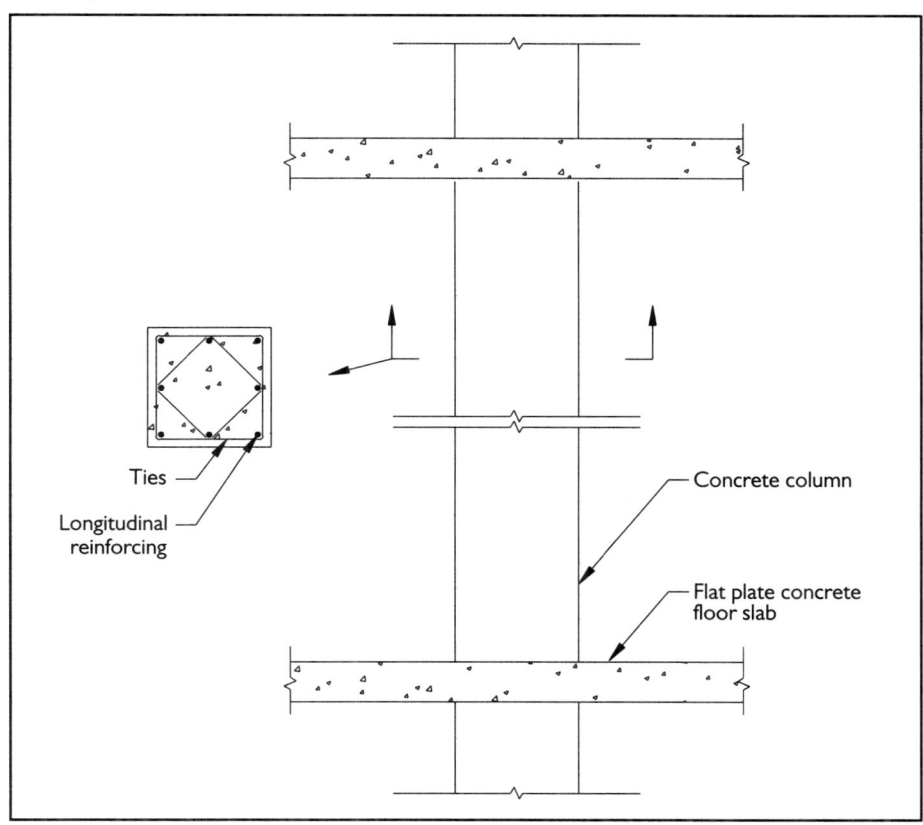

7-3-1. Existing column before encasement

lateral bracing. Typical concrete columns therefore have an effective length longer than their actual length. The large effective lengths and the effect of slenderness in compression design make increasing the radius of gyration or reducing the actual length of a column very effective methods of increasing strength.

A column can be made stockier by simply adding new reinforced concrete to the exterior (figures 7-3-1 and 7-3-2). As long as the new material is properly reinforced as a compression member, with its longitudinal reinforcing confined by ties, and the new material is connected to the old so that the two act together, the increased radius of gyration can be used. The new material cannot be assumed to carry any dead load, and possibly not any live load, but it will share in resisting moments. Encasing a concrete column within more concrete thus

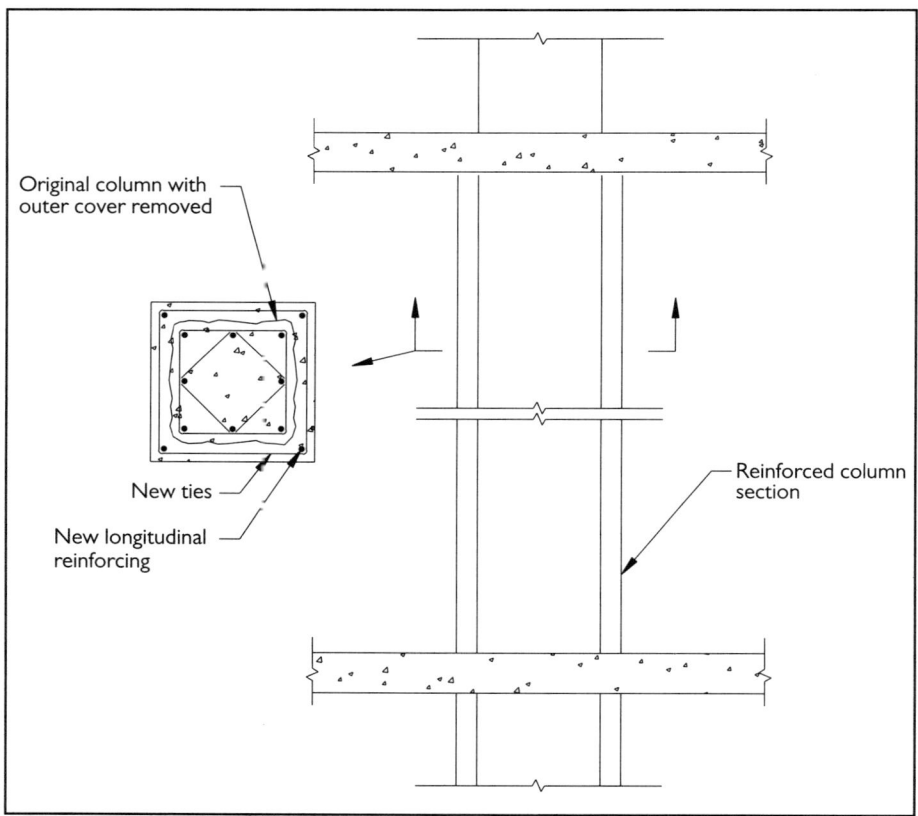

7-3-2. Reinforcing a column through encasement

increases the allowable stress by reducing the slenderness at the same time that it reduces the actual bending stresses from lateral loads.

In advanced seismic retrofit design, concrete columns are not only encased in this manner; they are occasionally wrapped in structural steel jackets. In addition to the beneficial effects described above, the added confinement of the jacket increases the ductility of the column.

Case Study 7-4: Creating Beam Splices

Because of the importance of continuity in concrete, many actions that are simple in steel require more intense planning and design. Steel beams can be extended by simply welding on a new piece, requiring only a design review for a longer span and a weldability check of the existing steel. Concrete forces must be accounted for, and transferred separately for both the concrete compression material and the rebar.

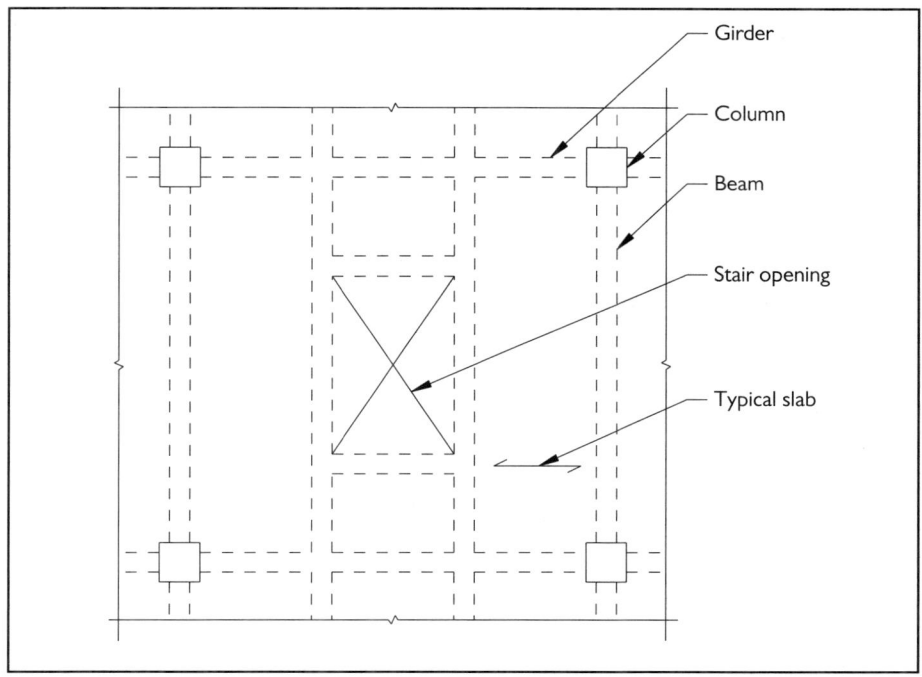

7-4-1. Existing plan at concrete floor stair opening

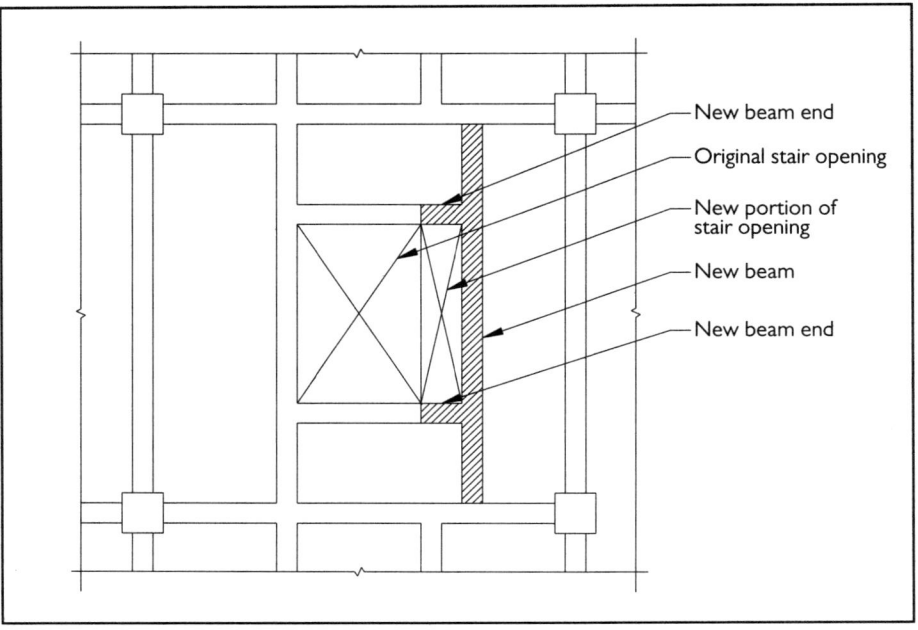

7-4-2. Revised plan at concrete floor stair opening

In this example, an existing stair opening in a concrete one-way slab floor is being enlarged. The stair opening was built surrounded by four beams, two major beams parallel to the axis of the stair that run to girders, and two minor beams that connect the major beams (figure 7-4-1). To accommodate the new stair configuration, one of the major beams will be removed and replaced by a new beam 2 feet (610 mm) farther from the beam to remain. The minor beams must therefore become 2 feet (610 mm) longer (figure 7-4-2).

A review of the original drawings showed that the reinforcing in the minor beams was the minimum allowed by code, but more than required for the loads and span. This reinforcing level would still be adequate for a longer beam. The problem at this point became one of constructibility and detailing rather than design.

Concrete for one end of each minor beam extension was to be placed with the concrete for the new major beam (figure 7-4-3). Reinforcing equal in size and spacing to the existing reinforcing in the minor beams was put in the forms, and mechanical splices were used to fasten the new to the ends of the old

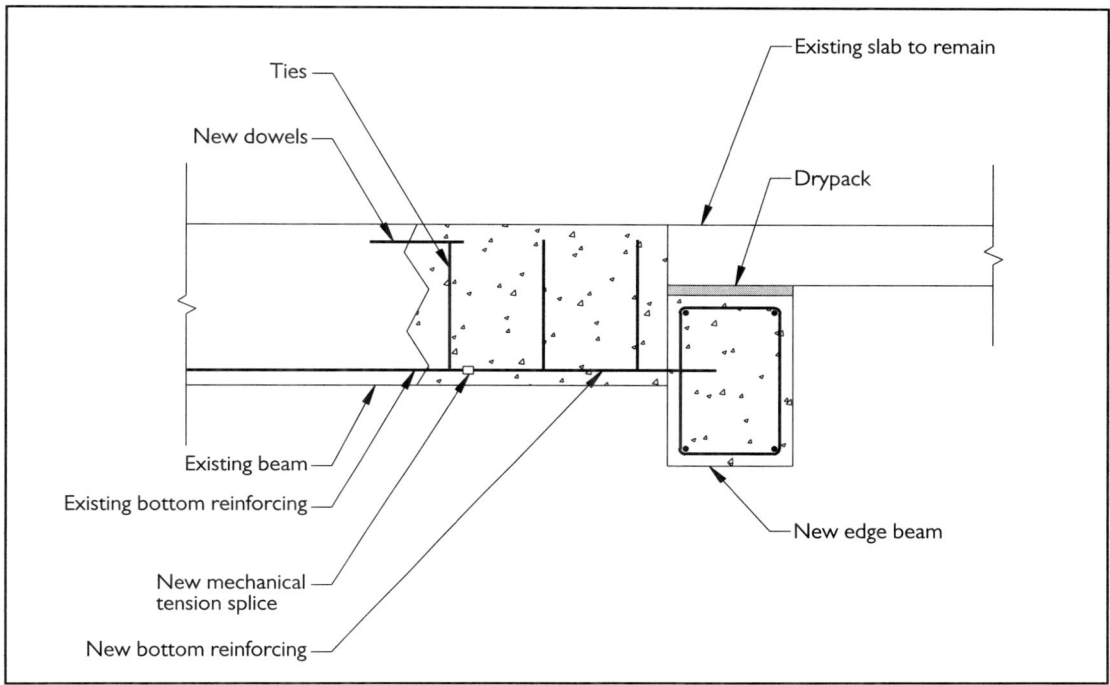

7-4-3. Detail at lengthened beams

exposed by the demolition of the old major beam. The end surface of the old beam exposed by demolition was left rough and coated with a bonding agent before the new concrete was placed. Finally, dowels were drilled into the end surface to create a tie between new and old concrete at the beam top.

Case Study 7-5: Two-way Slab Modification

Two-way slab alterations are either very simple or very complex, with little middle ground. Certain slab portions, specifically the middle-middle strips in the center of each bay, can be removed with little difficulty. These portions are treated as unimportant by the slab-design methods, required to support themselves, but otherwise seen as dead weight spanning to the surrounding column strips.

Column strips, by contrast, support not only themselves but the middle strips as well, and also serve as parts of the lateral load resistance. Technically, removing a large enough piece of the middle strip will affect the lateral-load frame, but removal must be extreme before the effect is noticeable. The importance of the column strip is shown by the extra reinforcing to transfer moments between the slab and the column often required where the column strip joins the columns.

Cutting holes larger than single, small pipe chases through the column-column strip of a flat slab or flat plate usually destroys the slab action. Even slots parallel to the main reinforcing destroy the transverse continuity, and so interfere with the load sharing that makes two-way action theoretically possible. The only practical method of dealing with such changes is resupport or reconstruction of the slab.

Column strips are also vulnerable to small changes when those changes interfere with load transfer at the columns. The limiting factor in many new flat slab designs and most new flat slab alterations (new openings or increased load) is the punching shear at the columns (figure 7-5-1).

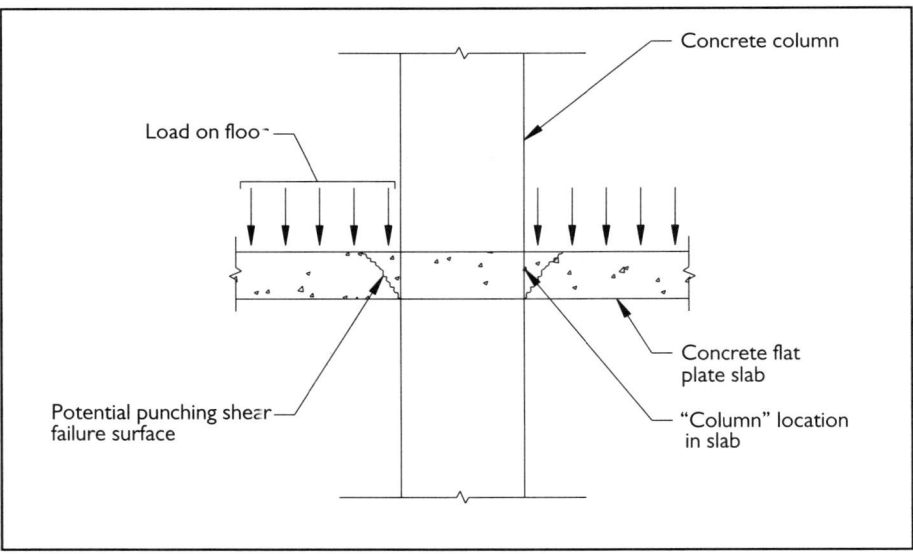

7-5-1. Punching shear diagram at flat plate column

There is usually some amount of reserve capacity in the moment design of the slab, but punching (two-way) shear is so limiting that it often determines the slab thickness in design. In alteration, if the moment capacity is adequate for the new loads, the shear problem at the columns can be dealt only with by adding external shearheads—steel or concrete supports below the slab that prevent the slab from ripping loose from the column and dropping.

Case Study 7-6: Sistering Concrete Beams

The methods described for strengthening concrete slabs all work, in theory, for concrete beams. The reality of concrete beams is that adding enough depth to make an effective difference in strength is rarely possible (an inch of added depth that might increase the strength of a 6-inch (150 mm) thick slab by 20 percent would only increase the strength of a 24-inch (610 mm) deep beam by 5 percent) and the existing amount of reinforcing is near enough to the maximum amount allowed by concrete design to prohibit any appreciable addition of external reinforcing. When large increases in load are imposed on an existing concrete beam, gross changes to the structure may be the most efficient and practical method of increasing the capacity of the beam.

The concept of sistering beams is familiar to most designers and contractors from wood construction. Because of the relative simplicity of wood connections, and the openness of wood structure, sistering a wood beam—effectively replacing it by placing an identical beam immediately adjacent—is common. The attributes of concrete construction are nearly opposite those of wood, in that concrete has integrated connections and is opaque and dense, but sistering is possible in a different form.

Continuity of concrete structure is required for lateral-load resistance and for the design of individual concrete members. If new gravity loads are to be taken by steel beams acting to effectively replace the concrete beam, the steel beams do not require continuity. Steel beams can easily be designed without continuity, and the concrete beam will continue to act as part of the frame, as it has in the past.

A typical steel sister to a concrete beam is sized to carry all the live load for the adjacent slab, and the concrete beam will continue to carry the dead load of the concrete. The steel beam may be installed on one side of the concrete beam

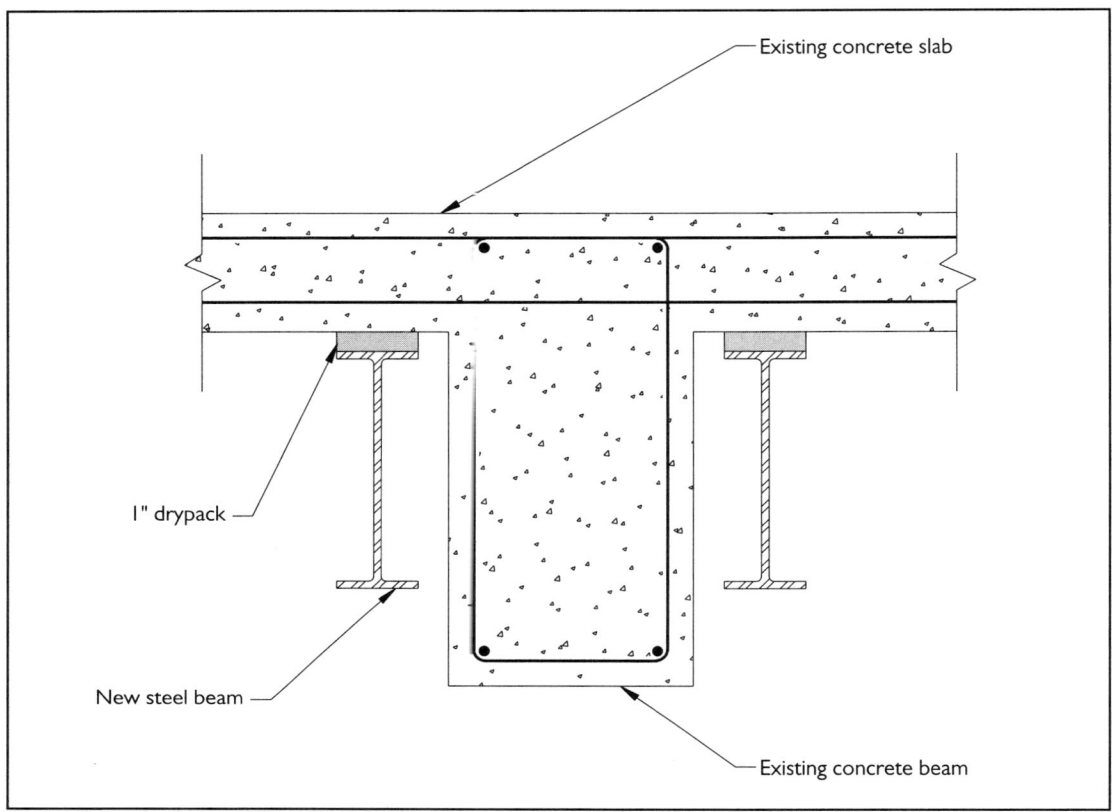

7-6-1. Sistered concrete beam

or as two smaller steel beams on either side of the concrete (figure 7-6-1). The steel is connected to the concrete girders or columns at the ends of the concrete beam with anchor-bolted steel connections.

Chapter 8

Wood Framing

Wood, more than any other material, has had its forms and methods of construction evolve from rules of thumb and verbal tradition. The combination of traditional information and modern research-based technique has produced a wide range of perceptions about wood and its practical uses. During renovation work, a designer not only has to determine the original design intent and the primary structural elements of a wood structure, a difficult task in itself, but also has to weed out popular techniques, both theoretically sound and not, to determine the best fix for the situation.

Compared to other structural materials, there is little standardization or field control in wood construction. The reasons include the common use of wood in light construction, frequently changed standards in both material grading and construction technique, new wood products that allow changes to tried-and-true designs, and finally, the general lack of interest in standardizing an industry that differs from county to county with material availability and local history and has generally less impact on public safety than steel and concrete construction.

Reviewing the evolution of every renovation technique is beyond the scope of this book, but defining the basic elements of wood construction helps explain its strengths and weaknesses. The underlying principles of wood construction can be applied to formulate an overall philosophy for each renovation job, guiding the design solutions in a way contractor and designers agree is the most efficient for that project. While they may debate the relative value of nails versus screws or new lumber versus an engineered wood product, everyone can agree on why certain elements of the building are reinforced and others are not.

The most important decision facing an engineer at the start of many wood renovation projects is the degree of rigor to be used in analysis. It is not uncommon to find conditions that cannot be proven stable but have worked because of redundancy and load redistribution. In some cases, fixing an apparently unstable condition may inadvertently cause a new, unstable condition elsewhere by disturbing existing load paths. Designers have to be especially diligent in determining the exact loading of an element before repair. In cases where a planned renovation does not change the loading or the material surrounding a questionable element, the best decision is to leave it as is. The justification for not taking action is that the condition has been in place for the life of the building and we may do more harm than good in changing it. However, this justification is very delicate, and the moment a new load, no matter how small, is applied, or the configuration of materials, such as walls or ceilings, surrounding the element is adjusted the element must be repaired to modern standards.

A designer must have a firm grasp of the characteristics of wood construction before commenting on the impact of a proposed renovation. With that in mind, note that the following principles are based on the issues that are most often touched on during renovation and are not an exhaustive list of every possible problem. Wood construction is so varied that it is impossible to generate office rules or standards that apply to every wood renovation job. It is even more difficult to create a library of typical repair details. "Typical" is an uncommon word in this field.

A designer of wood renovation should avoid trying to find typical solutions and instead learn the history and characteristics of wood construction. This chapter lays out a loose checklist of critical issues: the light weight and inherent redundancy of wood construction; the rigor with which new code provisions should be applied; the frame type; the balance of existing roofs and the effect of proposed alterations; the type and condition of the existing connections and the rigor that will be used in their analysis; and, finally, the possible introduction of man-made wood products into an existing timber frame.

The Nature of Wood Construction

Wood is capable of withstanding similar tension and compression stresses, making it the only natural material that can act efficiently in bending. However, it is weak in general when compared with other building materials such as steel or reinforced concrete, and weaker in specific comparisons than stone or unreinforced masonry in compression.

Wood has traditionally been the most common building resource. The design of preindustrial homes and barns depended on the work being performed by only a few people with easily obtainable materials. This meant each piece was relatively light, and it led to basic repetitive wood framing and barn structures. Even before mass-produced nails and 2x4s, wood structures had many small beams and posts. The change to balloon and platform framing, when cheap wire nails, studs, and joists became available, was natural.

Light, repetitive framing creates redundant structures. In other words, if one joist fails, the joists to either side can pick up the additional load with little impact on the overall building. The structural subfloor, whether planking or plywood, serves to distribute load from one joist to the next. This is generally not the case in steel or concrete structures, particularly when used in modern forms such as space frames, where the load failure of a girder or column can have disastrous consequences for the entire structure.

In a light-framed structure, the unintentional strengthening from nonstructural elements such as ceiling and wall finishes may be significant. For example, a typical wood house is designed to resist lateral loads using the shear diaphragms of the exterior walls. Because the interior partitions and exterior walls have similar stiffnesses, interior partitions often contribute to the overall stiffness of a house regardless of the designers' original intent. This effect is common in wood construction and rare elsewhere, although older steel buildings are sometimes stiffened by masonry partitions. Again, the partitions are of a similar lateral stiffness to that of the steel frames and contribute unintended stiffness.

A wall that can be removed by one person with a hammer and saw is not considered important to the structure of a house. This is a dangerous assumption, which leads homeowners to remove small parts of bearing partitions or remove nonbearing walls that are serving as lateral support during weekend do-it-yourself projects. They usually do not remove entire walls without checking with someone in the design field, but small alterations have an effect. Changes too small to result in collapse can cause small, sometimes imperceptible, movements that weaken the overall structural system and reduce the redundant degree of safety.

Plumbers are notorious among engineers for cutting through joists to place waste lines and piping. Their work, both during original construction and during renovations, is often performed after a house has been completely framed.

There are rarely provisions made in the framing for running pipe. Because of the inherent redundancy of wood construction, floors rarely collapse, but given enough of these cuts, a floor will deflect excessively and show other signs of incipient failure. Architects and engineers who have experience in renovation and have seen the effects of a badly coordinated mechanical layout always try to integrate mechanical systems into their design.

Because alterations are easy, repeated previous renovation work may have changed the load paths of a building. The designer must determine where the loads begin and where they are ultimately supported. A house more than twenty years old will very likely have undergone different rounds of alteration that have greatly altered the structure in ways that are not immediately obvious.

Designers must take stock of the existing conditions and fully understand the extent of previous alterations and the intent of proposed alterations. Wood construction is more closely related to living structure than any other material. It grows and shrinks and adapts. As outlined in chapter 5, a thorough series of probes and a subsequent understanding of the structural system are key components in determining the feasibility of proposed changes. Original drawings of a house or wood construction rarely exist, making a good probe program even more important.

Old Code versus New Code

In 1944, the National Lumber Manufacturers Association (now the National Forest Products Association) published the first National Design Specification for Wood Construction. This publication recommended design formulas, techniques, and bending values for various grades and species of wood. The values were based on tests from the 1920s. A 2x2 clear (knotless) piece of each species of wood was tested to failure. The tabulated values were adjusted from the tests to account for the presence of knots and natural characteristics inherent in each species. While the specification formulas were updated through the years to keep up with emerging technologies and new engineered products, the basic wood values did not change. The 1991 edition, however, represented a dramatic shift.

The 1991 "in-grade" design code is based on a research program conducted by the U.S. Department of Agriculture Forest Products Laboratory, in which 70,000 pieces of full-size structural lumber were tested to failure. The new code, while decreasing most allowable bending values, allowed for adjustments based on size (in most cases increases), moisture content, and flat use. These changes resulted in a general decrease in allowable bending values and stiffness. It is important to note that the decreased values were not due to the weakness of modern wood but rather to a new testing technique. This is an important distinction in discussing renovations.

The difference in the values is not extreme, and it is obvious that the old values resulted in adequately designed wood members. However, the new values represent a more thorough testing technique and are widely supported by the industry. During renovations it is obviously impractical to go through a house and reinforce every joist and girder not otherwise affected by alterations that does not work using the new code. It is, therefore, up to the designer's judgment as to whether the old code or new code shall apply.

General rules of thumb can apply in this situation: for any new construction, the new code applies; for existing construction that is not to be altered in any way, the old code applies; for any existing wood member that is to be reinforced for increased loading, the new code applies to both the existing wood and the new reinforcing members.

Framing Types—Balloon versus Platform

Excepting barn construction, there are two types of house framing that a renovation designer should recognize immediately: balloon and platform framing. The original type of framing in a house greatly affects design.

Balloon framing is an almost extinct design that is still found in some older houses. In balloon framing, the wall studs are continuous from the foundation to the roof. Ledger boards, sometimes called ribbands, are cut into the stud at each floor level, and the joists rest on the ledgers (figure 8-1). Obviously, this type of construction is difficult to alter, because of the greater length and continuous connections of the wall studs.

Platform framing replaced balloon framing as the popular way to construct houses in the first half of the twentieth century. In a platform frame, each floor is built on top of the floor below (figure 8-2). Each set of studs is capped with a full-width wood sill at the underside of each floor and the joists sit on the sill. A new sole plate is nailed to the floor sheathing and a new stud wall built on that for the next floor. The entire house is stabilized by the exterior wall sheathing.

122 WOOD FRAMING

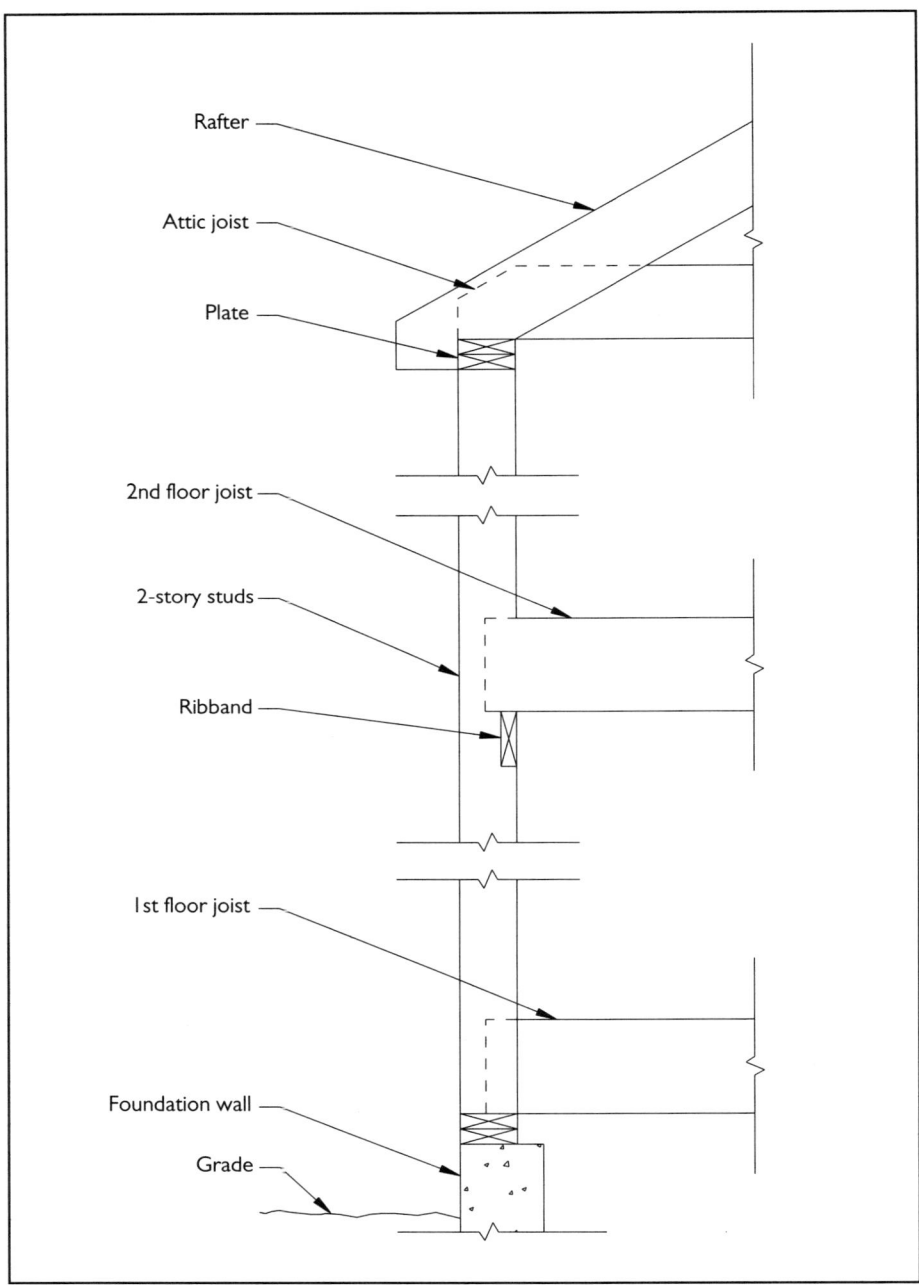

8-1. Balloon framing

Framing Types—Balloon versus Platform

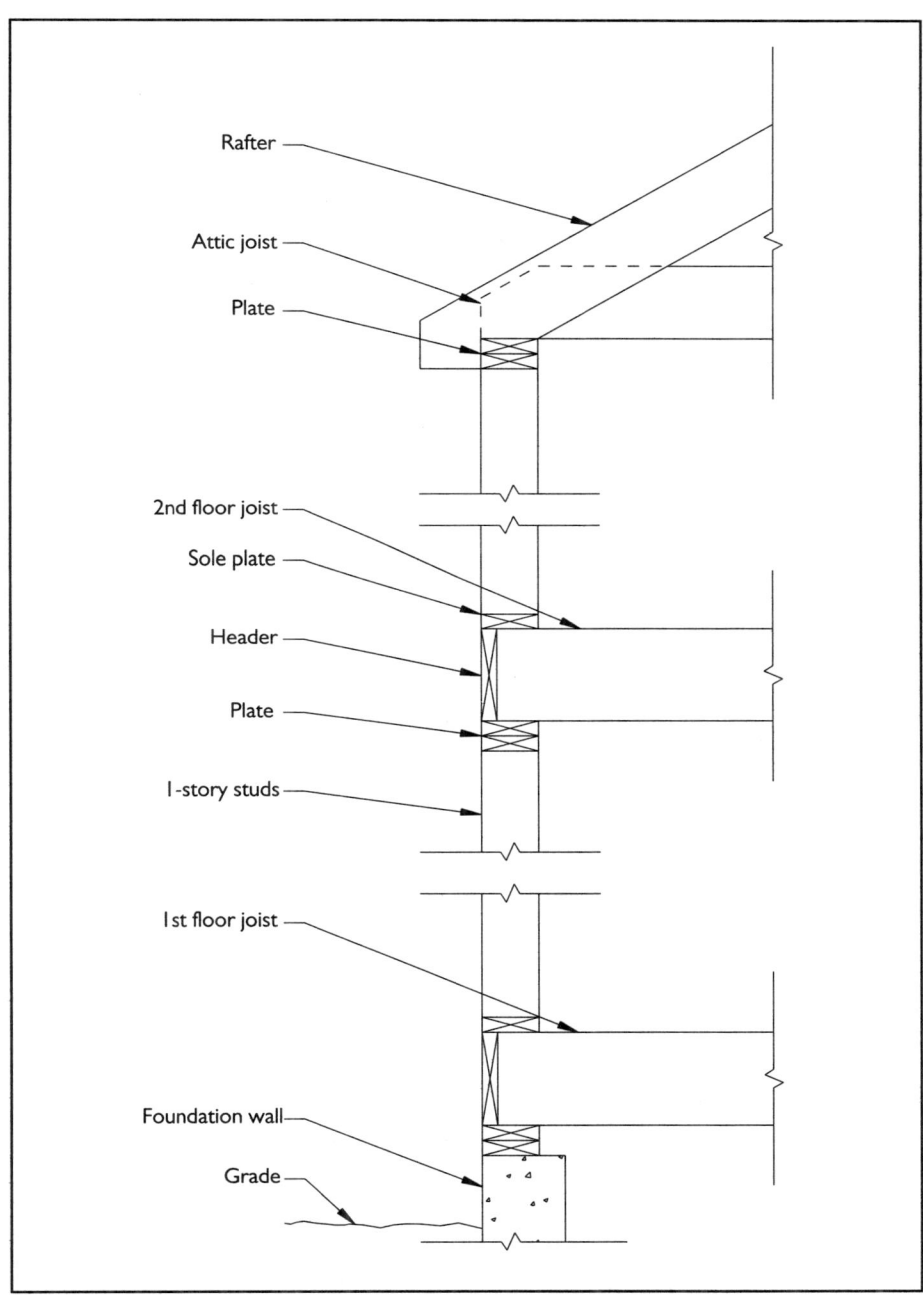

8-2. Platform framing

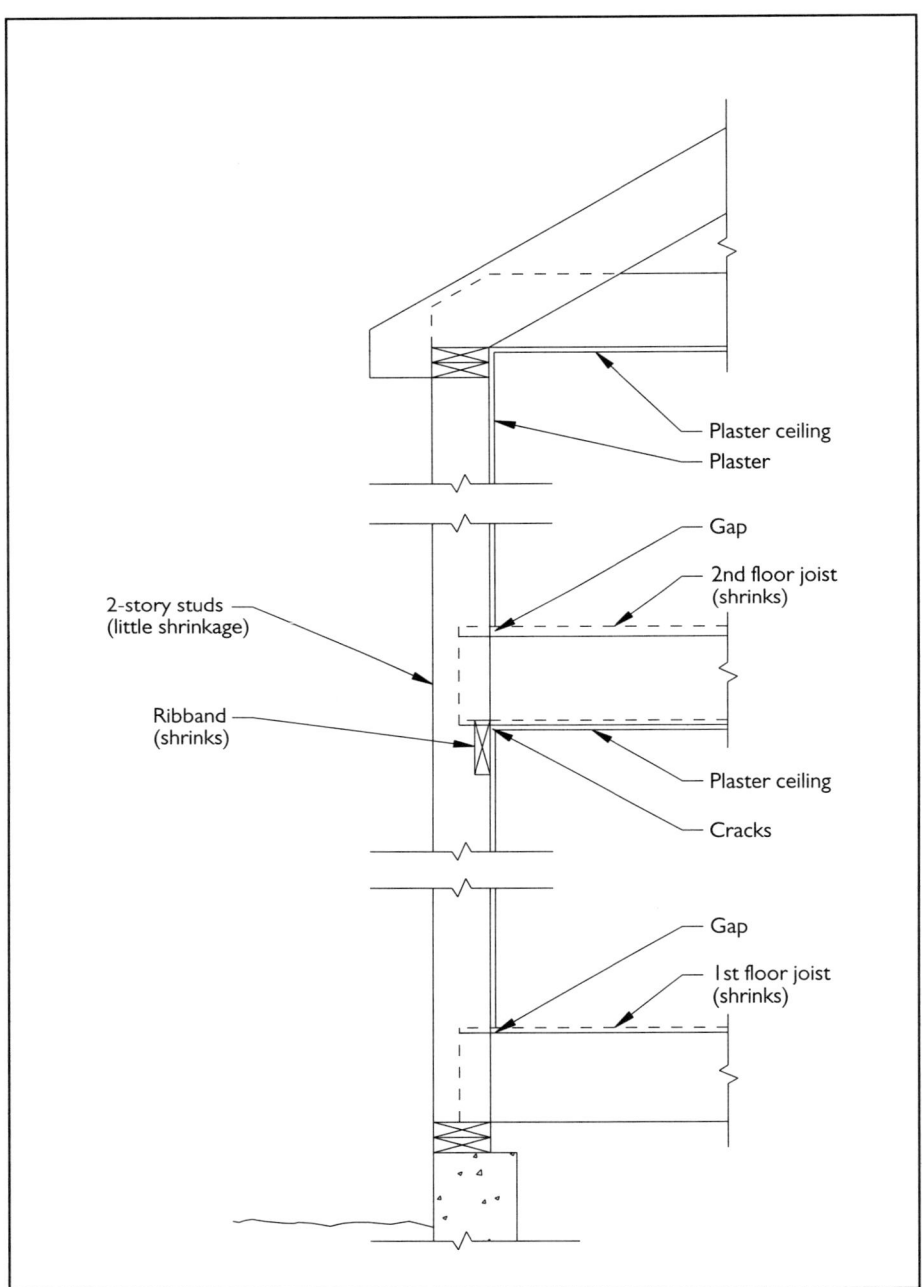

8-3. Shrinkage in balloon framing

Platform framing is easier to build and, more important, shrinks uniformly. In a balloon frame, the floor joists shrink separately from the wall studs. This can result in large gaps between a new floor and the baseboard molding nailed to the studs after a couple of heating seasons (figure 8-3). Each floor of a platform frame shrinks as a unit, with the floor above following the movement of the unit.

Knowing the framing type is especially important if the proposed renovation requires that a floor be demolished. Cutting a series of studs off at a floor level, as would be required with a balloon frame, is labor-intensive and will affect the integrity of the structure below. Removing a wall from a plate in its entirety, as is the case with a platform frame, is relatively simple.

Roof Types

Traditional house construction in temperate climates included a pitched roof to shed snow and rain and to prevent leaks in the winter months. Modern architectural design abandoned the pitched roof and suffers the effects of built-up snow and ponding rain. Postmodern architecture has continuously played with the roof line and added various pieces to the basic pitched roof. The resulting complex roof profile has disrupted the original load transfer. In recent years, architectural designers and homeowners have become enamored of grand spaces and cathedral ceilings that greatly alter the traditional roof load path. Moreover, revising the roof is one of the first means of making an architectural statement during a house renovation. These factors make the architects' understanding of the underlying principles of a pitched roof crucial, so that they may understand the impact of their proposed alterations.

Basic statics dictates that if an inclined beam is loaded vertically and supported vertically at only one end, a horizontal reaction is created at both ends of the beam. In a traditional gable roof, there is no line of support at the ridge, where the rafters simply meet at a ridge board that has no structural capacity, and bear at the outside ends on the exterior walls (figure 8-4). If there is a vertical support at the top end of the rafter (a ridge beam), no horizontal forces exist.

The equal horizontal thrusts normally take the form of an inward push at the ridge and an outward push at the base of the rafter. The base push is resisted by the attic framing and flooring, which provide a diaphragm to tie the rafters together. The push at the top is resolved by the opposed rafters on the other side of the ridge board pushing in. This system also relies on approximately equal

126 WOOD FRAMING

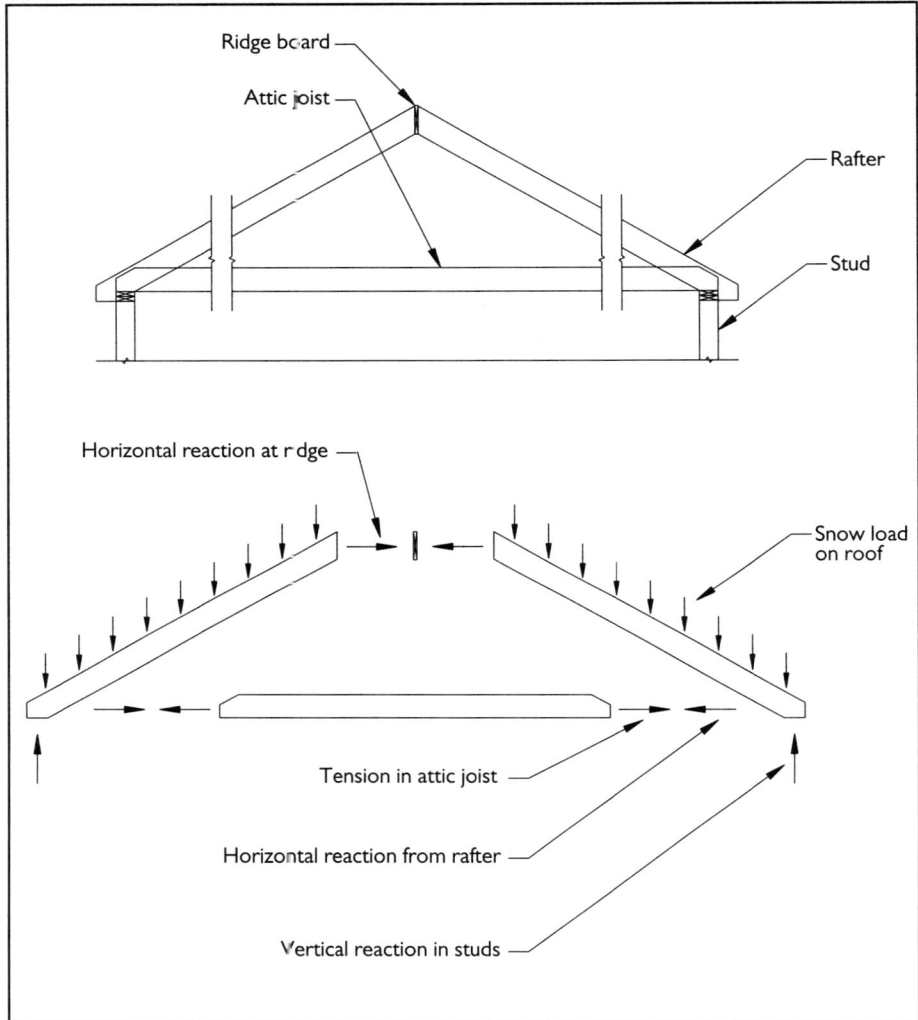

8-4. Gable roof truss and forces

rafter spans to either side of the ridge, as unequal horizontal reactions will produce an unbalanced push at the ridge and a "leaning" roof. The plywood sheathing across the rafters provides lateral stability to the roof system. Often, there will be collar ties at approximately every fourth rafter about a third of the way down from the ridge. These ties are meant to provide support against sag within the

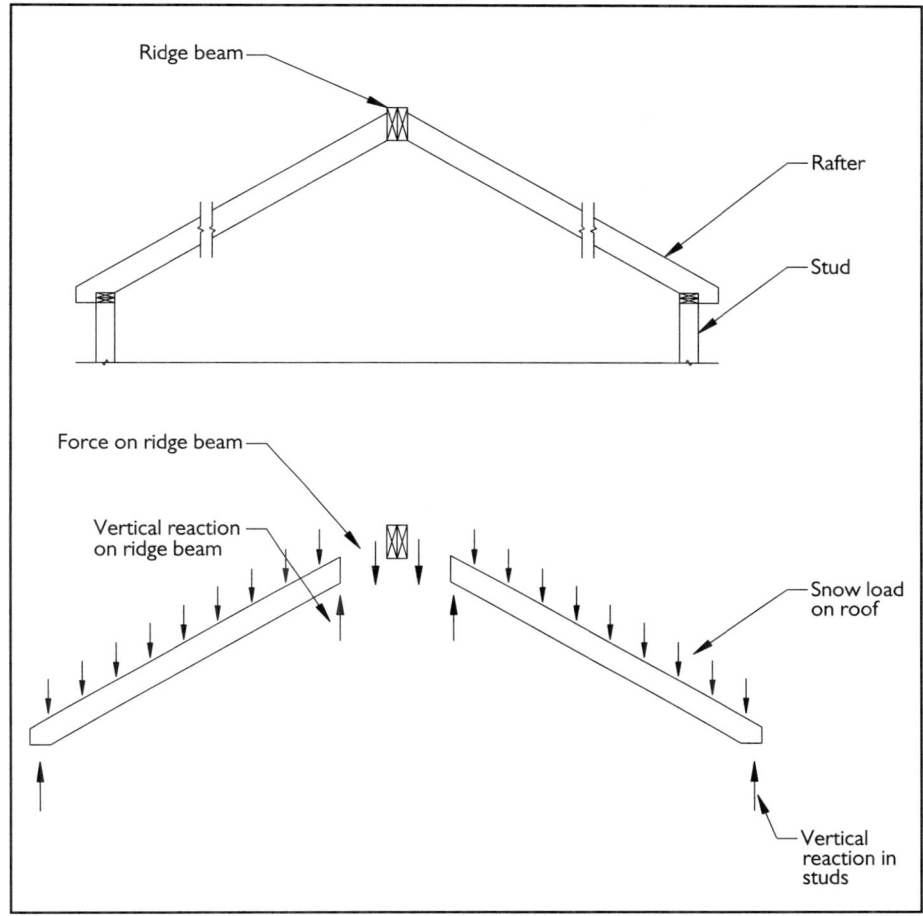

8-5. Cathedral ceiling roof and forces

length of the rafter and are not to be confused with elements used to tie the roof together.

If no attic floor exists, as in the case of a cathedral ceiling, or if the attic floor is raised above the bottom of the rafter, as in a "tray" ceiling, the rafters are not tied and there is no way to resolve the horizontal forces. Therefore, vertical support must be provided at the ridge to eliminate the need for horizontal support (figure 8-5). Ridge support is also required when roof lines are revised in a way that results in an unbalanced horizontal load at the ridge.

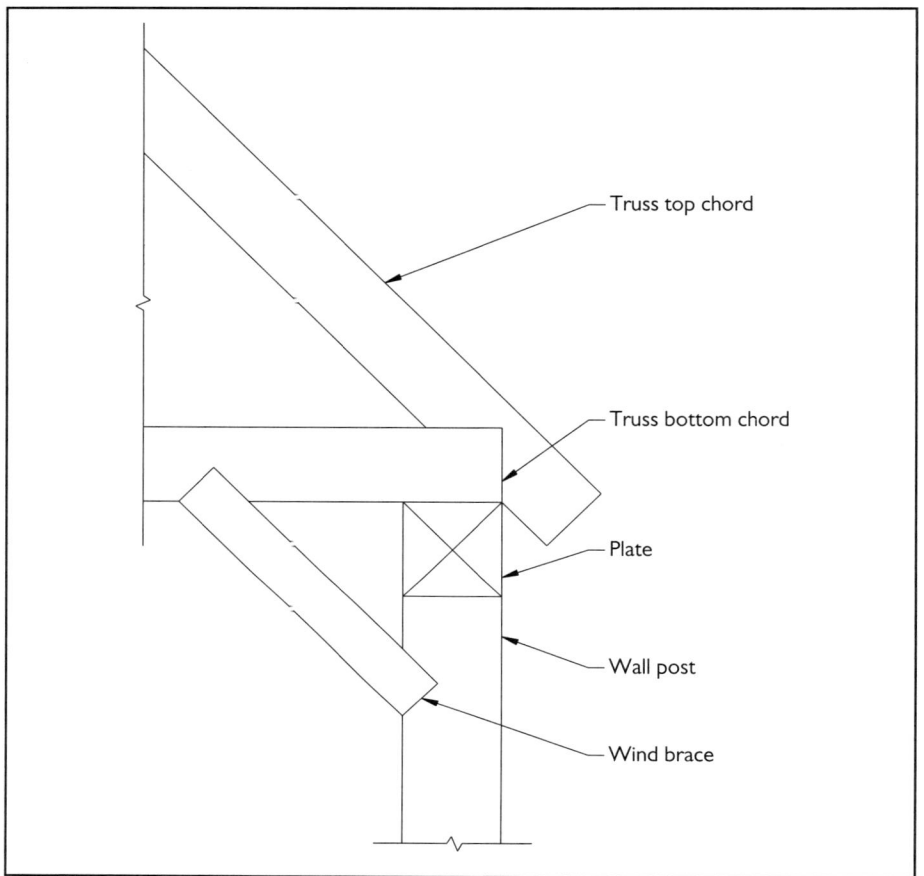

8-6. Barn frame eave connection with brace

In some cases, such as a small round or octagonal structure, the horizontal forces can be resolved by a continuous tension ring at the base of the roof to support the roof rafters' outward thrust. This type of structure also relies on a compression ring at the top of the rafters.

Designers must keep in mind the support of roof thrust when laying out a new roof on an existing house. A small addition and alteration may necessitate the introduction of support at the ridge, which must, in turn, be supported down to foundation. In other words, an alteration at one end of the house may affect the opposite end of the house.

A less delicate type of roof construction is the standard barn roof. Barns were constructed with less rigor and allowed to move more than houses. Their large beam and girder frames depended on braces for lateral stability, not the sheathing diaphragm of stud houses (figure 8-6). Concentrating lateral resistance in braces generally gives more stiffness than diaphragms, but when rotten or broken joints allow movement, there is no redundancy—as illustrated by the innumerable barns that are slowly leaning toward their collapse. The differences between braces and diaphragms are important to note as more homeowners and architects use a barn esthetic for their modern homes. Often this means larger and more intrusive connecting elements than before—for example, diagonal braces running though a room to connect beams to posts. It is important that homeowners and architects realize the severity of movement under wind loading in a barn-type structure with insufficient or deteriorated connections.

A typical barn roof had a supported ridge and no continuous ties at the attic or hayloft level. This allowed an open center bay for moving hay up and down. The supported ridge would frame to equally spaced wood trusses or posts, since the intrusion of a post or truss diagonals was less important in a barn than a house. The trusses would normally span the entire width of the barn.

The typical long, straight, rectangular plan of the barn, coupled with the absence of interior partitions, created the need for intermediate lateral support. This generally took the form of knee-braced, heavy-timber frames at each truss. Braces are found in both directions, parallel to the truss and parallel to the axis of the building.

In renovating barns remember that reinforcing may be required to reduce the larger than normal movements, as well as the advantages of a supported ridge.

Wood Connectors

Connections between wood members have evolved over the years from labor-intensive wood joinery to prefabricated light-gage steel, rapid installation hangers. Wood pins and steel spikes were replaced by the steel bolt and standardized nail. During renovation it is important to keep in mind that a steel bolt in wood often fails when the steel bolt crushes the surrounding wood. Very rarely does a steel bolt fail before the wood itself fails.

Wood joinery is an old and traditional method of connection and often produced elegant and efficient connection between two wood members in a heavy

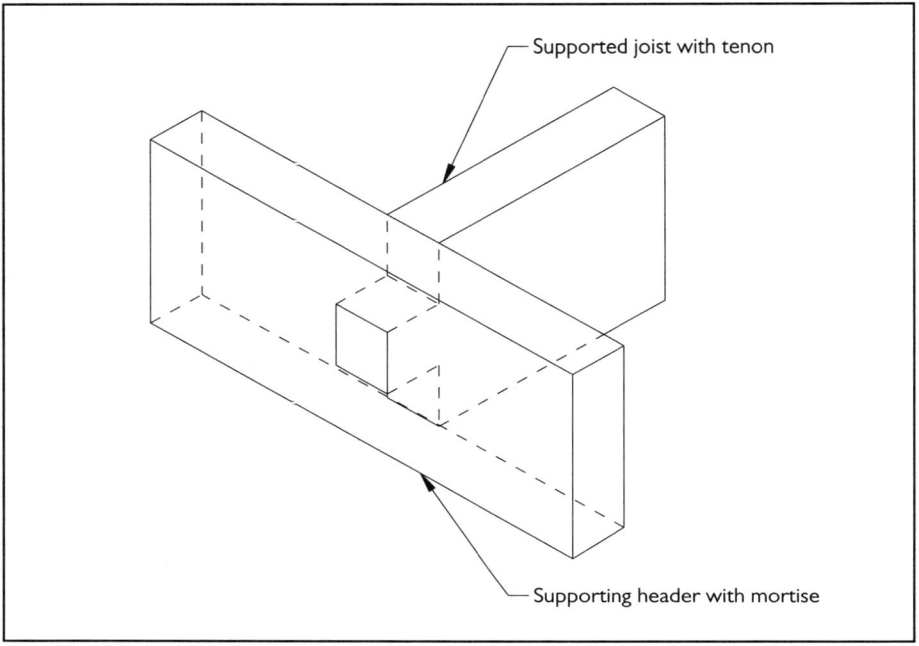

8-7. Mortise and tenon

timber construction. The most common of these connections was the mortise-and-tenon joint (figure 8-7). The mortise is the accepting component of the connection cut into the supporting girder. The tenon is the tongue created by removing material at the end of the supported member. A pin was sometimes placed at the end of the tenon to fix the connection in place. While the mortise-and-tenon connection can usually be justified in theory, in practice cutting the joints often created a local stress concentrator, which caused the wood to split. Renovation will often result in retrofitting newer, prefabricated hangers to mortise-and-tenon joints to resupport the members, since the joist hangers support the tenoned beam at the bottom. These cracked connections usually have not failed totally because the connection of the wood planking to both the joists and the girder transferred the loads.

Another all-wood joint that often fails is the outer end of wood trusses. Traditional wood trusses resolved the compressive force from the top chord into the supporting bottom chord by notching the bottom chord to seat the top chord.

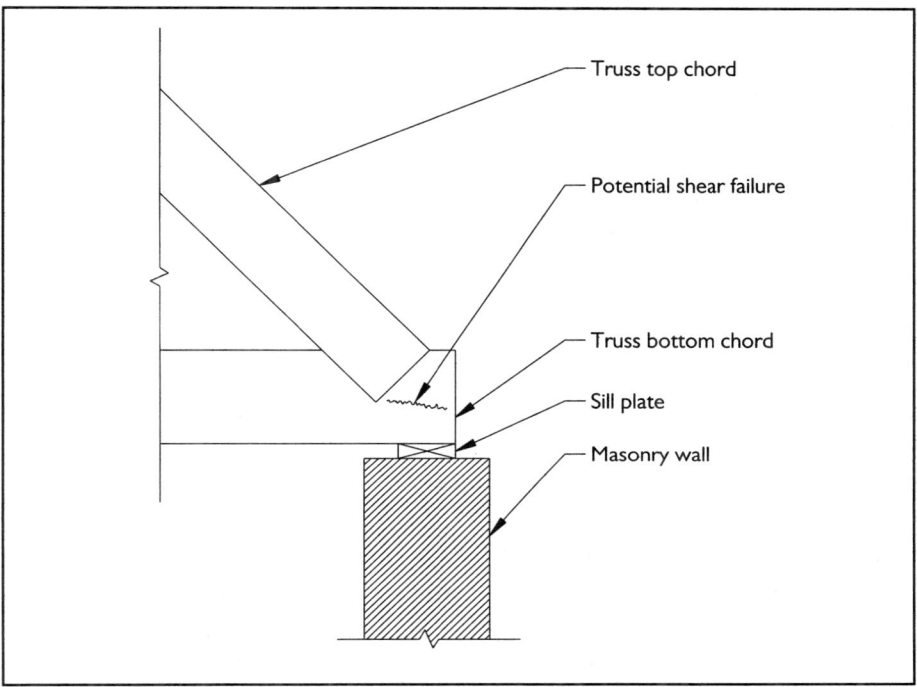

8-8. Roof truss eave connection failing

Unfortunately, the compressive force in the top chord almost always overwhelms the notched piece and the top half of the bottom chord is sheared off along the grain (figure 8-8). It is not unusual in an investigation of an old wood barn to find that the ends of the roof trusses have failed and that the top chords have slid outward, prevented from collapse by redundancy in the truss and the roof diaphragm. The easiest repair is the placement of new steel gusset plates on either side of the truss end and through-bolts between the three members. This solution is adequate if the aesthetic appearance of the trusses is not a crucial element of design.

When clean appearance is an imperative, a more expensive but hidden repair is possible—cutting a steel plate into the end of the truss. The steel plate and the chords are then drilled out in the same fashion as if through-bolts were to be used to secure the plate. Instead of bolting the holes, however, high-strength epoxy is injected into the holes to form hardened pins of a quantifiable strength. This technique is used by only a few qualified craftsman and is an extremely labor-intensive operation.

Shear failure as described obviously occurs at truss ends. However, in traditional truss building each connection was built with very few fasteners, which resulted in repeated notching and cutting. These are very clean connections on paper that are difficult to build cleanly in the field. The first step of any renovation job that involves trusses should be a thorough examination of all truss joints.

Wood Products

Laminated veneer lumber (LVL) was recognized as an engineered wood product by standard codes in the late 1950s and early 1960s. LVLs are wood beams constructed of veneers glued together to form a composite member that is stronger than the sum of the individual pieces, similar to plywood. Generally the producer is able to control the grade of veneer, creating controlled strength grades. Each manufacturer has different trade names for its LVLs, which are generally very similar in design and use. The veneers in LVLs can be stacked with the plies vertical (parallel to the beam depth) or horizontal (parallel to the beam width). Vertical stacking allows for curvature about the major axis, as well as placement of better material at top and bottom to produce an even stronger framing element. The glu-lam is the best-known example of a vertically stacked LVL. LVLs with horizontally aligned veneers are practically impossible to curve in the vertical plane and are generally mass-produced in the form of framing beams equivalent in size to but greater in strength than natural lumber.

Glu-lams enjoyed an architectural vogue in schools and churches during the 1960s and '70s and continue to be used. They are a relatively inexpensive and aesthetically pleasing way to create large open spans. The ability to curve this type of LVL enables the designer to take advantage of arching action and create large, very efficient spans in wood. Heavy tongue-and-groove decking can be used to allow for greater spacing of glu-lam arches and even more economy. Because these arches are generally dramatic and designers wish to expose them, fabricating is done so as to create a very aesthetically pleasing material. Often glu-lams are exposed to the elements as well, and the components are designed for weathering.

Mass-produced, horizontally aligned LVLs are not meant to be exposed, either to view or to the elements. These beams are generally heat-pressed together and may be distinguished by the vertical burns evenly spaced along their length. Although some producers of these LVLs have begun placing a protective wax coating on each beam, the beams deteriorate from prolonged exposure to water and should not be used as exterior elements or in a damp, unventilated cellar.

The mass-produced, slightly weaker, unsightly straight beams make up the vast majority of the LVLs used. Horizontally aligned LVLs are one of the best new tools to be introduced to renovation in the past thirty years. As a fabricated wood product, they are dimensionally stable, a tremendous advantage in renovation design where the surrounding natural wood is dimensionally stable only because it previously underwent shrinkage. LVLs were originally much more expensive than ordinary lumber. However, as the price of lumber has increased and the price of LVLs dropped, the cost gap has become much smaller. As the gap narrows and the advantages to construction and design are factored in, the use of LVLs in renovation is no longer a luxury but, rather, an efficient way to design.

Besides LVLs, there are other engineered wood products on the market that are dimensionally stable and effective. A product used extensively as a substitute for standard lumber and LVLs, in a repetitive joist application, is the prefabricated wood I-beam. If deflection criteria are carefully obeyed, wood I-beams can provide a suitable floor joist system for a large addition, less expensive than LVLs. Like LVLs, they do not shrink, and therefore the first couple of heating seasons will not produce a "lip" between original construction and addition. Their ability to span farther than most actual joists is helpful when the removal of interior partitions increases the unsupported room width.

Other wood-framing products exist, such as joists with wood flanges and trussed steel webs, but these often are less stiff than LVLs and framing lumber and produce a floor that is perceptibly and disconcertingly "bouncy" compared to a typical house floor. These products can be compared to the open-web steel joists used in mall and factory roofs.

The field that has seen the most growth in the past decade is that of engineered wood panels. These panels are stronger than standard plywood panels and designed to support heavier lateral stresses as fewer interior partitions are used in the design of a house and more lateral reliance is placed on the exterior walls.

In addition, many new wood products are made of reconstituted wood and glue, helping to preserve the wood supply.

Reinforcing Techniques in Wood Framing

Carpenters and homebuilders have long used the term "sistering." Unfortunately, the word has come to be used for any sort of reinforcing where new wood is placed next to an existing joist. This has included splicing wood joists, scabbing plywood on a joist, and reinforcing only a small portion of a joist for added capacity.

Proper sistering relies on the transfer of load through direct vertical shear. This should not be confused with reinforcing that works through horizontal shear transfer, such as welding a steel plate to the underside of a steel beam or screwing and gluing plywood to the bottom of a wood joist. In the latter cases, the transfer of horizontal shear creates a new, stronger composite piece. Horizontal shear transfer, as described in chapter 6, allows the full transfer of load from one individual piece to another.

In sistering and vertical shear transfer in general, the final composite beam is at most only as strong as the sum of the strengths of the two pieces, and sometimes less, as in the case of a flitch beam.

Simply put, you can increase the capacity of a sound joist by placing a new, full-length joist next to it and bolting the joists together. You cannot fix a discontinuous, deteriorated joist by bolting short lengths of wood to either side of it, even if you run the new joists a few feet beyond the splice-point to "develop" the splice, as you would a steel WT section. For that scenario to work, the connection between new and old material must carry not only the shear—the load downward—but also the moment at that point within the beam. This is theoretically possible, but the low capacity of individual wood connectors and the need to keep the connectors a minimum distance apart to prevent local overstress of the wood makes a full-moment splice that can easily be obtained in steel nearly impossible. Placing added material to the side as opposed to the top or bottom is a very different condition.

To avoid confusion, in this text "sistering" a wood joist refers to the placing of a new joist next to an existing joist to increase the capacity of the floor system (figure 8-9). The new joist is placed for the full length of the existing joist. The bolts between the two beams, in most cases, simply hold the beams together and are required for good practice, not stress. A more direct form of reinforcing, related to sistering, would be the placement of a new joist for every existing joist, without any connection between the two.

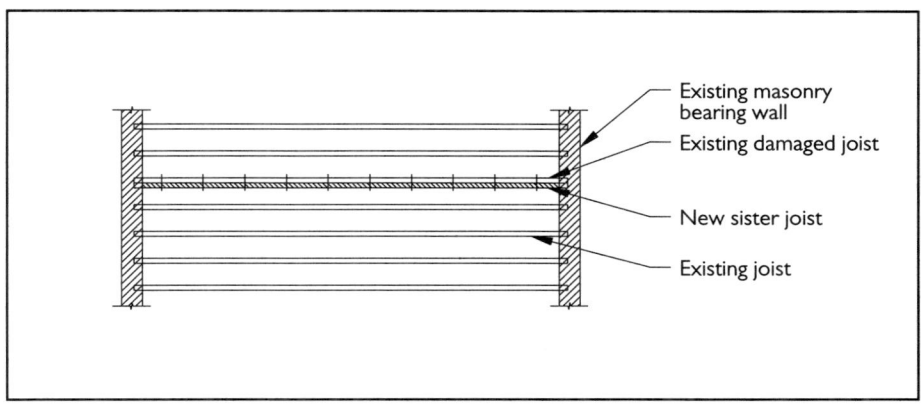

8-9. Sistered joist

In order for true sistering to occur, as opposed to simply adding a second joist, two conditions must be met: first, the flooring above must have continuous bearing on both the new and existing joists, to ensure that the floor load is transferred to both beams; second, bolts at each end must transfer the shear within the new joist to the existing joist. If the reaction of the new, sister, joist is transferred, via through-bolts, to the existing joist within a distance from the end bearing equal to the joist depth, the existing, sistered, joist only needs to be checked for bearing for the entire load. If the bolt group cannot transfer the vertical reaction of the sister joist within the end distance, the sistered joist must be capable of supporting the entire reaction in shear, bearing and bending.

In order to achieve continuous load transfer from the floor to both new and existing joist, the use of manufactured wood products is highly recommended. New lumber sistered to existing will, most likely, shrink away from the subfloor. Manufactured wood does not shrink, and therefore, continuous bearing will be assured through the lifetime of this repair. Shrinkage is especially noticeable when new joists are simply placed between existing ones, not sistered, to increase floor capacity. Over the first few heating seasons the new lumber generally shrinks and an undesirable waviness may occur in the floor.

If the original joist is not capable of supporting the entire reaction, the new joist must bear on the wall. This is simply additional joist placement. Separate bearing has never been difficult to attain in wood platform framing where new

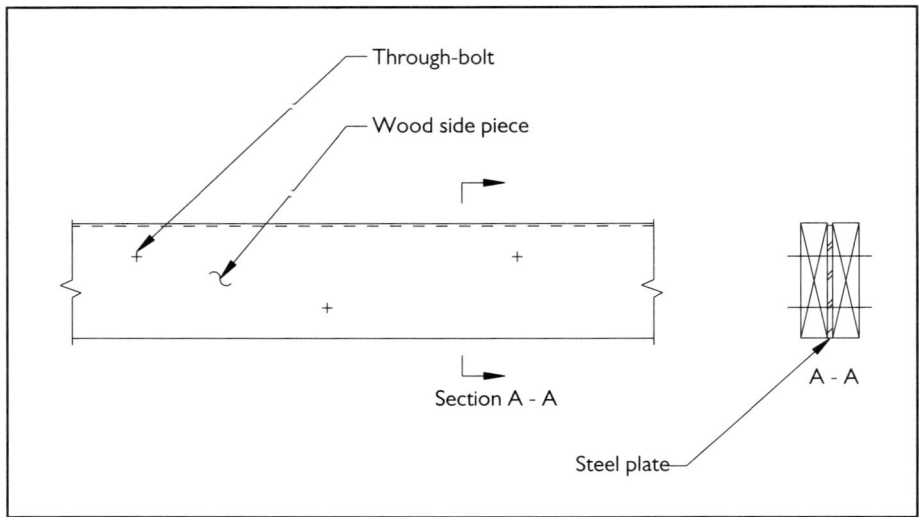

8-10. Flitch beam detail

joists can be slid into place next to the existing joists. With the advent of joist hangers and adhesive anchors, balloon framing and masonry walls do not pose as big an obstacle as they once did.

As noted above, the bolts between sistered joists are not required in most cases. Bolts are required when sistered joists are used to level a floor, as opposed to adding strength. In this case the new joist is continuously supporting the new, level subfloor and the bolts are transferring the load to the working, existing joist. No bolts are required to develop the load at the end of the span because the load has been transferred throughout the span. This is really a form of blocking, but by definition it is sistering, as vertical load is being transferred from a new joist to an existing joist for the full span length.

A more ambitious form of sistering is the flitch beam. Flitch beams flourished in the middle of the nineteenth century when wrought-iron plates were introduced as a construction material. The flitch beam is typically a combination of two heavy wood pieces with a center steel plate (figure 8-10). The steel plate dramatically increases the overall strength of the beam. The wood girders to either side of the plate add stability and provide ease of connection to this girder for other wood members. Today, the availability of high-strength wood products has lessened the appeal of flitch beams. However, flitch beams are still in use and are especially helpful when LVLs are difficult to obtain or when the need exists for high strength and stiffness in the smallest possible depth.

Like sistered beams, the flitch beam works by vertical shear transfer. The floor load is carried by the wood component and transferred to the steel plate by evenly spaced through-bolts. Theoretically, we assume that the entire beam will deflect in unison and the load carried by the wood or steel component will be based on their relative stiffness. As long as each component is capable of carrying the percentage of load it is responsible for, the flitch beam can carry the full load. Often, a flitch beam will bear on a wood post or sill and the steel plate alone would crush the wood in bearing. Therefore, the wood component is designed to carry all of the end reaction. As with sistered beams, the reaction from the steel plate is transferred to the wood side members by through-bolts at the end of the beam. If this method prohibitively increases the size of the side members, provisions can be made to bear the steel plate without crushing the wood support.

Plywood Tee Reinforcing

Unlike sistering, plywood tee reinforcing is based on horizontal shear transfer and is similar in design to the steel reinforcing techniques of welding plates to the bottom of steel beams. By transferring horizontal shear, a composite section is created that is stronger than that obtained by adding the two individual pieces together.

As with a composite steel beam or a reinforced steel beam, the horizontal shear at the intersection of the plywood sheathing and the wood joist is transferred by discrete fasteners, in this case wood screws or nails (figure 8-11). Unlike sistered beams, this reinforcing method can be used over portions of a floor, as long as it is "developed" at either end. Theoretically, this method can be used to splice a wood beam at midspan if plywood is used at both the top and bottom of the joist and the thickness of plywood and the fasteners' capacity are both sufficient to carry the full moment.

Unlike sistering, plywood reinforcing must be carried out with great care and should only be specified when no other alternative exists. The practical objections to this work include the difficulty of obtaining full contact between the plywood and the joists and the difficulty of obtaining full strength from the fasteners. New wood beams vary slightly in size, and existing wood beams vary

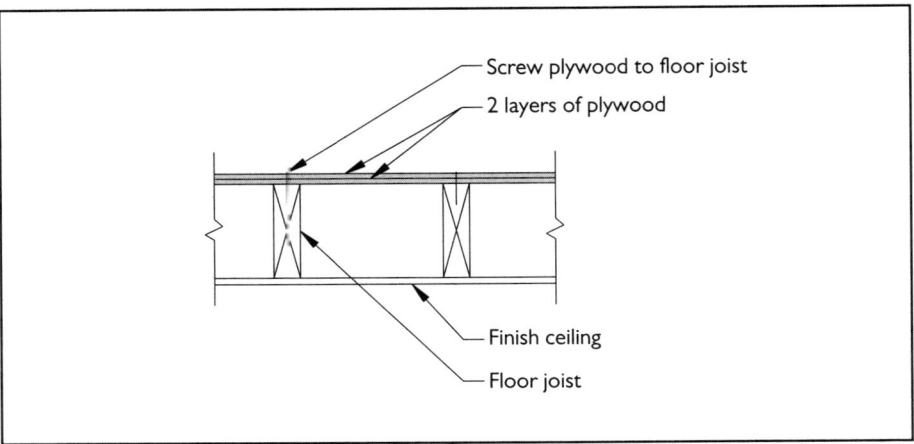

8-11. Plywood tee detail

even more, making full contact difficult. Fastening plywood to a joist is a blind operation where the fasteners will be accurately placed and attain full load strength only some of the time. Top and bottom plywood reinforcing is a doubly blind operation, and this is why splicing wood is highly discouraged.

While this technique is theoretically simple, and employs basic structural principles, it relies more on good craftsmanship than sistering does. While good craftsmanship is considered synonymous with wood construction and carpentry, the industry is less regulated than the steel and concrete industries. The designer has less control from paper to reality. For these reasons, this type of reinforcing is often recommended when only additional floor stiffness is required, and not additional strength.

Case Study 8-1: Sistering Joists 1

In this case study, a four-story rowhouse is being thoroughly renovated. On the third floor, the architect wants to move a 10-foot (3050 mm) length of a wood stiffening partition 4 feet (1220 mm) to the side, creating the need for sistered joists.

As is typical for urban rowhouses, the wood joists span the width of the building, in this case 20 feet (6100 mm). A wood-stud partition separates the stair hall from the rooms on each floor. Because of the framing orientation, this

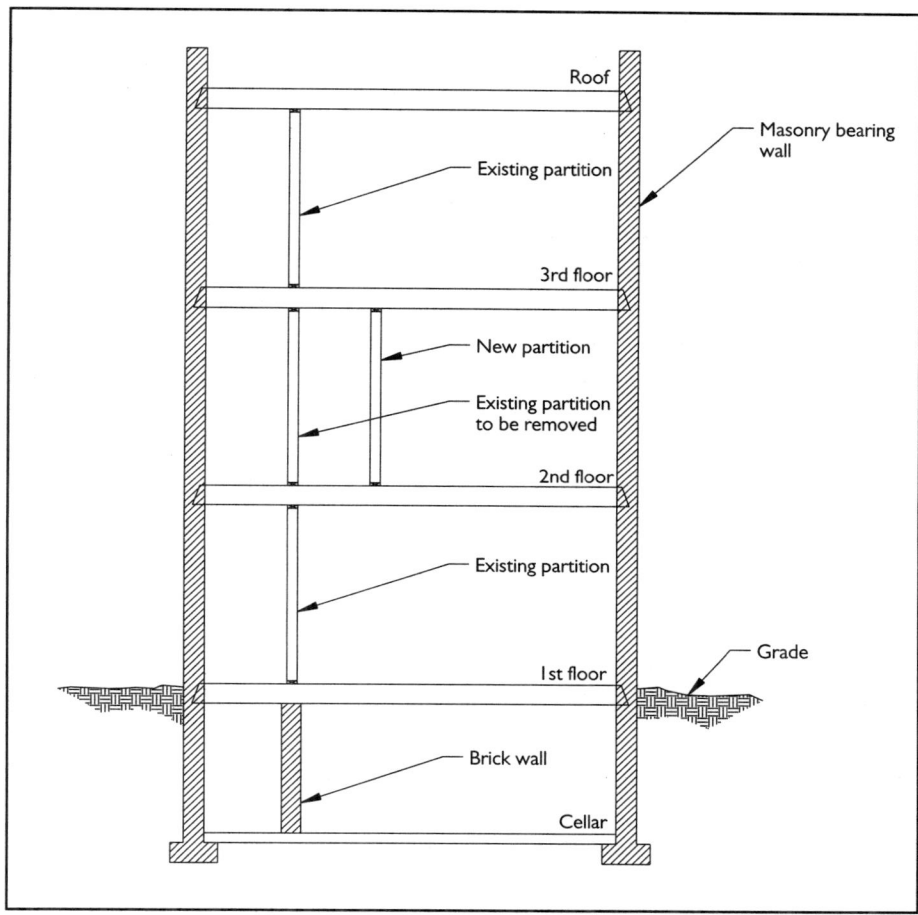

8-1-1. Building section of rowhouse with moved bearing partition

partition usually supports the joists, acting as a structural wall. Since it is not strictly a bearing wall and calculations often show that the joists can span the full building width, this is known as a stiffening partition: it stiffens a floor that is otherwise supported (figure 8-1-1). This type of wall is usually supported on a brick wall or metal beams in the basement, indicating that the original builders knew the wall would be supporting load. The nature of the partition is important to remember during renovations that change its location. Removing portions of these walls will not cause a floor to fail, but the floor may deflect excessively, cracking plaster and annoying occupants.

Early in the design phase the engineer opens probes at the ceiling of each floor and, if possible, at the intersection of the stiffening wall to the joists. In this case, each floor has 3x9 (75 by 230 mm) joists at 14 inches (355 mm) on center. (The spacing of joists at 12, 16, and 24 inches [305, 405, and 610 mm] did not dominate until the introduction of panelized wood sheathing, such as 4- by 8-foot [1220 by 2440 mm] plywood sheets.) The roof joists are 3x8s (75 by 200 mm) at 18 inches (460 mm) on center. The floor joists bear on the stiffening partition, but the roof joists do not. The stiffening partition ends at the ceiling of the fourth floor, while the roof joists step up in elevation toward the rear of the building to provide a drainage slope.

At the third floor, the architect's intention to move the stiffening partition will impose a point load on the existing joists that they were not designed to carry. With the new loading, the existing joists do not work for bending and must be reinforced. A new joist is to be placed next to each existing joist. Sistering the old joists and not bearing the new joists will ease construction, so each end of the existing joists is checked for bearing and shear with the new, increased load. The reactions are different at the two ends of the joists because the stiffening partition is not centered in the house width. It is found that the end of the joist bearing on the stiffening partition is overstressed, while the end bearing in the masonry wall is not An LVL of equivalent stiffness is sistered to the existing joist and carries roughly half the load. Through-bolts are sized for the half-reaction and placed within the first 9 inches (230 mm) of the joist at the masonry wall. The LVL is slid onto the existing sill at the stiffening wall and toe-nailed into place. The two joists are through-bolted together at 24 inches (610 mm) on center with ½-inch (13 mm) diameter bolts. This is repeated for each joist in this area. Before placement of this detail, the entire ceiling is removed and the engineer checks that each existing joist is adequate and stable. Any joists in disrepair are replaced with a new LVL capable of carrying the full new load.

The final construction does not change the overall load distribution, so there is no need for new lines of bearing or new foundations.

Case Study 8-2: Sistering Joists II

This case study involves the same rowhouse renovation as Case Study 8-1. On the second floor of the building, directly over the original living room, the owners want to level a section floor that sags noticeably.

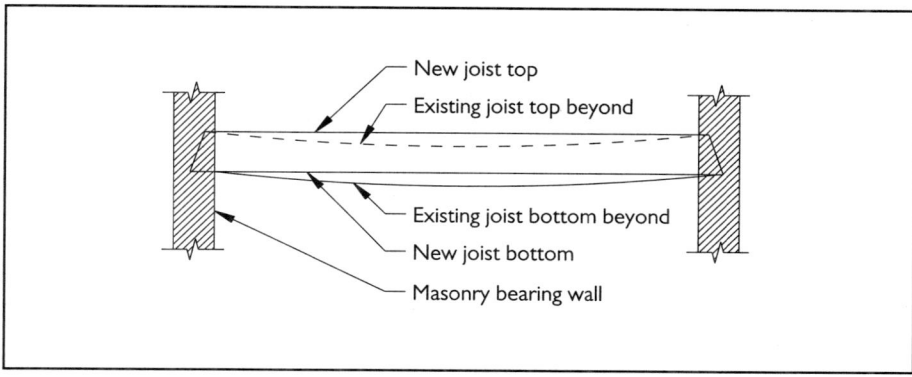

8-2-1. Building section showing deflected joists and new joists

The joists are found to have crept in a very uneven manner over the hundred-year life of the building. The cause is the absence of a stiffening wall below: the first-floor living room is the largest open space in the house. The absence of cracking in the ceiling below is a good indication that the ceiling was most likely patched at some time, and that the movement has greatly subsided. Calculations show that the joist can support the floor load with only normal deflections. Based on these facts, new joists can simply be sistered to the side of the existing ones (figure 8-2-1). Evenly spaced through-bolts transfer the floor load from the new joists to the existing joists. The loads on the existing joists have not changed, so the existing capacity is adequate by inspection. The only real difficulty is the existing 14-inch (355 mm) spacing, which requires custom-cut plywood panels when the floor is replaced above unless the original floor planks are salvaged and reused. This work does not change the overall load distribution at all.

Case Study 8-3: Barn Renovation

Structural engineers sometimes work on buildings that are not easily analyzed. A traditional, late-nineteenth-century New England barn can present complicated problems in analysis and design.

The roof is supported by heavy timber trusses spanning the full width of the barn at approximately 8 feet (2440 mm) on center. Wood purlins, at 2 feet (610 mm) on center, span the 8 feet (2440 mm) between trusses and are covered with wood planking. The trusses bear on heavy posts that sit on a perimeter foundation wall. The walls consist of wood cladding on infill studs with cross-bracing.

While there is some noticeable structural deterioration, the wide open lower level will work well for the storage of equipment and cars and the owners decide to proceed with a full renovation to make this a usable storage space. The renovation will include the repair and upgrade of the roof structure and the introduction of HVAC systems to heat and cool the space. The most efficient HVAC system found works from above, suspending mechanical equipment and ductwork from the bottom chords of the existing trusses.

As with almost any barn structure, it is probable that no design drawings were created; certainly, none exist. In order for the renovation to be accurately priced, investigation and program analysis are called for before renovation. The investigation takes a few weeks and requires two phases of analysis. First, the existing sizes and configuration of roof structure are recorded and the roof analyzed as if it were new and in good condition. Once it is determined that the basic structure works for the proposed loading, the existing condition of the structure is reviewed and repairs recommended as required.

Structural investigations are often performed in one visit, making gathering the proper information crucial. In this structure, the necessary information includes: truss configuration and dimensions; roof pitch; purlin and joist dimensions and spacings; purlin and joist bearing points (to determine if truss chords are in local bending); truss member connections; and the condition of panel points connections. The panel connections are probably the most important data. An efficient way of recording conditions is to use a key plan numbering the trusses, together with an elevation of a typical truss lettering the panel points (figure 8-3-1). Each condition note or photo can then be labeled with the truss number and connector letter. This prevents connections that are obvious in the field from being forgotten in the office.

The trusses in this barn are traditional Pratt trusses with 6x8 (150 by 200 mm) diagonals and chords. Each connection is mortise-and-tenon, and compression members are notched into the top or bottom chord. The purlins are connected to the top chords with mortise-and-tenon connections as well. The ceiling structure consists of joists bearing on the bottom chord of each truss and planking spanning between the joists. The roof pitch is 4 inches per foot (18 degrees). A small piece (¾ x 1 x 3 inches [19 by 25 by 75 mm]) removed from a truss and sent to the Western Wood Products center for evaluation is found to be yellow pine.

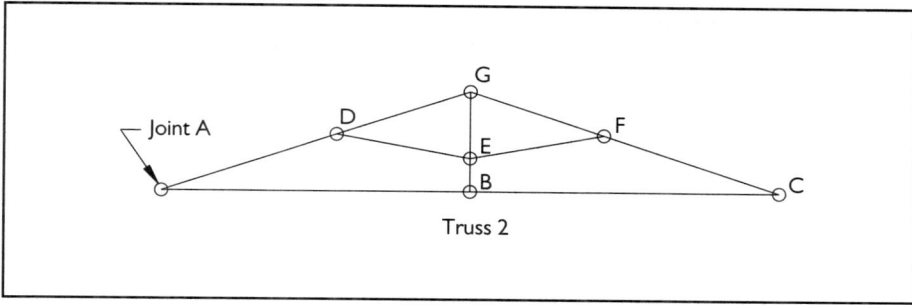

8-3-1. Roof truss with connections numbered

The panel point connections have shifted in some locations and are failing at each end where the top chord is notched into the bottom chord. In some instances the bottom chord has failed in shear and the top chord has slid out. Before a repair can be specified, the proposed loading must be calculated to determine the appropriate fix.

The barn is 64 feet (19,500 mm) in length (five trusses with no end trusses), and the trusses span the clear width of 30 feet (9145 mm). Initial calculations will involve the roof purlins and ceiling joists to determine their load capacity and the feasibility of supporting mechanical equipment on these members. While the roof purlins are sufficient to carry the required dead and live loads, it is found that they do not have extra capacity to support mechanical equipment. The joists and the trusses as units are capable of supporting additional loads, but the bottom chord of the truss cannot support these additional loads in local bending from panel point to panel point. Any mechanical equipment, therefore, must be supported on new structural members that will frame into truss panel points only.

The proposed loading, with the exception of specific areas of mechanical loads, is not significantly different from the existing loading. Equating the mortise notches with wood knots, it is found the percentage of material lost is acceptable for a Number 2 grade yellow pine and the truss members are adequate. As expected, the compression notches at the ends of each truss are not structurally adequate.

This information defines the scope of the renovation. New mechanical equipment is to bear on new beams that will frame into the panel points of the trusses. A new walkway will be supported on the truss panel points and occupy the center bay of the trusses. The shifting of the truss members will be alleviated by placing new bracing members from truss to truss to prevent the members from shifting out of plane while allowing them to continue to work as designed. Lastly, the truss ends must be reinforced with steel plates and steel through-bolts.

Case Study 8-4: Plywood Tee Floor Stiffening

A house on the ocean, designed as a summer house and built of generally light construction, is to undergo renovation to become a year-round dwelling. This means the placement of insulation throughout the house, an upgrade of general mechanical systems, and the placement of new windows. Among the general improvements, a stone floor will be installed in the bathrooms and kitchen.

Accurate original drawings exist. The contractor wants to use foam insulation installed through access holes in the floor, not remove finishes, if possible. The engineer finds that the existing floor joists have the capacity to carry the added stone weight. The joists will, however, be undesirably flexible and will probably cause cracking in the stone floor. Without removing the ceiling below the bathrooms or kitchen, the simplest way to stiffen the floor is to remove the

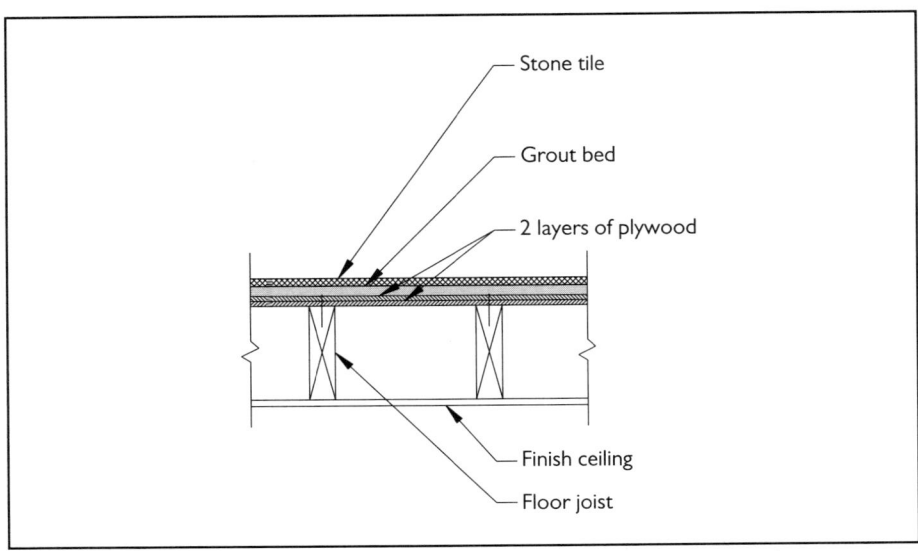

8-4-1. Plywood tee with stone finish

flooring in the work areas and replace the old flooring with stiffer plywood that is glued and screwed to the existing joists (figure 8-4-1). The result will increase the stiffness due to horizontal shear transfer between the joists and plywood through the glue and screws. The new plywood, setting bed, and stone will create a small step up. However, this is expected with a new stone finish and an unchanged ceiling.

Case Study 8-5: Attic Opening

A two-story wood-frame house, constructed as a platform frame with a gable roof, is to undergo renovation. The house is a rectangle in plan, measuring 60 by 30 feet (18,300 by 9150 mm), with a small number of dormers and chimney openings in the roof. The attic framing directly connects the bottom of the roof rafters, properly tying the roof. The owners of the property wish to add light and height to a new "grand" entrance. The architect suggests removing the roof, attic, and second-floor framing directly above the foyer to create a light-well. The design calls for a new skylight centered above the foyer and walls from the underside of the skylight down to the second floor.

The roof is tied together by the attic rafters, which prevent the rafters from spreading apart under load, as described earlier in this chapter. Removing a portion of the framing will disrupt this balance and, while immediate damage may not occur, the roof may start to spread apart under heavy ice or snow loading. Shifting of the framing, in turn, will cause gaps and leaks at the skylight. Depending on the size and location of the skylight, there are two possible techniques for reinforcing the roof.

If a small skylight is located immediately adjacent to the front wall, the best approach to reinforcing would take into account the tying action of the attic framing and the strength of the roof diaphragm. The roof diaphragm can act as a horizontal beam to carry lateral loads to the perimeter shear walls. In the same way, the portion of the roof remaining between the skylight and the ridge can act as a horizontal beam and transfer the thrust of the opposite side of the roof out to the new trimmer beams that frame the opening (figure 8-5-1). These beams will then be tied with reinforced attic framing, creating a small triangular truss (figure 8-5-2). As with any reinforcing technique, it is essential that the forces are resolved and, in this case, that the connection between the new trimmers and the reinforced attic framing is adequate.

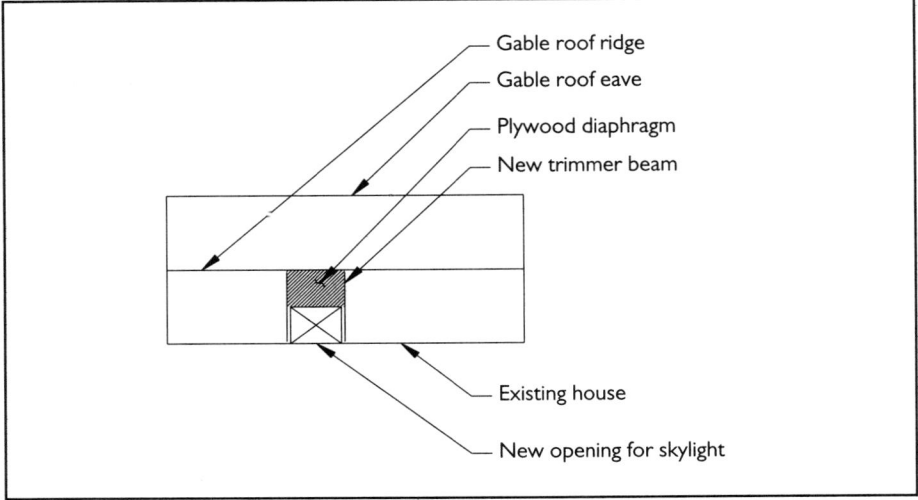

8-5-1. Roof plan with opening, diaphragm, and new trimmer beams

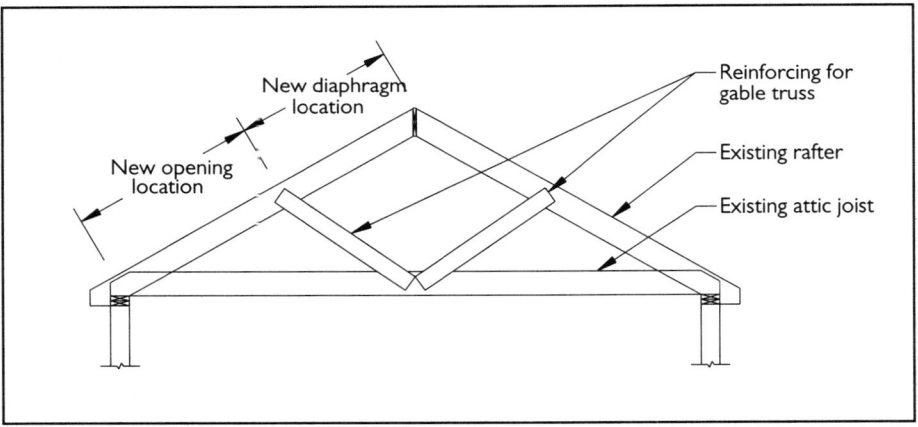

8-5-2. Roof sections showing truss and reinforced tie

For larger openings the primary method of reinforcing would involve converting the existing ridge board into a ridge beam. Posts would be placed under the ridge board at the perimeter of the opening (figure 8-5-3). The ridge board would then be reinforced as required to carry the vertical reaction of the joists.

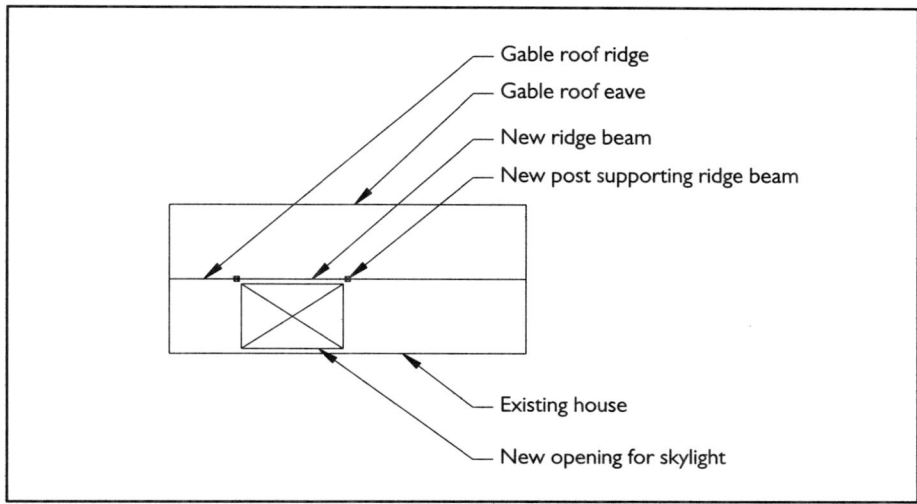

8-5-3. Roof plan showing opening, ridge beam, and posts

This reaction would not exist at the ridge if the gable were properly tied at the attic level. These posts then have to be carried down, either to reinforced interior floor framing or to a new footing in the cellar.

The second technique is the more straightforward of the two and allows for more flexibility in the placement of the skylight. However, this method will produce a rigid portion of a relatively flexible structural system. If the gable roof is sound and well built, this hard spot should not cause a problem. If, however, the roof line has begun to sag noticeably, the reinforcing work may cause a hump to develop in the ridge line. The problem is primarily esthetic; however, it may, at its worst, disrupt the waterproofing and may cause leaks in the future. These problems can be alleviated by converting the entire length of ridge board into a ridge beam. In an ordinary size gable roof, this may require only two interior columns, not a large price to pay for the flexibility of multiple openings.

Case Study 8-6: Roof Addition

In this example, a two-story house is expanded. The rectangular house, 50 feet (15,240 mm) long by 30 feet (9150 mm) wide, will gain additions at the rear and one side. A 30-foot (9150 mm) long extension will connect to the side of

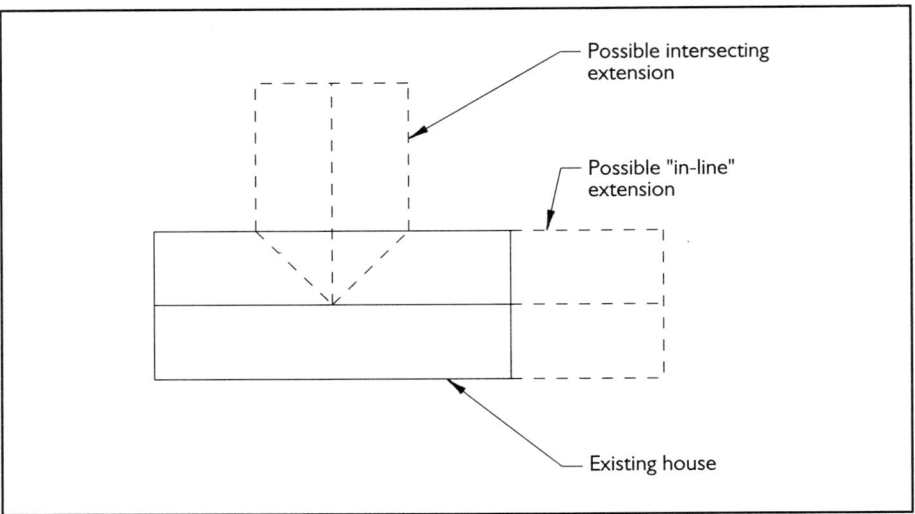

8-6-1. Roof plan showing roof additions

the house and a 20-foot (6100 mm) long by 20-foot (6100 mm) wide room will be added to the rear (figure 8-6-1). The existing ridge line will continue over the side extension and the new ridge at the rear extension will run perpendicular to the existing ridge, creating valleys at the intersection of the two roofs. The interior plan of the existing house will remain unchanged.

The existing house sits on good sand and has not shown any signs of foundation problems. The new additions therefore are placed on identical footings. The walls and floor are platform-framed, like the existing house, except that manufactured wood products are specified to avoid gaps and warping due to shrinkage. Rough lumber will be used at the roof, where shrinkage will affect the overall structure less and the members are smaller (shrinkage occurs as a percentage of overall size).

The existing roof is a standard tied gable roof, with 2x8 rafters at 16 inches on center and a 2x10 ridge board. The attic is unoccupied, although there is ductwork throughout the space.

At the side extension, the roof structure is simply continued onto the new roof. While the original exterior side wall, now an interior partition, is not serving as a bearing wall, it is left in place to keep the lateral stiffness of the house. If it were necessary to break through this wall, the roof diaphragm would have to be analyzed for the new, longer span between exterior wall diaphragms, and the existing exterior wall at the opposite end of the house would have to be analyzed to accept a larger load due to the increased length of the house. For this project, only small cutouts are made in the wall for new doors and ducts.

The plans call for the ceiling at the second floor of the rear extension to follow the roof lines, requiring that the existing rafters be cut at the newly introduced valley beams rather than simply building the new roof over the existing. The valley beams run from the intersection of the new and existing ridge to the exterior wall. Like a typical rafter, the valley beams are supported vertically and horizontally at the exterior wall and horizontally at the ridge. The beam must be capable of spanning between the ridge and exterior wall, and the roof diaphragms must be capable of supporting the horizontal thrust of the valley at the roof because the thrust is not a "balanced load" parallel to the new roof line.

Chapter 9

Masonry Buildings

Masonry design, like wood design, requires a working knowledge of the material's history and use to enable efficient design. Masonry, both clay (brick and terra cotta) and concrete (block), is strong in compression but weak and brittle in tension. Individual units may sometimes be nearly as strong as concrete or stone, but the strength of a masonry structure relies on the grade and type of mortar, which forms a system different in capacity and ability from concrete or stone.

The inherent qualities of masonry have led to its common use in wall construction, where the compressive forces dominate. Where flat or true arches can be formed, masonry has been used in floor construction. Familiarity with the history of masonry is especially crucial during renovation in urban areas, where old buildings may contain masonry used in ways that are not now common.

The importance of determining the purpose of a specific masonry structure within a building slated for renovation cannot be understated. A masonry wall intended as a shear wall that is misinterpreted as a curtain wall can be dangerously weakened by the introduction of expansion joints. Similarly, a curtain wall mistaken for a bearing wall will continue to deteriorate and crack if expansion joints are not introduced.

In general, masonry is one of the simpler materials in terms of pure design. Masonry acts primarily in compression and any calculations are generally a matter of computing simple stress. In fact, much of the current masonry code continues to rely on empirical guidelines for design, although formulae and more rigorous designs have been developed. Therefore, the detailing and proper interpretation of in situ masonry is at the core of efficient renovation design.

Properties of Masonry Construction

Masonry building elements are strong in compression and weak in tension in large part because they are systems of masonry units and mortar. These properties make unreinforced masonry walls very capable but not versatile. Unreinforced masonry is capable of supporting substantial compressive loads, so that the dimensions of a building are usually limited by the overall lateral stability rather than strength. As with concrete, the addition of reinforcing bars greatly increases the tensile and flexural capacity of a masonry wall. However, the introduction of bars requires filling the hollow cores of the units with mortar or grout, often a costly endeavor.

Urban construction, beginning in the early nineteenth century and continuing through the twentieth century, relied on solid clay brick units. By the middle of the nineteenth century, hollow clay terra-cotta units were introduced, primarily to build partition walls and arch floor systems in fireproof buildings. The clay material and thin shells make terra-cotta tiles fragile, so they were rarely used as a substitute for brick at exterior bearing walls. The early twentieth century saw the introduction of gypsum block as a substitute for terra-cotta in partitions. Finally, in the 1930s, hollow-core, concrete masonry units (C.M.U.) were introduced. This form of masonry combined the relative strength and capacity of brick with the hollow construction of terra cotta. The hollow core allowed for large, still manageable units to be fabricated, and this in turn decreased the amount of time required to build masonry walls. C.M.U. continues to be the preferred bearing-wall construction material. Unfortunately, hollow-core clay units and, to a lesser extent, hollow-core concrete units, are especially susceptible to point loads. Flat-arch terra-cotta floors were constructed with a concrete topping slab to protect the tops of the tiles. Similarly, hanging loads from the underside of arch floors was strictly prohibited.

A unique feature of masonry renovation is the presence of an entire industry devoted only to masonry anchors. Mechanically interlocking bolts (with expansion or wedge inserts), widely used in concrete renovation, are not suitable for clay masonry. The expansion of the wedges at the bolt base, meant to provide the bolt's strength, will simply split or crush brick or terra cotta, destroying in the attempt to strengthen. Relatively new high-strength adhesive anchors, first introduced in the 1970s, are generally specified for brick connections. These anchors work by the bond of a high-strength adhesive, usually epoxy, between the masonry and steel bolt. While the anchors often are capable of relatively high values in tension, it is very difficult to justify connections other than simple shear in a masonry wall because the wall cannot carry local moment.

Masonry Bearing Walls

During the first three-quarters of the nineteenth century, brick bearing walls were almost always used in urban construction. The inability of masonry to resist tension restricted the height and width of the building. The lateral reactions of tall and narrow buildings were supported by masonry bearing walls acting as shear diaphragms. The lateral reactions of low buildings were small enough that the walls' dead load more than compensated for any tensile or uplift force generated by the shear diaphragm action. Building codes gave specific rules for masonry wall construction based on past experience and rules of thumb. They specified maximum wall heights, minimum wall thickness, and maximum clear spans. Brick bearing walls, if constructed properly and in stable condition, are usually capable of supporting much greater loads than those currently imposed on them. This is very important to remember when designing renovations to floors supported by masonry walls. Transferring loads to the exterior bearing walls is usually advantageous.

Wall continuity is crucial to stability in bearing-wall buildings. Since there were no other structural elements with appreciable lateral stiffness, the buildings tended to move as a piece, so that expansion joints were not required. In fact, the structural integrity of a masonry bearing wall is severely damaged by any sort of discontinuities or joints in the wall.

Since brick bearing walls are often limited by stability and not strength, substantial cracking and movement are usually a sign of foundation failure and not material overstress. Demolition of wall finishes during renovation will often uncover noticeable cracks in a masonry bearing wall. A first step in determining the severity of the crack is to try to find its origin, if possible, to gain insight into the direction and degree of movement. It is equally important to determine whether the crack is active or dormant. If the crack is located in a relatively hidden location, a crack monitor can be affixed over the crack and the crack monitored over a period of time. If this is not possible, the crack can be examined for soot and dirt and roughness. If the crack is relatively jagged and clean, this is a good sign that it is relatively new.

Masonry Curtain Walls

Starting with the advent of steel and concrete construction in the late nineteenth century, and spurred by the inherent height limitations of masonry bearing walls and the increasingly high relative labor costs of masonry construction, heavy masonry construction declined in favor of nonstructural masonry. Masonry use in curtain walls had a new set of requirements, some of which directly contradicted previous guidelines.

Masonry curtain walls are not required to carry the gravity and lateral loads of the entire building. Curtain walls carry wind loads between floor diaphragms in simple bending, similar to beams, and thus act in combined tension and compression. As noted previously, the tension that a bearing wall is asked to support is usually offset by the dead load that it is carrying. When curtain walls replaced bearing walls in design, a thinner wall was allowed by both codes and logic. Coupled with the decrease in compressive load from both the weight of the wall and applied floor loads, thinner walls greatly reduced the factor of safety inherent in empirically built masonry bearing walls. Construction quality and proper design became more important than before.

Early masonry curtain walls lacked expansion joints. The difference in relative stiffness between the curtain wall and the building frame subsequently caused substantial cracking near external corners. The lack of joints also resulted in cracking throughout the wall as a result of temperature expansion and contraction. With the masonry spanning in one direction and bounded by each floor, continuity of the structure horizontally and vertically was no longer required. Discontinuities, prohibited in masonry bearing walls, are crucial to the survival of masonry curtain walls.

Expansion joints also are crucial in discontinuous curtain walls because of the tendency of baked clay products to expand throughout their lives as they absorb moisture. Horizontal expansion joints became even more imperative with the advent of large concrete frame buildings. Concrete columns have a tendency to shorten over time. The combination of the masonry expanding and the concrete shortening overstresses the curtain wall as it is forced into carrying vertical loads (figure 9-1).

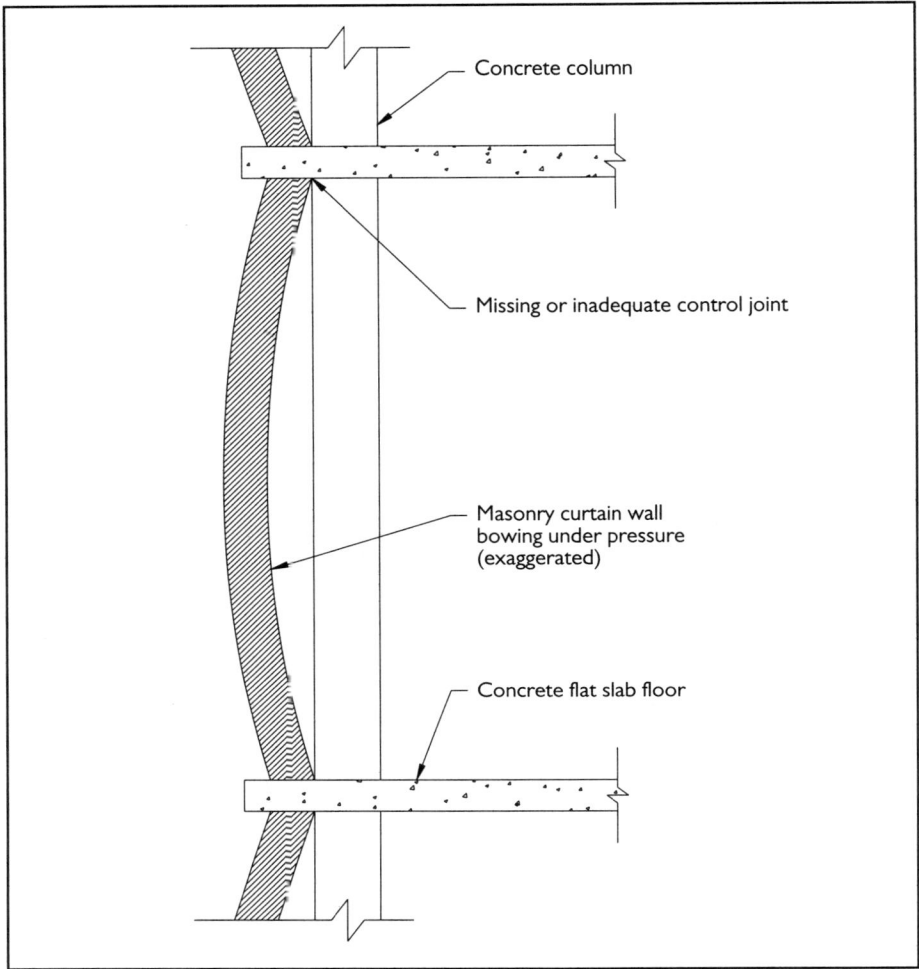

9-1. Concrete frame shortening stressing curtain wall

The development of curtain walls proceeded faster than the development of the individual pieces of material needed for their construction. At the time when true curtain walls were first being built, in the 1880s, the only connectors for attaching brick to steel were steel straps bolted to the steel frame, which were awkward to use. Better mechanical fasteners did not appear before the use of welded ties for steel frames and dovetail inserts for concrete frames after World War II.

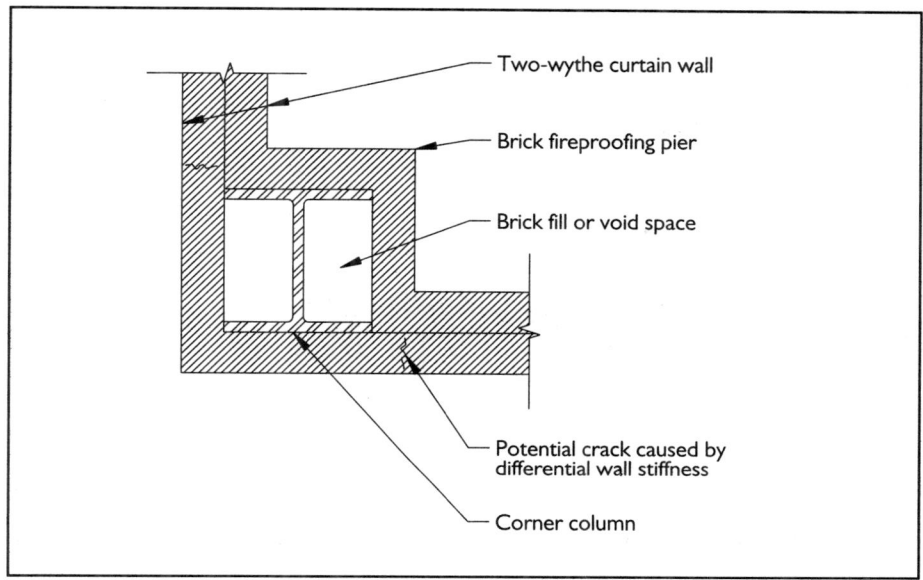

9-2. Curtain wall restrained at column piers, with cracks

Without mechanical fastening, the only feasible method to ensure solid lateral connections between curtain wall and frame was to encase the spandrel columns in masonry piers built integrally with the wall. In such a scheme, vertical expansion joints at the typical modern locations—the corner columns and other columns with a spacing of 20 to 30 feet (6100 to 9150 mm)—were impossible, since wall stability required full continuity between the brick pier and the wall on either side of the column. Integral piers seemed to be a solution of great efficiency, as the masonry piers fireproofed the columns in addition to stabilizing the wall. In reality, this method of tying together two different materials exacerbated the problems caused by the lack of expansion joints. At the very point where expansion and contraction demanded free movement of the wall, the relatively inflexible pier prevented the wall from moving (figure 9-2).

Wind blowing on a building with its curtain wall braced by piers has caused the same pattern of failure on hundreds of buildings. The unbraced expanses of exposed wall are the most flexible element present, and bow inward on the windward side in rectangular panels bounded by two floors and two piers. The building frame moves laterally under the wind load, while the faces of wall parallel to the wind direction are less flexible, and lag in movement behind the

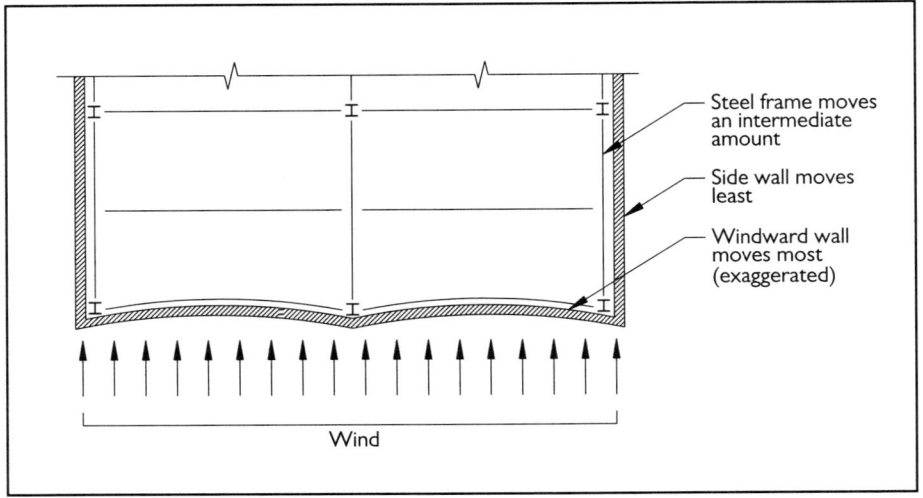

9-3. Differential movement of windward curtain wall, frame, and parallel curtain wall

frame (figure 9-3). The windward and leeward walls fail at the edge of the corner piers, where the brick is stressed by both the differential movement of the two walls across the corner and by the movement of the unbraced panel. The end result is a set of parallel cracks through the masonry on each wall face, running more or less from the top of the building to its base, between 1 and 3 feet (300 to 900 mm) from each corner of the building. These are the locations of the most important expansion joints in a modern curtain wall.

When new vertical expansion joints are cut in an existing masonry wall, the locations chosen must balance the ideal location against the location of internal structure that can be used to brace the cut edge. Even if the wall is analyzed and is capable of spanning vertically between the floor slabs, it is not advisable to leave a freestanding masonry pier at the corner.

New Connections

When new beams are added to a bearing-wall building, they are typically attached to the existing walls. In renovation, as previously mentioned, bearing walls have the great advantage that they are almost never stressed near their full

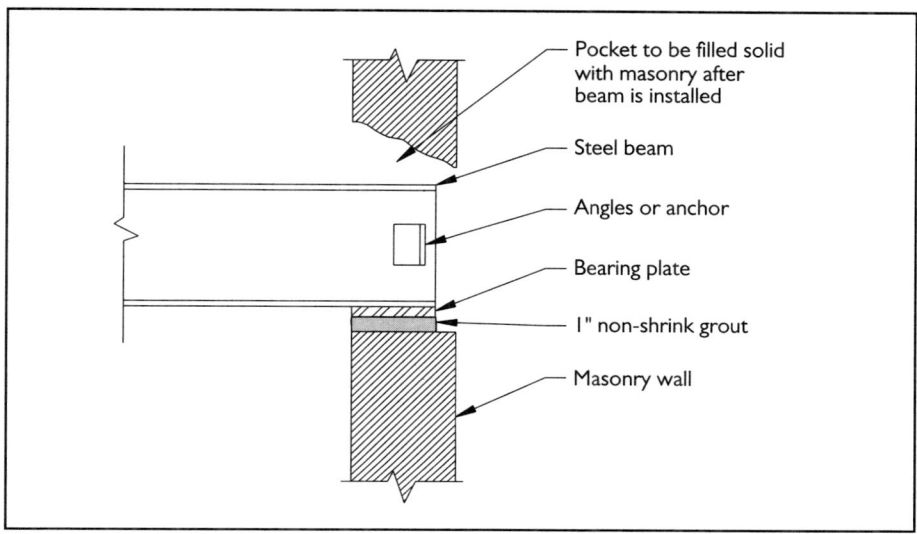

9-4. Beam pocket in wall

capacity by existing conditions. Little examination of existing wall design is necessary to decide whether new structure, such as a new beam to frame a stair opening or a new building level, can be added to a masonry bearing-wall building. At the same time, the economic advantage of simply reusing the existing vertical structure is so great that it takes very special circumstances to not use it.

There are two basic methods of attaching new beams to masonry. One is to remove enough masonry to permit the installation of the new beam bearing on the wall, in the same fashion as the original beams (figure 9-4). The inherent arching action of the wall and the shear strength of the mortar holds the small, unsupported soffit of masonry in place above the new beam bearing pocket, until the beam is in place and the pocket filled in. The second method is to provide a connection member on the face of the wall to serve as a bridge between the new beam and the old wall without disturbing the wall (figure 9-5).

Beyond ensuring that the local bearing stress below a new beam does not exceed the capacity of the wall material, there is little difficulty in designing a newly embedded connection. All building codes either specify an allowable bearing stress for masonry or refer to the ACI masonry code. These values are

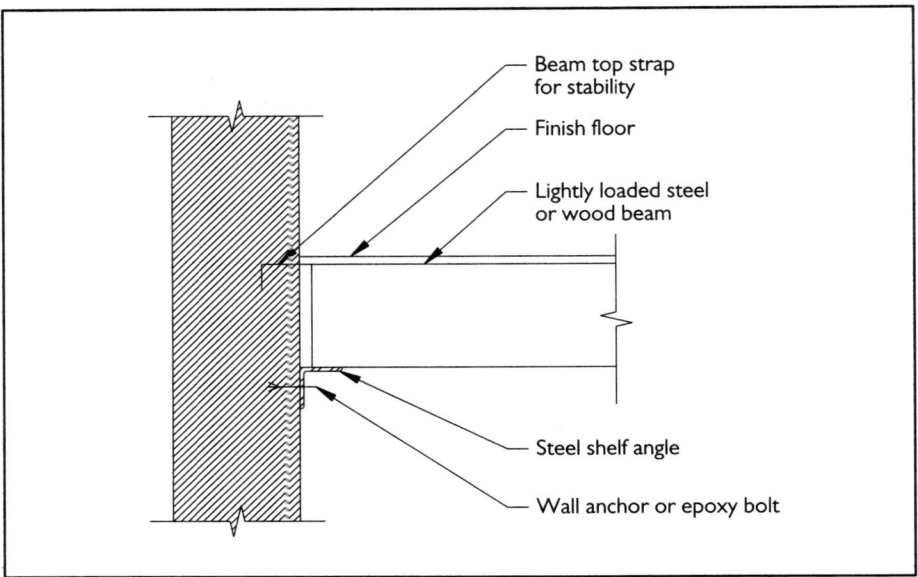

9-5. Shelf angle attached to wall

for new masonry, and an engineer must use judgment as to what value is to be used for existing masonry. In general, a well-maintained masonry wall is capable of supporting approximately 200 psi in bearing.

Attaching steel posts to the top of an existing masonry wall is similar to attaching a beam to a wall face. Assuming that the wall has been analyzed for the load the post will impose, the effects that must be considered in connection design are the local bearing pressure and the base shear, if any, of the post. Since unit masonry walls are incapable of withstanding any appreciable moment out of plane, the post base cannot be designed as fixed against rotation perpendicular to the wall. In theory, the post could be designed as fixed in the plane of the wall, but in practice this requires anchors deep enough to engage large amounts of masonry, or else the top courses will simply pull out. Almost all posts attached to the top of existing masonry walls are simple gravity supports, and thus can be designed with pinned bases, and have negligible base shears. The base-plate size is determined by the bearing capacity of the masonry. Base shear out of the wall plane may require reinforcing the wall face, but again, this is not common. Adhesive bolts are generally the best type of anchor.

Replacement or Removal

Replace-in-kind repairs in solid masonry construction are very simple. Existing joints are cut apart and masonry units, from individual bricks to large ashlar blocks, removed. New material is toothed in and new joints created by cutting existing units. This method has been around for centuries, and its boundaries are well defined. Even if the walls carry structural loads, this is work defined by architectural details for finish masonry, not by structural concerns. The engineer's responsibility in such work is often limited to sequencing and shoring.

Rowhouse renovation often requires the removal of portions of the masonry bearing wall, generally at exterior walls to allow more light into the building than was originally provided. In some instances, the openings are created at interior bearing walls to enlarge living space.

Typically, these removals are done by shoring the masonry wall above the proposed opening, inserting a steel lintel designed for the specific span and load, and removing the shoring. This method is troublesome and not very efficient. Shoring, a common construction method, is inefficient because it is a support built to be demolished upon completion of construction. In rowhouse layouts it is also often difficult to "thread" the shoring down to suitable bearing, as required. A substitute for this type of repair is a lintel system that can be installed without shoring.

A chase can be cut into a well-constructed masonry wall without damage to the wall's stability, because of the shear interaction between the wythes of the wall. Typically, an exterior wall is at least three wythes of brick (12 inches [305 mm]) thick. Floor joists in rowhouse construction generally frame side to side, so that the front and back walls generally have no floor loads or point loads. The fact that the building stability relies partially on the diaphragm action of the front and rear walls will be discussed later in this section.

By taking advantage of temporary removal in a wall, a contractor can "chase" in a single channel or I-beam that is less than 4 inches (100 mm) wide. Once this piece is securely in place, the wall can be considered as solid as it originally was and an identical channel or I-beam can be chased into the other side of the wall. After both channels are in place, they are bolted together to sandwich the middle wythes. Now the opening can be created, and the channels become the supporting lintel.

Many factors affect the actual detailing of this design, but the basic scheme never changes. In applications where the opening is large, creating a large span, deflection of the lintel may be a problem, especially given the very stringent deflection criteria usually used with masonry-supporting lintels. In this case the lintels can be predeflected by placing wedge plates through the wall at the deflected distance below the lintel. The channels can then be drawn down to the wedge plates by the tightening of bolts. The middle wythe is sandwiched between the lintel and the induced bending in the lintel will, theoretically, "unload" the masonry below before it is removed.

In a more complex case, the lintel can be part of a steel frame introduced into the wall to replace the lateral stiffness that the removed portion of wall provided. Here columns can be chased into the wall in the same way the lintel previously was and connected to the beams before the wall replacement.

Stone Lintels

In the past stone was used in ways that are no longer considered good practice. While all masonry design codes allow some flexural tension in ashlar blocks, the levels of tension are so low that they preclude many of the old uses. Granite that is allowed roughly 50 psi (7 kPa) in bending stress cannot be designed to act as a lintel over double windows or doors, but was commonly used in this way before 1900. The extremely low tension values allowed prevent the formation of cracks that will propagate unchecked through the brittle stone (figure 9-6). Many old lintels show exactly this condition. The stone has cracked, leaving the broken pieces and the masonry above supported by the window frame or by their own inherent arching action. In these cases, the stone must be replaced either entirely or effectively.

If such a repair does not conflict with preservation goals, a complete replacement in precast concrete can provide a substitute that is fairly close in appearance, structurally sound, and easy to build. Most of the time, however, "fairly close" is not good enough. Legal landmark status, esthetics, and the desire to retain original material all prevent the use of a precast lintel. In this situation, the solution is to replace the stone lintel as a structural member by adding a hidden steel lintel. Depending on the size of the steel lintel required and the configuration of the masonry opening and the door or window frame, there are various locations for the steel. Hollow door and window frames can sometimes hide new steel lintels.

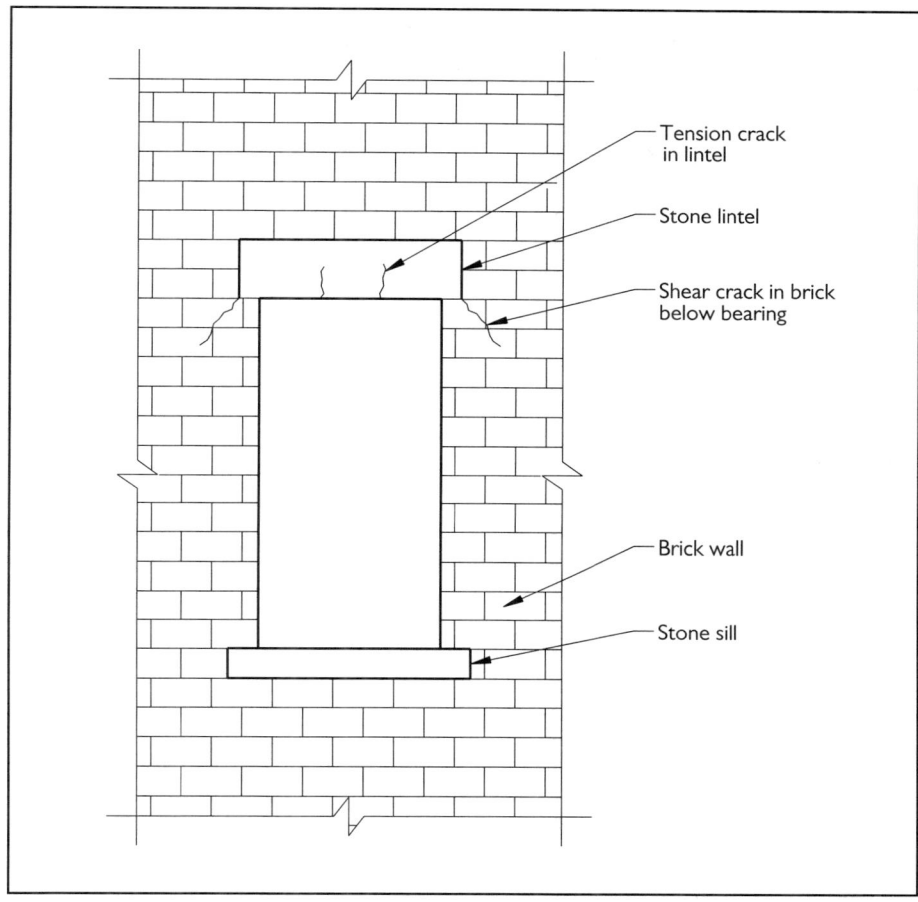

9-6. Stone lintel

Masonry Floors and Partitions

Masonry floor systems were used as early fireproof floor structure and evolved in different forms. Arches were the only way to create a horizontal surface out of material that could not carry tension. As with walls, terra cotta and brick were both used for this construction. Common to almost all forms of masonry floors are two properties: they are one-way systems, with arches spanning from beam to beam in one direction; and there is generally a topping material of some kind above the arch.

New openings usually require the demolition of an entire strip of the arch, since it is nearly impossible to support a half-arch during construction. Usually an entire panel of slab must be removed, and the slab area to remain must be infilled around the new opening. Tile arch floors perform very well, but are almost incapable of sustaining alterations without damage.

True masonry arch floors are an archaic form of structure rarely found in the United States outside of some monumental buildings such as churches or governmental buildings. Modification of the arches is so time-consuming and expensive that the floors are nearly almost removed if alterations are required. This work is similar to the description above for solid masonry alterations, and rarely requires the attention of an engineer except for shoring.

The problems created by gypsum block and tile partitions are similar to those with tile arch floors. Gypsum block and tile partitions were used extensively during the 1920s, '30s, and '40s for interior space creation in all sizes and types of buildings, typically with gypsum block used for ordinary partitions and tile used for fire separation and wet walls. These partitions are as fragile as tile arches, and even more expendable, since there is no better economic basis for attempting to save them than there is for attempting to save gypsum board over metal studs. It is unfortunate to lose these partitions when it is not necessary, however, since they are more solid to the touch and more soundproof then their modern counterparts, but they are inevitably removed when they are in the way.

Case Study 9-1: Chased-in Lintels in a Masonry Wall

Light is often a rare commodity in urban rowhouses, which may be rich in character, finishes, and esteem, but often were constructed to the minimum of light and ventilation requirements. This is partly the result of nineteenth-century ideas about ventilation (many townhouses were built in the Victorian era) and partly the result of the house designers' keeping their construction simple.

One of the primary goals of many rowhouse renovations is to increase the amount of light by enlarging existing window openings and adding new window openings. Because rowhouses are built side by side, this work is usually confined to the front and rear masonry walls. These walls generally run parallel to the floor framing and are nonbearing. They support only their own weight and any imposed lateral forces, and so are only 12 inches (305 mm) (three wythes) thick.

If it is determined that the removal of masonry will not reduce the lateral stability of the wall (compare Case Study 9-2 where it does), all that is required is a new lintel to span the enlarged opening. The time-tested method for creating new openings in masonry generally includes shoring the masonry above the new opening by placing small beams through the wall (needle-shoring), cutting the new opening, installing the new lintel, and removing the shoring. For smaller openings the shoring work often is not included in the original estimate and, unfortunately, often is not performed. The contractor may try to replace the lintel quickly, while there are no supervisory personnel around. Often there is no serious damage because a masonry wall, by its nature, will inherently form an arch over new openings, but this procedure poses some threat to the stability of the surrounding wall and should be avoided. A licensed design professional cannot depend on the infrequent occurrence of collapse and must make every effort to provide for proper shoring during construction. The requirements of speed and efficiency often come to a head with the requirements for safety in this type of renovation, where smaller contractors and tighter budgets are prevalent.

One compromise combines the permanent lintel with the temporary shoring requirements. By dictating the installation process of the lintel, the design professional can ensure safety while avoiding the relatively large costs of temporary shoring. Keep in mind that this procedure is recommended only for relatively small openings in nonbearing walls. The process may be used in larger openings, but with additional precautions and much more control.

The technique involves sandwiching the inner wythe of brick with the halves of a double-channel lintel. Enough brick is removed only to place a single lintel, and the lintel is secured into the wall; the second lintel is placed by the same procedure. The two lintels are bolted together through the masonry wall at approximately 16-inch (405 mm) spacing, creating a combined steel and brick lintel (figure 9-1-1). The brick below the new lintel is then removed; in some cases, plates may be placed beneath the channels to ensure that the center bricks do not shift over time.

The brick above the single-wythe chase is held in place both by the arching of the brick over the opening and by the shear strength of the masonry between the wythes of brick. Obviously, this type of work should only be performed on solid and stable walls. In addition, while it can be performed on bearing walls as

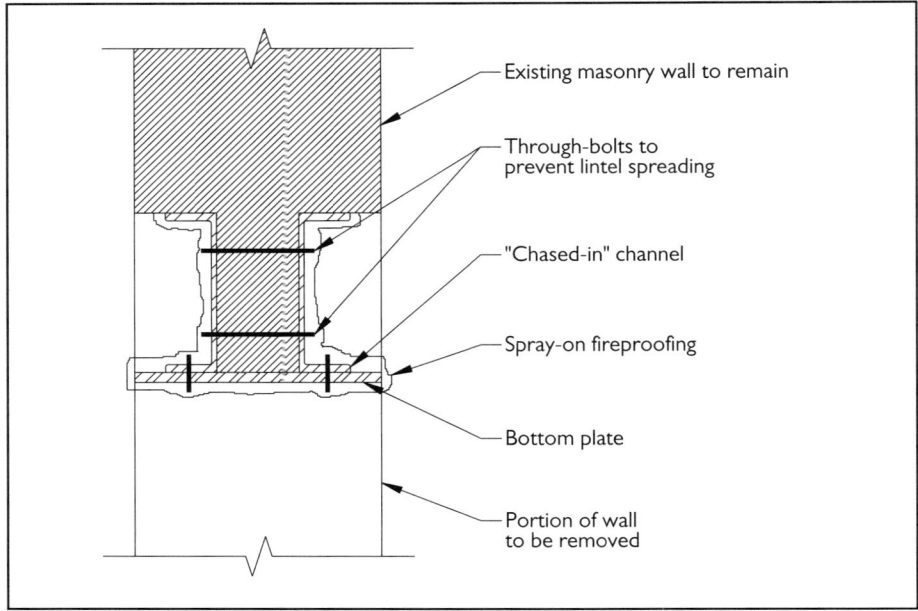

9-1-1. Chased-in lintel detail

well as nonbearing walls, all joists that frame into the wall at the opening must be temporarily shored. In the case of larger openings the lintel may have to be predeflected to avoid unnecessary immediate deflection of the lintel and associated cracking in the wall above.

Case Study 9-2: Rigid Frame in Shear Wall

As with Case Study 9-1 this example involves a new opening in the rear or front wall of a rowhouse. However, the proposed opening here is large enough to affect the lateral stability of the structure.

As outlined in this chapter, masonry bearing-wall buildings rely on the strength and stiffness of the perimeter walls to provide lateral stability. In general, the front and rear walls of rowhouses are only 16 to 25 feet (4880 to 7620 mm) wide (figures 9-2-1 and 9-2-2). A large opening in a wall this wide can quickly destroy the lateral strength of the wall and requires a rigid frame—

Case Study 9-2: Rigid Frame in Shear Wall **165**

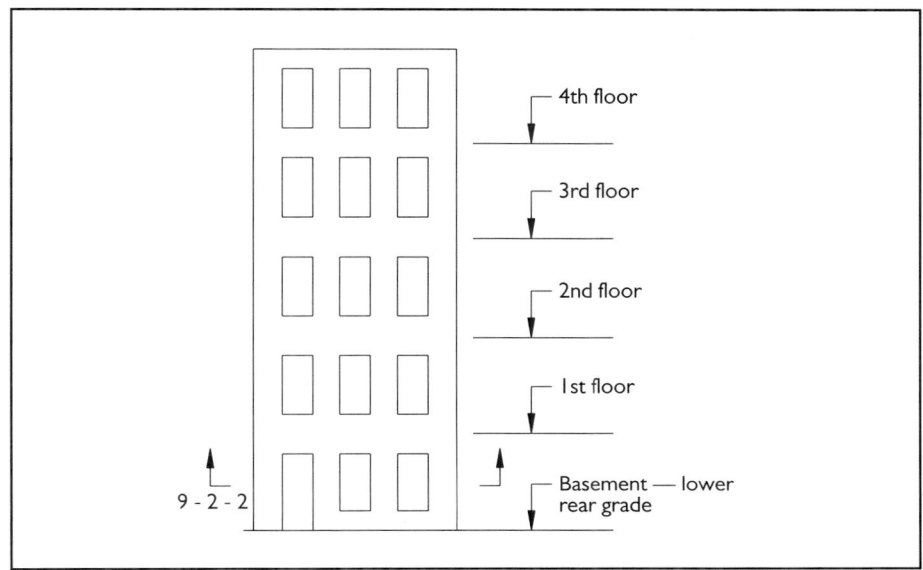

9-2-1. Original rear-facade elevation

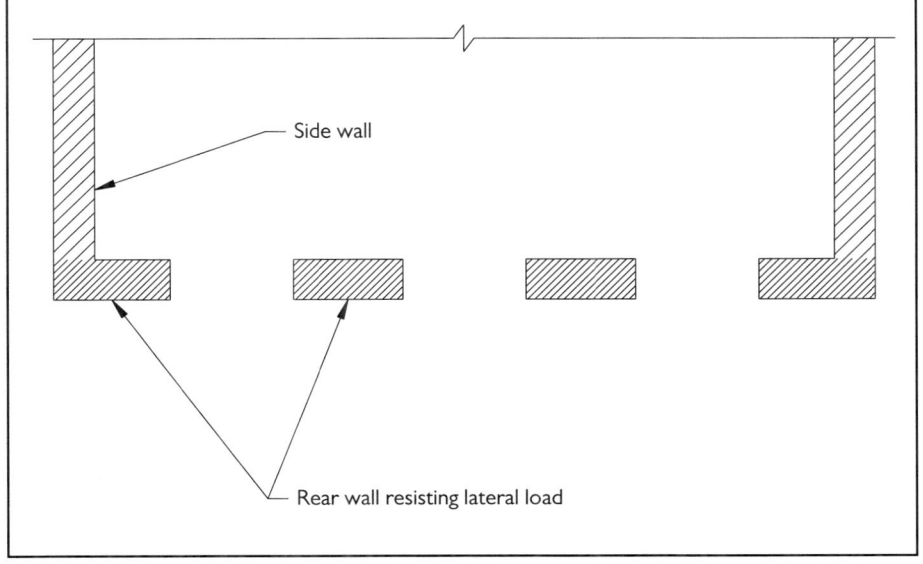

9-2-2. Original wall section

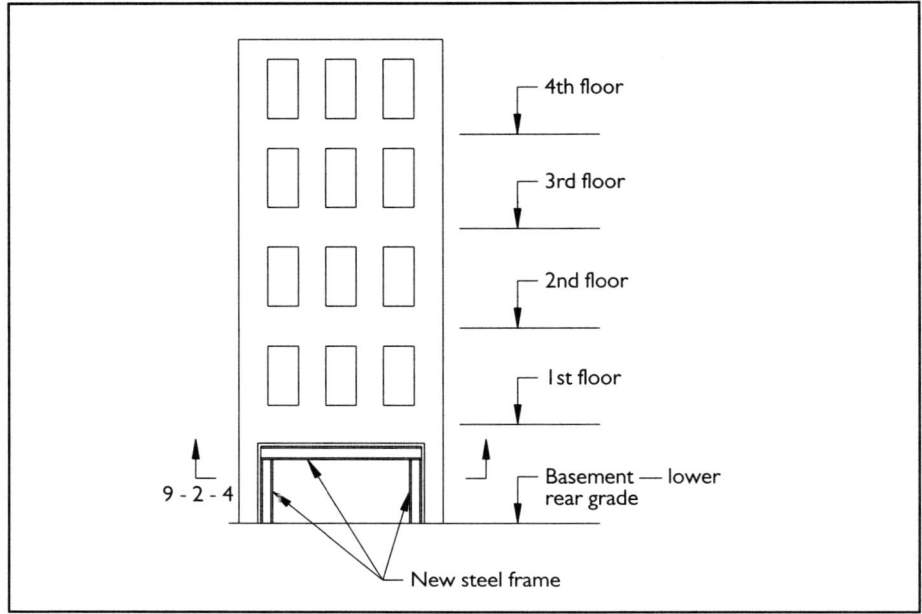

9-2-3. Rear-facade elevation with rigid frame

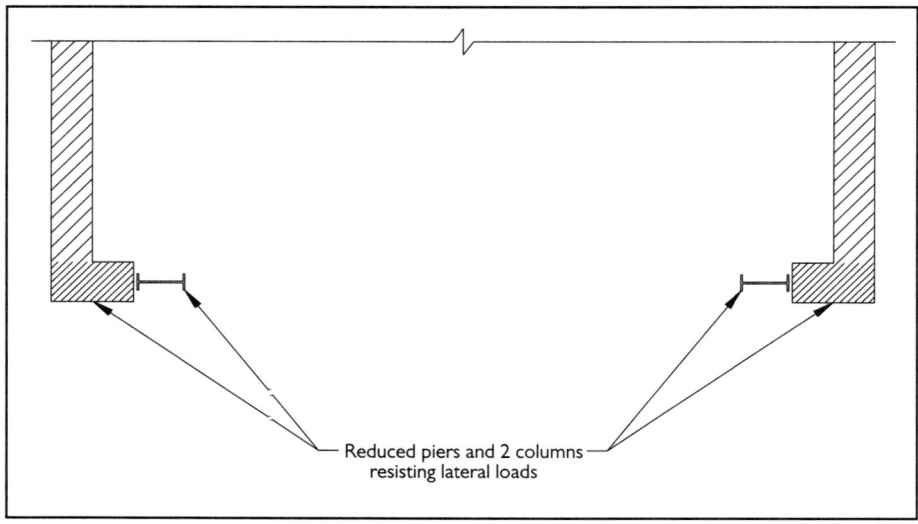

9-2-4. Wall section with new frame

normally steel—to replace this strength. As with any renovation, the key to a good design is to replace, in some form, whatever structure is removed.

Typically, a structural removal of this scale in relation to the overall stiffness of the frame requires a full analysis of the remaining lateral support systems and the replacement of the removed strength with an equivalent system. Fortunately, the lateral system is very simple in this type of construction. The front and rear walls each support half the wind load of the building. Unfortunately, not only are these walls often insufficient to support the full load, but the floor diaphragms also are insufficient to carry the full loads out to the front and rear walls. Rowhouse building structures were not explicitly designed and have survived despite their theoretical structural weaknesses because of the redundancy present in a row of connected buildings.

A frame to replace the sections of wall to be removed designed for the full loading would be prohibitively large, both in size and cost. In this case the designer is justified in replacing only what is removed—that is, designing the rigid frame for the capacity of the masonry wall removed and not for the full wind loading.

In instances where there is very good on-site supervision, the quality of work is excellent, and the wall is sound and stable, the technique described in Case Study 9-1 can be adapted to this installation. The entire frame is placed, piece by piece, in the wall and tied together, and the opening created without shoring the wall (figures 9-2-3 and 9-2-4). Since the on-site conditions are rarely ideal, the frame is usually installed after needle-shoring is in place and the masonry opening has been created.

Case Study 9-3: GFRC Substitution

Traditional masonry construction is based on bearing. Masonry walls were used to carry loads; masonry arches, to carry floors and roofs; masonry partitions that carry no other loads carry their own weight through direct bearing. Ornament on buildings, regardless of the type of construction, is basically nonstructural, and often part of a veneer of stone applied to the structural masonry. Changes to the structure of a wall, usually a solid core of ashlar or common brick, are performed as described earlier in this chapter. Changes to the veneer portions of a wall, though not affecting the building structure, require local support and design.

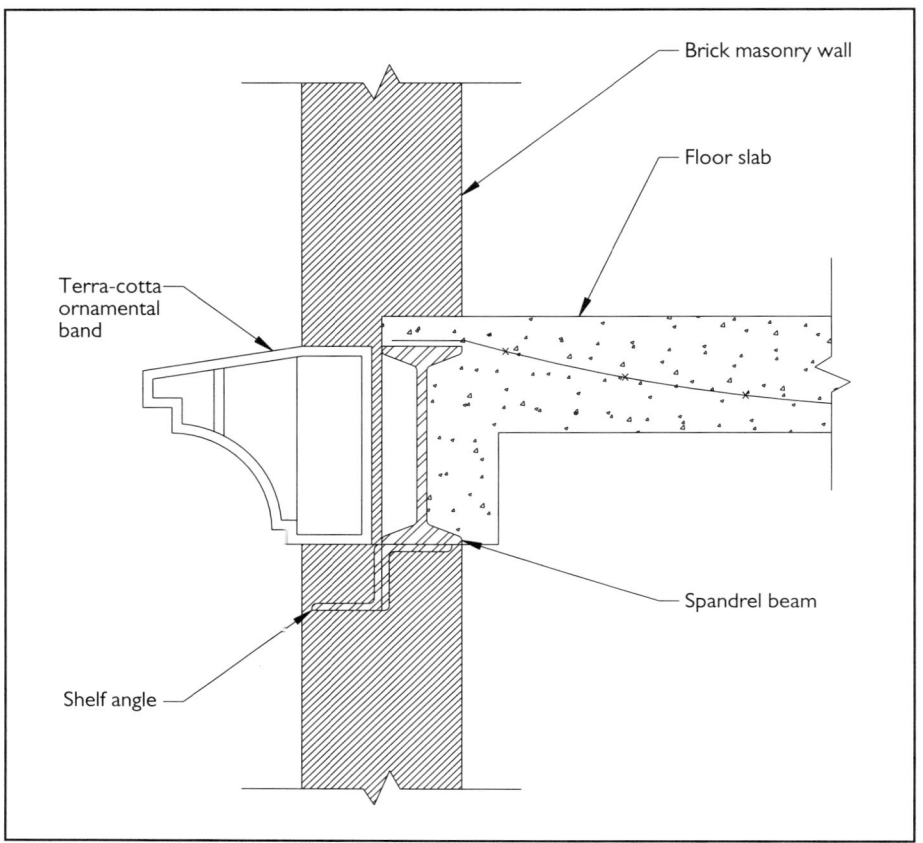

9-3-1. Original string course of terra cotta

From the 1880s through the 1930s, terra cotta was widely used for exterior decorative trim on buildings. Originally seen as an inexpensive substitute for cut stone, terra cotta was popular for a long time because it remained an easy way to produce large amounts of complicated ornament. The supports used for terra cotta varied with the location of the individual element: flat wall decoration, such as string courses or window heads, was simply built in with the masonry (usually brick) that made up the bulk of the wall; projecting elements, such as cornices, were supported on simple steel substructures; and hung elements, such as the soffits of decorative balconies, were hung from steel substructure specifically designed for the occasion. The difference between projecting and hung supports is subtle but real. In small buildings, particularly bearing-wall

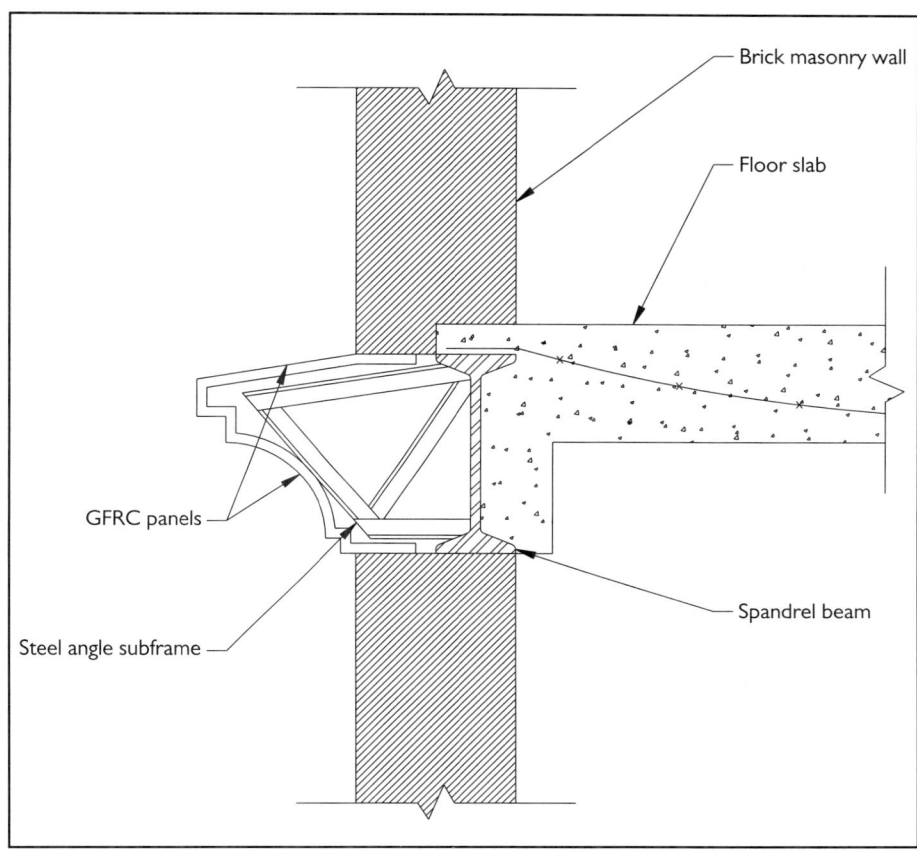

9-3-2. New GFRC string course

buildings, terra-cotta cornices were sometimes built using the terra cotta itself to cantilever part of the total projection, and loose steel supports embedded within the wall to cantilever the remain distance. This is not necessarily a flawed design, but it is difficult to analyze, and therefore difficult to repair if either material should become damaged. More stringent designs, such as those used in the cornices of steel-frame buildings, usually had steel cantilevers tied back to the beams within the exterior wall or entire frames of secondary members supported by the exterior wall beams.

Because terra cotta is brittle itself and is waterproofed by a brittle coating of glaze, pieces that have been subjected to long-term movement and weathering, such as the ornament under discussion, tend to develop cracks and spalls. In the course of facade repair, badly damaged pieces are often replaced when they cannot be patched. When large areas are damaged, a substitute material such as glass-fiber reinforced concrete (GFRC) is installed. GFRC comes in large panels less than an inch thick, and requires very different supports than terra-cotta blocks, which are hollow, rectangular prisms roughly as deep as they are high (figure 9-3-1).

GFRC is denser than terra cotta, but since less of the new material is required, the weight stays the same or declines slightly. The existing building frame and ornament substructure do not need to be reinforced for load, although they may need to be reinforced if they have weathered. New substructure is required, however, to meet the connection requirements of the new GFRC cladding (figure 9-3-2).

Case Study 9-4: New Control Joints

There has been little change in pure masonry design during the twentieth century for the simple reason that the material has been used and well understood for hundreds of years. Most of the innovation in masonry design has been its use in nontraditional ways, for example, reinforced masonry and masonry curtain walls.

The use of masonry a heavy bearing material, as a curtain wall supported by structure became practical on a large scale only with the development of the modern frame during the 1880s and '90s. This new use took place before there was a theoretical basis for it: as soon as iron and steel technology and design theory developed to the point where complete frames carrying curtain walls became possible, such buildings were built. At that time, little research had been performed on the stresses within curtain walls and the interaction between curtain walls and structure.

All early curtain walls, many built in the 1940s and a few built later, have too few expansion joints. The lack can cause the exterior walls to carry a portion of the structural loads as well as exaggerate weathering from cracks caused by movement forced on stiff, brittle masonry walls by a limber steel frame.

In a typical case, a steel-frame, fifteen-story building from the first half of the twentieth century with individual windows whose area constitutes roughly 25 percent of the wall area displays brick cracking at plan corners and brick bulges over the spandrel beams. During the course of investigating the damage,

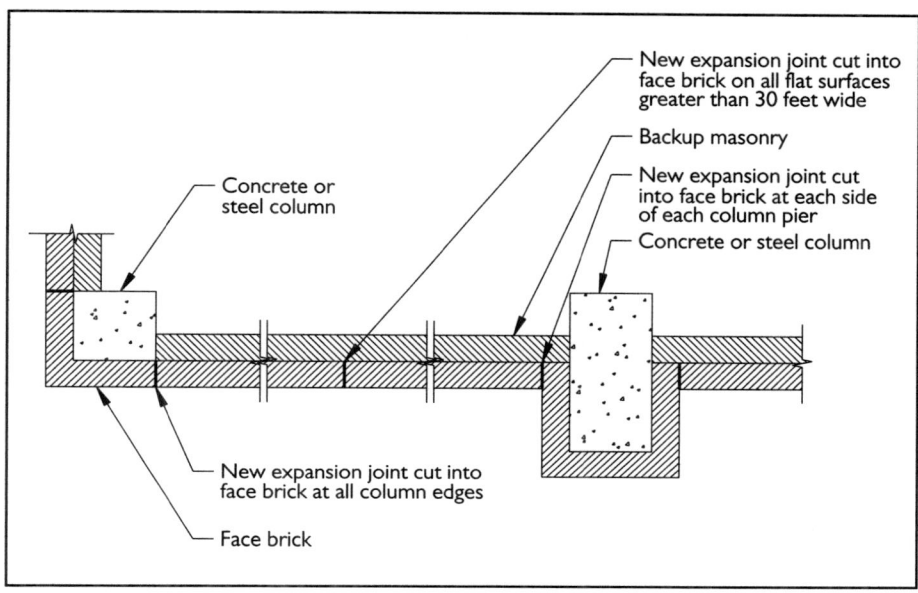

9-4-1. Location of new expansion joints in existing wall

which includes rust on the nonwaterproofed beams (typical of the time) and damaged loose lintels, the decision is made to add expansion joints during the repair process. This is not necessarily a large expense, since the cracked and damaged masonry will be rebuilt regardless of other work.

While the brick wall was never intended to be structural, it may not be properly connected to the frame to act as a curtain wall. Before new joints can be cut in, probes were made to determine the type of connection from the masonry to the frame. New connections will be provided, in the form of two-piece wire ties, one part welded to the building columns and beams and the other embedded in the new masonry. The location of the vertical expansion joints is determined by the location of the existing columns and the architectural details of the wall itself (figure 9-4-1). Because there are no extraordinary conditions, horizontal joints will be located directly below the spandrel beams that carry the wall.

Chapter 10

Other Materials

The common structural materials already described occupy most of a renovation designer's time. The relatively rare occurrences of other materials can pose serious problems, since there are fewer options for analysis and the design of alterations available. To most engineers and architects, a lack of direct personal experience is the limiting factor in choosing details and design methods. The basic principles of design are the same regardless of the material, but material characteristics, such as available methods of connection, greatly influence the feasibility of any given alteration. Some of the structural materials that may be found are discussed below in rough chronological order of original use. There are a limited number of material types; any material can be loosely compared to another, possibly more popular material.

Cast Iron

The use of structural cast iron had stopped by the time that systematic testing and research of the type that has led to the current steel and concrete codes became common. As a result, there is little theoretical base for comparison of the dozens of formulas for allowable loads in cast-iron columns used before 1920. While most of those formulas had some relation to the theory-based column formulas used in steel today, they were all modified by empirical data. Structural iron is no longer cast on a production scale, making it impossible for a researcher to recreate the conditions of the old empirical experience. Current research into cast iron typically uses testing data that are one hundred to one hundred and twenty years old. All information now available is based on the limited amounts of old published research data or modern empirical experience. This tends to make attitudes toward cast iron use more conservative than they might be otherwise, but for this brittle material, conservative design is a good idea.

Unless research can show that an existing cast-iron column is loaded well below its capacity, the amount of load present should not be increased. Cast iron is subject to numerous defects, most of which are invisible without X-ray inspection. The presence of one hidden crack or one improperly thin wall is enough to cause a catastrophic collapse. Since the budget of a renovation is rarely capable of including the X-ray inspection of a series of columns, the presence of flaws must be assumed. The justification for accepting the presence of a flawed material then is that the structure has survived for some time (cast-iron columns almost always date from before 1910) with no signs of distress; therefore, the columns are adequate for the loads to which they have been subjected in the past. If this seems an overly conservative method of examining a structure, two factors must be considered. First, during the period of active cast-iron use, the allowable stresses were revised downward in successive building codes to a degree unique among structural materials, until the metal was finally dropped from use. If the people who used cast iron regularly found reason to distrust it, we must now give their opinions considerable weight. Second, cast iron fails without warning and in a brittle fashion. Just as we would approach a slender unreinforced concrete pier with trepidation, we cannot assume that cast-iron columns are safe.

Even counting the spandrels in iron facades, cast-iron beams are far less common than cast-iron columns. The earliest systematic research into the use of structural metals during the 1840s and '50s revealed the large disparity between tensile and compressive strength in cast iron. The recommended shapes for cast-iron beams from this time forward were inverted Ts or inverted Us. These shapes ensured that enough extra material was provided for the lower, tension flange to balance the fact that the tensile allowable stress was calculated to be between one-sixth and one-tenth the compressive allowable stress (figure 10-1). The asymmetrical distribution of stress means that loading on a cast-iron beam must be kept in roughly the same distribution as it has always been: the beams are so specifically designed for a given load distribution that they cannot readily accept other loads. This limitation is similar to the limitations imposed by the distribution of reinforcing bars within reinforced concrete.

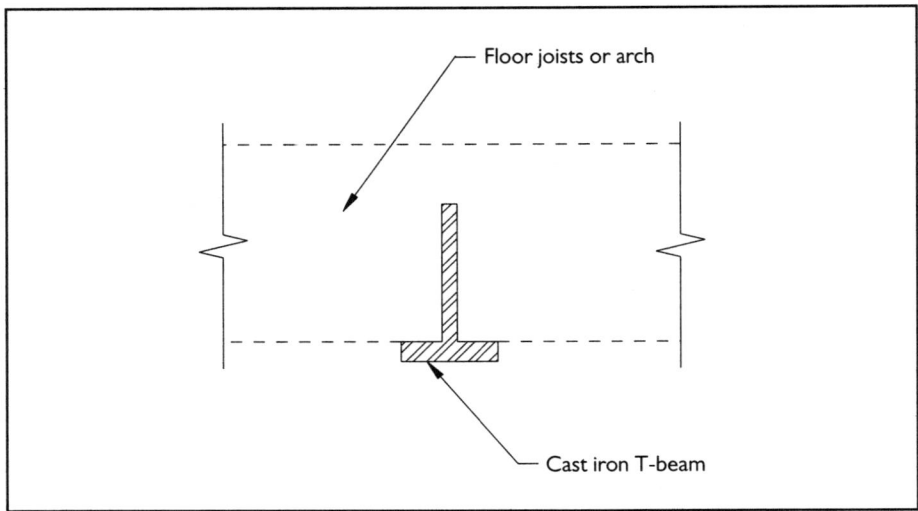

10-1. Cast-iron inverted T-beam

Making new connections to existing cast iron can be extremely difficult. It is barely possible, but not recommended, to weld to the metal. Its high carbon content interferes with the creation of a solid weld bead, and the permanent stresses induced within the metal by the heating and cooling of welding are likely to crack it. Finally, the restraint caused by welded connections is greater than that created by bolts, and causes additional local stresses that may break cast iron. New bolted connections can be made at existing brackets and bolt holes, although high-strength bolts should not be torqued down to create slip-critical connections, as this also creates local stress concentrations. New holes should only be created with rotary drills, as the forces created by impact drills may destroy a cast-iron member wall.

When rolled wrought-iron beams became readily available during and after the 1850s, designers jumped at the chance to use them instead of cast beams. The record left in the form of constructed buildings shows that cast iron was not used for ordinary floor construction after the introduction of wrought iron. Cast iron lingered on in flexural use in two isolated areas, facade spandrels and sidewalk vault and courtyard framing, until roughly 1885. The rationale for the use of cast iron was based in one case on architectural fashion and economics and in the other on a peculiarity of the metal's material properties.

Iron facades were already past their peak of popularity by 1875. Various fires had disproved the idea that an iron facade made a fireproof building, and had literally exposed the weakness of iron in a fire. With the building codes encouraging masonry use, and the cheapness of common labor, cast iron was relegated to a few niches of the construction market. By 1885, its use for structure, even for the simple self-supporting facades popular ten and twenty years earlier, was largely over. Before that date, however, some industrial and commercial buildings were built using the facade perfected by Daniel Badger and James Bogardus in New York, and cast in foundries in every major city. The facade system was a dense grid of columns and spandrel beams bolted together from behind and decorated with cast trim screwed or bolted to the main members. The majority of these facades are parallel to the interior floor beams or joists, and carry only their own weight. This system had proven itself in terms of quick, easy, and inexpensive construction, easy maintenance, and structural adequacy; there was no perceived need to tamper with success until the issue of fireproofing killed the system entirely. Iron facades typically have very short spans between columns, in the range of 4 to 6 feet (1220 to 1830 mm), and the spandrel panels that serve as beams are often 2 feet (610 mm) or more deep (figure 10-2). Beams that are relatively so deep for their span develop relatively low bending stress, reducing the possibility of failure. Since cast-iron facades are valued for their historic nature and appearance, they are not ordinarily modified except for restoration. A normal iron facade restoration will not alter the existing layout, but simply replaces or repairs broken members.

The use of cast iron for subgrade structure seems to have been motivated by cast iron's resistance to rust. Unlike wrought iron and steel, where surface rust flakes off, exposing a fresh surface to rust, and building up layers of loose, delaminated rust, surface rust on cast iron stays adhered to the base metal, protecting it against further rusting.

Sidewalk vaults and basement areas below courtyards tend to be continually damp. In addition, ancillary spaces in a building, especially those below grade, received less maintenance than the building does on average, both in the nineteenth century and later. Cast iron's inherent resistance to rust meant that a good coat of paint was sufficient for long-term survival in the damp. In any case, reexamination of many existing beams will require reinforcing or, more realistically, effective replacement.

Sidewalk support beams differ greatly from facade spandrels in analysis. Cast-iron beams used in sidewalk vaults, courtyards, or as lintels are similar to

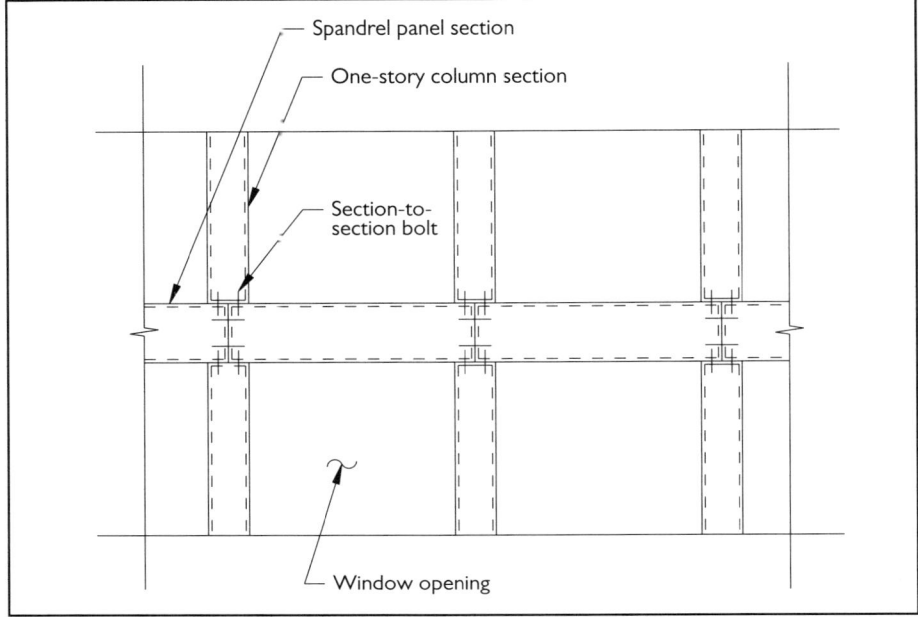

10-2. Cast-iron facade elevation

most beams of any material in that they are relatively shallow for their span, ordinarily in the range of one-eighth to one-twelfth as deep as they are long. These beams develop high bending stresses, and a modern analysis will often show them to be overstressed and in need of reinforcement. Unlike the facade spandrels, which are rarely damaged by stresses, many cast-iron beams used for ordinary structure need to be replaced because they are not justifiable by modern analysis and they have failed under previous loading.

Wrought Iron

The amount of surviving wrought-iron structure is fairly small. Structural use of the metal was common for roughly twenty-five years, from the late 1860s until the early 1890s, when it was permanently supplanted by steel. The buildings containing wrought iron were in large part the first wave of skyscrapers, most of which were torn down during the second wave after 1900 or during the third wave in the 1920s and 1930s. Cast-iron columns were more widespread, being used in low buildings with wood joist floors as well as in conjunction with steel floor beams. Wrought-iron beams were used in low-rise buildings during the brief period of popularity but, again, in relatively fewer buildings than cast iron or steel.

With the exception of welding, wrought iron can be treated in the same manner as steel. The difficulty is that the majority of techniques used in renovating steel make use of the flexibility of welded connections. Welding wrought iron is possible, but requires low-hydrogen electrodes, low temperatures, and more careful control than ordinary steel. Fortunately, wrought iron shares steel ductility and homogeneity. Wrought-iron beams can be loaded in varying patterns and directions, and even reused in entirely different locations.

While the exact values vary, good wrought iron after 1870 can usually be assumed to have a yield stress of 24 ksi (3.5 MPa) and allowable stress in the same proportion to the yield as steel. As with any old metal, coupons should be tested for yield stress and chemical composition—particularly sulfur and other welding inhibitors. If the tests show that the material is not weldable or contains impurities that reduce ductility, other types of connections must be used and more careful analysis of loading may be required.

In the twentieth century, wrought iron is very rare, although the material still surfaces, usually for semiornamental architectural work. The metal called wrought iron today is often chemically indistinguishable from A36 structural steel, although fabricated under uncontrolled conditions. This material is rarely, if ever, permitted in structural use.

Light-gage Steel

Despite the enormous differences in material and technology, the design of light-gage stud and joist structure is analogous to the design of wood stud and joist (figure 10-3). This is an intentional effort on the part of the manufacturers encouraging light-gage frame use and designers who favor the material. The easiest way to gain acceptance for a new material or system is to make it a straight replacement for an existing material or system. Many of the issues previously discussed in the renovation of wood-frame buildings are applicable here.

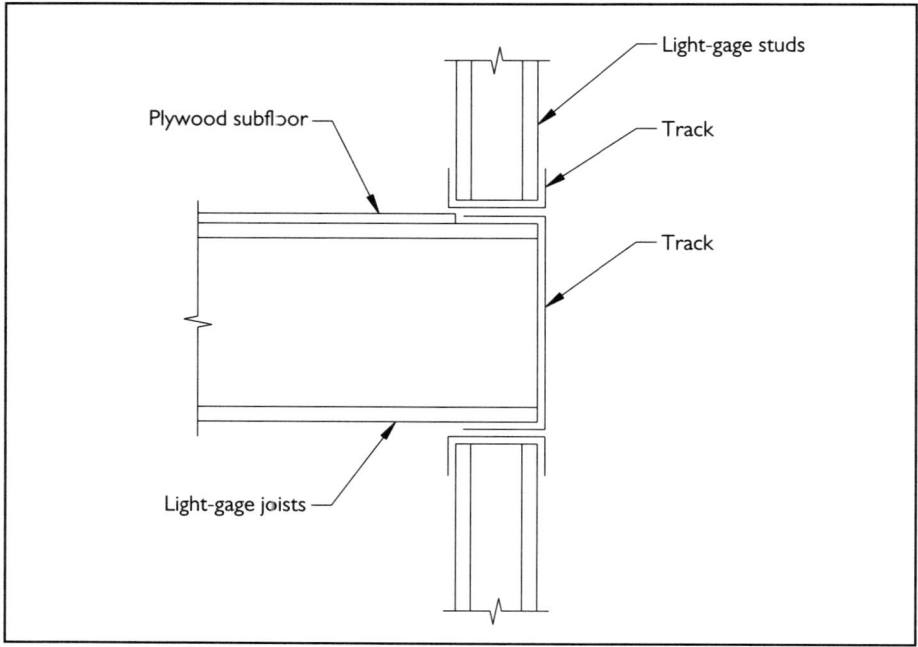

10-3. Typical light-gage joists over light-gage studs

Not only does light-gage framing greatly resemble wood framing, but the available sizes are similar to wood. The external dimensions of light-gage members are in the same range as wood members, and the difference in material strength between steel and wood is roughly balanced by the fact that the open sections of light gage have much smaller moments of inertia and section moduli than the solid sections of wood. A 12-inch (305 mm) deep light-gage joist is roughly similar to a wood 3x12, for example.

The most important difference between wood and light gage is the ability of the steel to accommodate complex connections. While welding light gage is sometimes difficult because of the danger of burning through such thin material, it is possible to make complicated connections of provable strength through the use of self-tapping screws. Moment connections, which are difficult to create in wood, are therefore reasonable in light gage.

All materials have their weaknesses, and light-gage steel is more vulnerable to water than any other. In addition to interior bearing walls in small buildings, light-gage steel studs are used as backup in brick or precast concrete curtain walls, and in low-rise buildings for walls protected by stucco or its modern equivalents.

Light-gage steel rusts at the same rate as any other steel, but when exposed to water, light-gage members are damaged more quickly, since the loss of $1/10$ inch (2 mm) of material, which would not be significant in a rolled steel beam, constitutes most or all of the section of a piece of light gage.

In examining the condition or design alterations to a curtain wall known to be backed by light-gage studs, the first step is to replicate the original design calculations as closely as possible. There are two main approaches to the design of this type of wall: assuming that the masonry acts in concert with the studs, and assuming that the masonry is simply a veneer that relies on the studs for all lateral stability. Walls of the first type are extremely difficult to modify without some form of lateral shoring or protection from wind loading. Walls of the second type may be treated as ordinary stud walls, except that extreme care must be provided in waterproofing details.

Aluminum

Structural aluminum is common in new construction in storefronts and curtain walls, locations where the higher allowable stresses of steel are not required. As a ductile metal, aluminum is generally similar to steel in design and detailing, but its material properties have so far prevented its use in most large-scale structure. Aluminum weighs only roughly one-third as much as an equivalent volume of steel, but has allowable stresses that are roughly one-third those of steel. Aluminum can be welded, but the process is more difficult and requires more accurate control than steel welding, and is best performed in the shop, not on site.

To most designers, the most important material property of aluminum is its resistance to rust. Like cast iron, aluminum rusts without delamination, so that the surface of aluminum oxide acts to protect the metal below. In this regard aluminum is superior to cast iron, since aluminum oxide is almost indistinguishable in appearance from the base metal. This property allows the metal to be used unpainted in exterior applications.

In structures where extreme light weight is important, aluminum has been used for base structure, but it is simply not strong enough for many applications. In order to gain the necessary strength, an aluminum beam would have to be proportioned much larger than the appropriate steel beam, reducing or eliminating the weight advantage. This fact, and the difficulties in working aluminum alloys that do not exist with steel, have relegated aluminum to minor roles.

The actual design of alterations or additions to aluminum structures is almost identical to that used with steel. The difficulties in welding do not eliminate the use of the details described for steel, but make field quality control more important.

Glass Curtain Walls

Unlike the other procedures described in this book, the alteration of glass curtain walls cannot be easily classified. The other materials and assemblies reached fairly modern forms at different times, with concrete having the "youngest" modern design techniques. The design of metal-framed curtain walls with the amount of glass approaching 100 percent is still evolving and is still the topic of research and debate. Much of the discussion since the 1960s has been devoted to the benefits of "stick" construction, where individual mullions and panels are erected, versus the benefits of panelized construction, where prefabrication reduces the amount of in situ assembly. This debate has relatively little impact on renovation and restoration of these structures, since the construction details, as built, are relatively similar between the two systems.

Every curtain wall is not unique, but since the mullion layout and configuration is often designed by an architect or by a team consisting of the architect and curtain-wall manufacturer specifically for the building, there is far less repetition of design than there is in structure. If original design and shop drawings are not available, complete field measurement of the existing mullion system is called for to ensure that no vital information is missed. The margin for assumption is far smaller than for structure. Because of the nature of curtain walls, there is no facility for accidental load sharing. The load paths defined by the original design are the only load paths possible.

Modern curtain-wall designs, many of which hold the glass in place with adhesives, can be vulnerable to the deflection of the mullions under wind load. A common design is to have the glass fastened with adhesive to the main body of the mullion, and then "snap-in" sections of mullion attached to prevent outward movement from wind suction. Early glass-panel design concentrated more on the stresses within the glass than on the deflection caused by the wind. Both stress and deflection are complicated by the fact that the glass in many designs is spanning to all four of its edges, creating patterns of stress more complex than ordinary one-dimensional beams. Excessive deflection of the panels, possibly not predicted during design, can cause degradation of adhesive strengths and, in rare cases, movement of the snap-in mullions.

Perhaps more than in any other renovation, simplicity is necessary in repairs to curtain walls. Any change to be made will be repeated hundreds of times, usually requiring the removal of wall and ceiling finishes. If the entire curtain wall is to be removed and replaced, often the mullions and other frame elements are completely removed, leaving only the clips to the base structural frame intact. If the glass is being replaced, often all of the mullion frame elements are kept and reused. Midway between these two possibilities is the partial alteration, which must depend on examination of the loads within the existing frames and the use of welding, self-tapping screws or some other easily repeatable form of connection to extend and change the existing members.

Case Study 10-1: Cast-iron Beam Analysis

All renovation cases that involve cast iron begin with the material present in the existing structure. As cast iron is no longer used for building structure (although fences, trim, and other ornamental pieces are still occasionally made of cast iron), most alterations involve maintaining the existing stress levels in the iron or replacing it. "Replacement" can be defined by true removal and replacement with new members, or effective replacement through the installation of new members.

While cast iron was originally used in both beams and columns, beam use was quickly superseded by wrought iron, and later steel, beams. One of the few locations where cast-iron beams were used after the introduction of wrought iron was in sidewalk vaults. Cast iron's relative resistance to corrosion was apparently the deciding factor in its use in vaults, where water entry from above is always possible.

A cast-iron beam used in a sidewalk may have never been stressed to its design capacity. Sidewalks are rarely loaded to their design loads, because the design load represents a truck pulling up onto the sidewalk. Therefore, even a vault that has performed structurally for many years could be dangerous if it were unable to carry the design load. Just as important, truck weights, and therefore code load requirements for sidewalks, have increased substantially during the course of the twentieth century.

182 OTHER MATERIALS

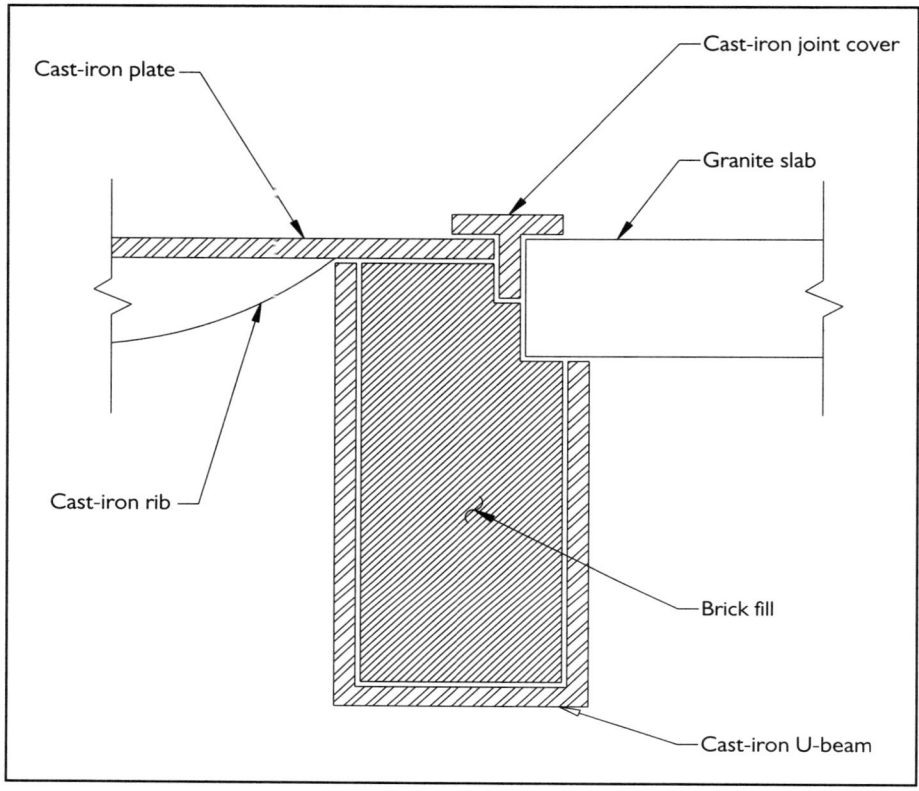

10-1-1. Vault sections showing cast-iron beam

A typical vault beam is a cast-iron U, 1/2 inch (13 mm) thick all around, 12 inches (305 mm) wide, and 18 inches (460 mm) high. Such beams were filled with brick, and the flat brick top surface used to support the sidewalk. Such a beam would span roughly 9 feet (2740 mm), supporting a thick granite slab on one side and cast-iron vault lights on the other (figure 10-1-1). The original design live load, as per pre–World War II standards, was 300 psf.

The iron must be carefully examined for damage from overstress and weathering. Even though cast iron resists rusting, decades of leaks through the sidewalk may have destroyed portions of the beams. Because the material fails brittlely, by cracking at the point of highest tension, past overstress is usually visible in the form of broken beam webs and bottom flanges.

Assuming that the beams are examined and found to be in acceptable condition, their continued use in the original configuration is ultimately a judgment call. Some notice to prevent modern loading, such as "Hollow Sidewalk" signs, is required as the least effort to protect the public against the potential of a collapse under the load of, for example, a moving van.

If damage is found, or the capacity of the sidewalk is to be upgraded to resist modern loading, the sidewalk structure can be directly supported by new beams and posts, or the cast iron continuously supported from below, reducing its role to that of a bearing plate between the sidewalk and new beams and posts.

Case Study 10-2: Wrought Iron

During the examination of a small office building for interior renovation, including the installation of a new elevator and fire stairs, the age of the building caused structural questions. The exact age was not certain, and original drawings were unavailable, but architectural sourcebooks described the construction date as various times between 1890 and 1895. The alterations required the installation of new beams to frame out the floor openings, and consequently the creation of connections between new steel beams and the existing beams.

Steel was in use during the 1880s, and wrought iron was occasionally used as late as the 1900s. The rough date of the building's construction is not sufficient information to pin down the material used in the frame. After the completion of building department documents, a testing lab was directed to take coupons from typical floor beams for testing to determine the percentage of carbon and impurities and to review the microscopic structure of the metal. These tests showed that the metal was wrought iron with relatively high silicon and sulfur content. Since it is almost impossible to create acceptable welds with such base material, the ordinary detail of welding the new beams connections to the existing beams had to be abandoned.

Bolt holes of acceptable quality can be created by using mechanically guided drills, most often magnetic drills that clamp to the metal being drilled. The connection details were redesigned using high-strength steel bolts in holes field-drilled in the existing beams. The connection redesign included oversizing the connections to account for the lower allowable stresses in the iron, most importantly the bearing stress of the bolts on the beam webs at the new bolt holes.

184 OTHER MATERIALS

Case Study 10-3: Aluminum Ornament

Because aluminum does not deteriorate from normal weathering, it is a popular choice for exterior ornament and trim of different types. Even ornament requires enough strength to support its own weight. Depending on its shape and size, the structural design of ornament may be what is referred to in engineering schools as "nontrivial."

The "structure" being examined in this case is a trellis that extends around three sides and forms a canopy over an exterior balcony. The adjacent interior space was converted from a manufacturing loft to a branch library, and the terrace, which had previously been unoccupied, was altered for the patrons' use. Because the terrace was in the rear of the building, facing a courtyard surrounded by similar loft buildings, the trellis was used as a way to screen the view. The trellis, while a purely decorative element, spans roughly 20 feet (6100 mm), and could conceivably be loaded by people (probably children) hanging from the canopy (figure 10-3-1).

Different metals react in different fashions to the heat of welding. Even steel, which is considered a weldable metal, may require preheating or special welding electrodes under some circumstances. Aluminum is more affected by the

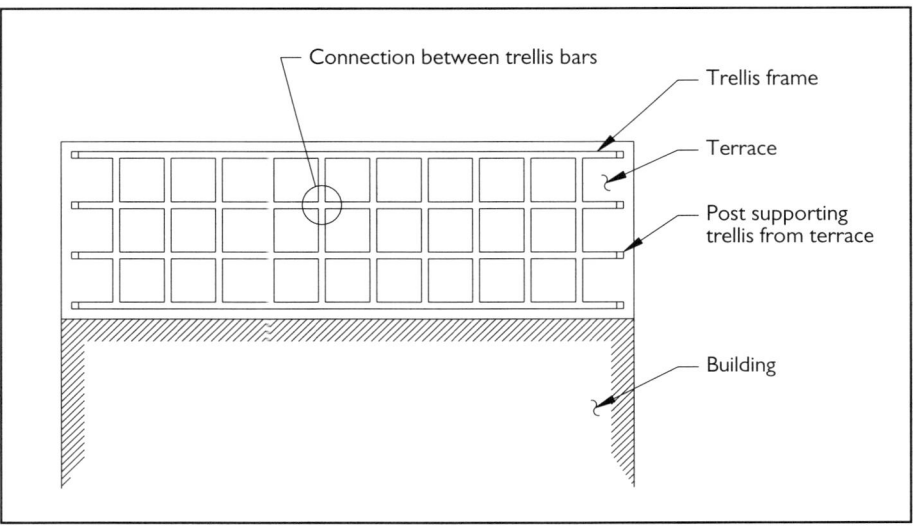

10-3-1. Trellis plan showing grid connection locations

heat, and so the aluminum codes require the use of lower allowable stresses in welded structure than are used in bolted structure.

Analysis of the trellis structure showed that the welded joints that were used for a clean appearance and to prevent water from being trapped made the canopy substantially weaker than had first been assumed. The canopy was redesigned to the lower stresses with a larger "main" structure supporting the actual plant-carrying trellis bars.

Case Study 10-4: Glass Curtain Walls

Mostly glass curtain walls are reexamined for two reasons: significant alterations are planned to change the appearance of the building, or there are performance problems. Poor performance of the waterproofing seals is not a structural problem, but frequent breakage or loss of glass panels usually is. The investigation of glass panel damage in a curtain wall will include many possible causes, some of which are related to the structural performance of the building as a whole, some to the structural performance of the curtain-wall system, and some not related to structural performance at all.

The last category includes breakage from causes such as "missile damage": if an adjacent building has a roof with loose gravel as ballast, high winds may pick up the gravel and propel it at the building under examination. Damage caused by missiles or wind "hot spots" created by the configuration of adjacent structures can often be identified by its patterns. If the damage follows patterns that vary from one building face to another, or that shows sharp lines of demarcation between damaged and undamaged areas, nonstructural causes are likely (figure 10-4-1).

Overall building structural performance can affect the curtain wall in various ways. In some cases where the patterns of damage include the frequent loss of intact panels, the cause has been determined to be the overall flexibility of the building. The amount of allowable movement allowed in the design of curtain walls is fairly constant from one building to the next, while the amount of movement that a building undergoes when loaded by wind varies greatly with the frame design and the wind exposure. Since retrofitting to reduce the amount of building sway involves disruptive changes within occupied spaces at all floors within the building, this problem has traditionally been dealt with by changing the expansion joints of the curtain wall. This is not a painless operation, but is less intrusive in an occupied building.

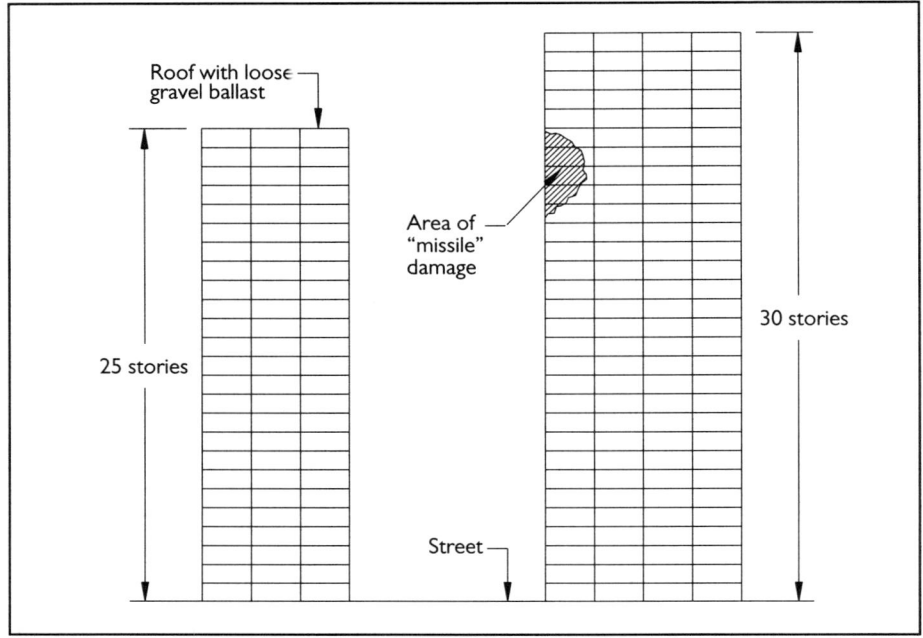

10-4-1. Elevation of two buildings showing missile damage

Finally, there is the potential for problems in the design of the mullion and glass system. In the early days of glass wall design, the late 1940s and '50s, the structural design criteria for wind loading of glass panels were less strict than those adopted in the 1960s and '70s. Advances in building design that have taken place simultaneously with the evolution of curtain walls include the use of wind tunnels to give reasonably accurate information about the local wind conditions, materials testing of the action of glass and adhesives under long-term exposure to high levels of stress and weathering, and gradual advances in the actual mullion design. The older a curtain wall is, the more likely it will have damage from local stress patterns caused by obsolete or incorrect design. Damage patterns that include breaks in specific positions in the glass panels or increasing amounts of damage with the age of the panel, or that can be cured by simply substituting the next thicker size panel during replacement, are indicative of local structural problems.

Chapter 11

Foundations

The construction of the foundation in new buildings comes first, and is literally the base for all work. Renovation designers, by contrast, work very diligently to omit this area of construction entirely. Unlike new construction, where the involvement of the excavation and concrete trades is unavoidable in the construction of foundations, economy in renovation work depends closely on limiting the number of different building trades involved.

The vast majority of above-grade renovations do not require changes to the foundations. Cases where the overall building load is increased enough to require heavier foundations are rare. Often when a schematic proposal results in a requirement for foundation work, the scheme is either altered or new columns and foundations are added so as not to affect the existing foundations. Load increases at only one or two floors in a tall building can often be absorbed in the overall load that the foundation supports through live load reduction. Similarly, conversion of industrial buildings to residential use often results in excess foundation capacity. The industrial live load per floor greatly exceeds the residential live load requirements.

Foundations, more so than concrete or masonry, are part of "closed" structural systems. Without original drawings it is very difficult to determine the full extent of foundation work without large areas of destructive testing. While it is possible to determine layout, depths, and soil bearing values, it is nearly impossible to determine reinforcing size and location. Making matters worse is the fact that foundations in smaller structures (houses and rowhouses) are often constructed with less quality control than any other area of the building. Spread footings are often "trench" poured (no formwork), and reinforcing that may be present is pushed into wet concrete, not set prior to the pour. A single exploratory test pit often does not tell the whole story.

This is not to say that foundation work is avoided altogether during renovations. A large portion of preliminary design, however, will often be spent analyzing the impact of a proposed design on existing foundations.

For these reasons foundation work during renovation is often driven by factors different from those driving the balance of the project. These factors may include: foundation failures that require repair before repairs for the damage it has caused; lowering the bearing depth of existing foundations that would be undermined by adjacent construction; and lowering the bearing depth for legal reasons (local code requirements). Most of the methods used to repair foundations can be used to give them extra capacity if required after a feasibility analysis.

This chapter explores general soil properties and foundation types, repair techniques, and some reinforcing methods. Rather than discussing the full scope of geotechnical engineering, we provide here an overview of foundation renovation.

Soils and Foundation Types

The capacity of a bearing surface is determined primarily by the composition of soil at the site. In general, soil is a collection of particles and voids. The smaller the voids, the more dense and usually the stronger the soil. The presence of water can adversely affect the capacity and stability of soil, so determining the water table is a key to any geotechnical investigation. For any large project, a series of test borings are drilled and the core samples tested and analyzed and finally classified by a geotechnical engineer. For smaller projects, a test pit, dug to the proposed bottom of footing depth, will often give a geotechnical engineer enough information to classify the bearing material. National and local building codes list allowable bearing capacities based on soil classification. In very general terms, the classifications range from clay and silt (lowest capacity) to sands to decomposed rock to crystalline bedrock (highest capacity). Clay is the most difficult bearing material to classify and can range widely in capacity.

During renovation work, as opposed to new design, it is more important to determine the classification of the soil that the existing foundations bear on rather than the classification of the best bearing layer. Placing an addition or new foundation on a different soil than that of the existing foundation can cause substantial damage as differential settling occurs.

There are two groups of foundations: shallow and deep. Shallow foundations are generally spread footings and piers; deep foundations are generally piles and caissons. The simplest type of foundation, spread footings are probably the most prevalent type and are found under most house and rowhouse-type construction as well as a substantial number of larger buildings. They are designed to spread a column or wall load onto the supporting soil. Spread footings are used when adequate soil is located near the optimum bottom of the footing, and additional excavation can be kept to a minimum. Piers are another form of shallow footing, placed in an excavated hole rather than drilled. If good soil is located lower than is practical to place spread footings but not deep enough to justify piles or caissons, individual piers are dug down to good soil. Concrete grade beams spanning from pier to pier are then placed.

Piles and caissons are used when adequate soil or rock is located below a feasible line of excavation. Piles are driven to capacity, while caissons are generally poured in drilled holes. Of interest to the renovation engineer are minipiles, low-capacity piles that can be driven with substantially smaller equipment and are often used during renovation when new foundations are required inside the building.

Foundation Failures

Foundation failures occur for many reasons. Like all forensic studies, looking at foundation failure can encompass a large percentage of the investigation phase of a renovation. Forensic foundation work relies on in situ conditions and history more than any other material does. Original records, new and existing borings, test pits, patterns of failure, local geotechnical information, original stream and river records, and more can assist in determine the cause of failure.

As noted earlier, the capacity and stability of soil is based on the balance of particles and voids. The failure of a foundation can usually be traced to the change in this balance during the life of a building. Foundation failure can occur in many ways, including the movement of the entire building down, sideways, and in some rare circumstances, up; the movement of a portion of the foundation; the loss of soil under a concrete slab on grade; and movement caused by freeze and thaw action in the soil.

Consolidation failure occurs when load causes the soil particles to compress into the void space, the result of either an underdesigned footing or a misclassified soil, both resulting in an overburdened layer of soil. In some cases a layer of especially weak soil will consolidate under its own weight. This may occur under a concrete slab on grade, causing large voids to develop. Although it is impossible to predict, a relatively stable soil may consolidate under a foundation to the required capacity and then stabilize. In this case, repairs at the foundation may not be required.

In some cases, soil particles will shift into the voids as a result of vibration. Movement from failure caused by vibration resembles failure due to consolidation but occurs faster, and with sometimes disastrous results.

The presence of water alone is not necessarily damaging to the stability of soil. The action of the water, whether it is static or dynamic, creates the danger. Water flowing from a broken water main or an underground stream can pass through a bearing layer, causing the soil particles to migrate and shift, and sweeping the bearing layer out from under a foundation. In this case, an investigator might look for evidence of water movement in the neighborhood surrounding the building. This type of dynamic movement may also occur when adjacent construction requires dewatering (the lowering of the local water table during construction to allow for a dry concrete pour). Often one of the first questions raised by a geotechnical engineer concerns recent construction activity nearby.

Building codes specify a minimum depth of exterior foundation to protect the foundation from freeze and thaw action. During the winter, any water present in the voids of a top layer of soil will freeze. The effective depth of this layer varies with geographical location. As the water freezes, it expands, causing the soil to expand, and as the water thaws the soil contracts. This cycle occurring beneath a spread footing can cause damaging movement. This movement can always occur and depends only on the severity of the winter.

Soil relies on the surrounding soil to remain stable. If soil is exposed on one side, the particles tend to "slide" along a line of failure or incidence. The classification of the soil can assist in predicting the angle of incidence. New excavation adjacent to an existing foundation may expose the soil on which the foundation bears. If this soil is not stabilized by sheeting or other methods, the soil may slide and undermine the foundation. A design that is adjacent to an existing foundation must make provisions or excavate far enough away so as not to undermine the existing foundation.

Failure of piles and caissons occurs less often, since these foundations are driven to more stable layers of soil, which are rarely affected by vibrations or the dynamic presence of water.

Methods of Repair and Reinforcement

Consolidation failure can be abated in many ways. Each method either extends the existing foundation down to a more capable and stable layer or stabilizes the present bearing layer.

The simplest design method, although the most labor intensive, is underpinning, which generally refers to the downward extension of continuous foundation walls. Underpinning can be used to correct any of the failures previously described by extending an existing foundation down to a more stable layer of soil. Underpinning can be used to lower footing bottom elevation when proposed adjacent construction is threatening to undermine the existing foundation, or when the capacity of the foundation is to be increased by extending to a stronger layer of soil.

While underpinning is a tried-and-true method of construction, it is one that must be carried out with patience and care. In general, underpinning is performed in 3-foot (915 mm) wide strips so as not to undermine the foundation being worked on. One strip is excavated and the concrete wall poured. Because this process is carried out in sections, the new concrete cannot be a continuous beam and therefore relies on the continuous support of soil (figure 11-1). After the first strip is poured, another section 6 feet (1830 mm) away is excavated and the underpinning set. Not until the first section has set, and the load transferred from the original foundation to the underpinning, is the soil excavated adjacent to it. In this way no portion of the original footing is ever unsupported for more than 3 feet (915 mm) of length at a time without at least 6 feet (1830 mm) of soil to either side.

When underpinning is not feasible, more advanced techniques for shoring up existing foundations are available. Like pile work, these methods involve drilling and are "blind" operations. An experienced geotechnical engineer is required during this type of work to monitor the progress and verify the suitability of work.

Injection grouting is used when consolidation failure has occurred but the soil is otherwise stable and there are no large voids present. The intention is to

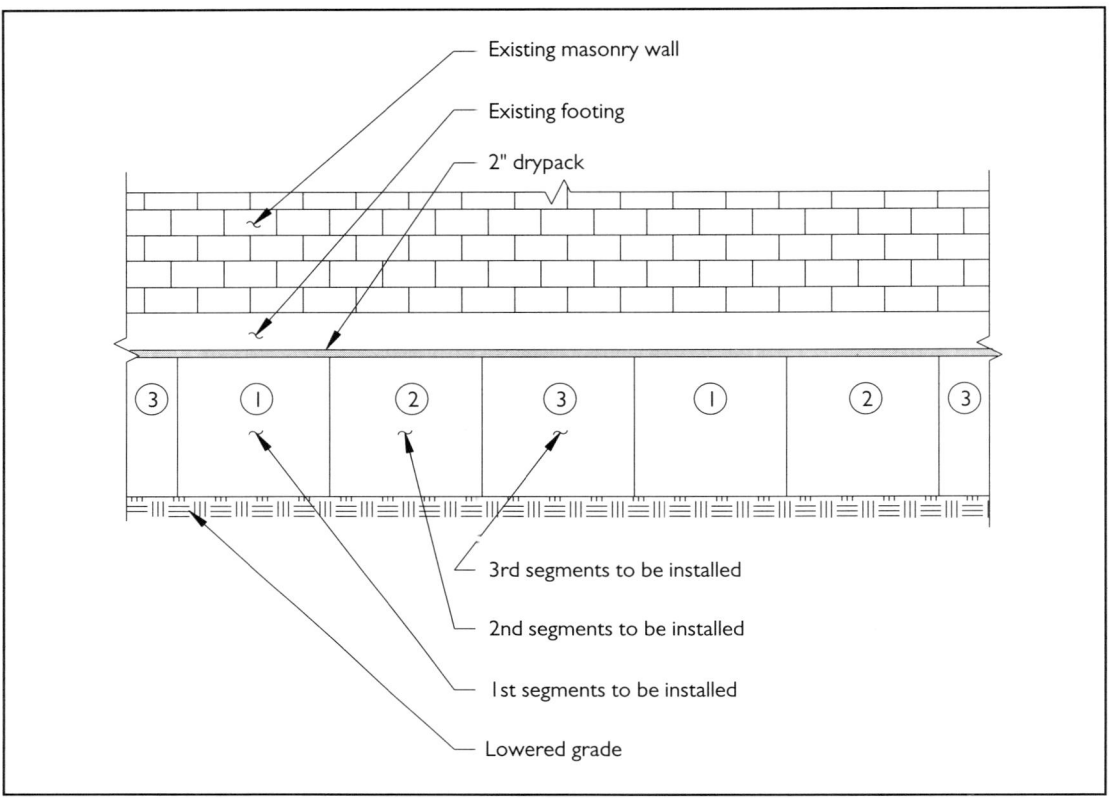

11-1. Underpinning

fill each small void in the soil with cementitious grout, thereby halting the movement of particles into these voids. This is carried out by drilling a grid of small access holes in the cellar or basement slab throughout the building and pumping grout into each hole. The engineer knows that enough grout has been pumped, and the small voids filled, when grout exits from other access holes during pumping. Unfortunately, an abandoned uncapped pipe, not discovered during preliminary investigations, can give the grout a flow path of greater volume than the foundations, leaving the contractor waiting for grout to exit from other grout holes. This makes original and current utility plans and records extremely crucial to this type of design.

If the original foundation was built on unsuitable bearing material and good bearing soil is too deep to allow for underpinning, grout columns may be recommended. In this operation, grout is used to create new columns from the new bearing layer to the underside of the original foundation. A small pipe is driven down to adequate bearing and slowly lifted through the unsuitable layer. As the pipe is lifted, grout is pumped through it, forming a column in the soil. If these columns are spaced properly, they will consolidate the soil around them and create a continuous layer of bearing beneath the original foundation. As with injection grouting, this operation is "blind" and can be damaged by abandoned pipes or large voids. The grout pipes are relatively fragile and can break off or bend at boulders. If borings predict the presence of boulders, the geotechnical engineer may recommend that a stronger pipe be placed around the weaker pipe to escort it through the soil.

Cellar slabs are often placed on less suitable fill than the building foundations as an afterthought to overall construction. For crawl spaces or cellars within houses this may be sufficient. However, in larger and more heavily used buildings, poor fill can cause noticeable settlement and damage. The simplest repair is to remove the existing slab and fill to reach a layer of suitable bearing material. The resulting pit is then refilled with clean, properly compacted fill and a new slab is placed on top. This repair cannot be guaranteed to support substantial wheel loads or machinery, and in some cases the soil failure was caused by washout that may occur again. The only way to guarantee stability involves converting from a slab on grade to a supported slab, which involves designing a series of grade beams and footings (or piers or piles) to support a reinforced slab. The slab and beams are designed as they would be for an upper floor, with no reliance on the soil. The footings, piles, or piers act as columns. The soil under the slab is required to support only the wet weight of the concrete during construction. Consolidation or washout will not affect the shape or stability of the slab.

Deterioration

Modern foundations rarely deteriorate simply from exposure. While concrete immersed in water will eventually deteriorate, and the rebar within eventually rust, this does not happen often. Modern foundations are waterproofed on their outside surfaces, and provided with drains to keep the surrounding soil from saturation. Only in rare circumstances are building foundations continually immersed in water; ordinary spread footings and foundation walls are above the permanent water table.

As late as World War II, foundation walls were still sometimes built of brick masonry. The practice of using unreinforced masonry for cellar and basement walls is hundreds of years old. Before 1900, the bulk of below-grade masonry was rubble or coursed rubble, with the remainder common brick. (Rubble is randomly shaped metamorphic rock such as granite or schist, usually in roughly flat pieces; coursed rubble is similar stone squared off so that the joints are of constant thickness and roughly horizontal and vertical.) After 1900, concrete became more common, the use of rubble ceased, and brick faded gradually.

There are two causes of deterioration in masonry foundations. Many mortars undergo changes in composition when exposed to water for long periods of time, and brick or soft stone will erode when wet. The first danger is the leaching of lime out of mortar. Unlike cured cements, lime dissolves in water and travels with the water through the wall. When there is consistent vapor pressure in one direction, as in foundation walls, lime gradually leaves the mortar and builds up on the drier inside surface. It is common to see the entire surface of a masonry foundation wall covered with the whitish residue of lime, whose absence has reduced the joints to packed sand. Even when the bulk of the wall is next to well-drained soil, the base of the wall has a tendency to pull water upward through wicking action, usually referred to as "rising damp."

Rising damp is simply a large-scale mechanism for water to move through masonry. The voids within brick and mortar are small enough to allow water to move by capillary action, where the cohesiveness of the fluid and its adhesion to the surrounding material pull it forward. Since the earth next to a foundation wall tends to be wetter the farther below grade you go, the capillary action tends to pull water upward, so that the wall is relatively more damp than the earth immediately adjacent. This completes the "circuit" by allowing vapor pressure to pull the water from the upper reaches of the wall into the earth. The last step is not always present, since in extreme cases, rising damp will pull the water 10 feet (3050 mm) or so above grade.

The presence of water does not harm the hard rock usually used for rubble, but is inherently destructive to brick. Water present from the exterior earth or from rising damp eventually spalls off the face of the brick and reduces the interior to powder. The mechanics of brick deterioration are well documented, and operate no differently in foundations than in facades. Once the brick and mortar material has deteriorated, there is no way to repair it short of replacement.

Conclusion

Foundation work and related shoring and stabilizing can be the most expensive portion of renovation work. In addition, reworking only a portion of an existing foundation can have an adverse effect on the remainder of the building as new support locations and load paths are developed. For these reasons, the feasibility of foundation work is carefully analyzed before proceeding. In some cases it is unavoidable.

If constructed correctly and properly monitored, foundation-renovation work can be successfully carried out. More so than any other renovation work, foundation work requires great patience and an understanding of the soil involved.

Case Study 11-1: Footing Encapsulation

During the renovation of a large steel-frame building, storage areas are replacing office spaces. This change requires an increase in live load capacity of the affected structure. The structure to be reinforced includes the steel columns and the foundations (see Case Study 6-4 for the steel-column reinforcing).

It is not ordinarily feasible to shore the existing structure, remove the existing footing, and pour a new, larger footing. This work requires the disruption of the space above for shoring, often all the way to the building's roof. Installation and inspection of the shoring are slow processes. The work can be speeded by increasing the area of the existing footing while keeping it in service.

In this case, the existing footing is encapsulated within a new footing. Without existing drawings or removing all load from the footing for probing, it is impossible to determine the exact reinforcing in the existing footing (figure 11-1-1). Under these conditions, the footing cannot be loaded beyond the capacity of its original design. These factors control the new footing design.

The new foundation must spread the column load throughout the entire footing area. The final design involves two new concrete structures to accomplish this: a concrete "donut" poured around the existing footing, and a reinforced-concrete slab poured over the existing and new footings to spread the load over the two (figure 11-1-2). The concrete for these two pieces may be placed simultaneously, but the pieces' roles are distinct. Shear plates and

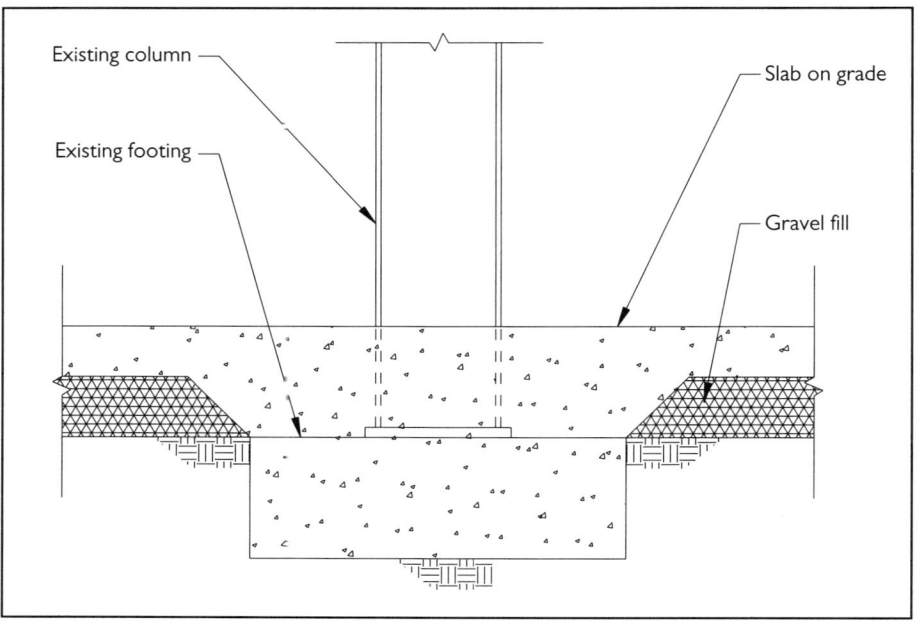

11-1-1. Footing before encapsulation

reinforcing are placed in the slab to transfer the new column loads out to the new concrete donut. The existing load remains in the footing, which has the capacity to support it.

The earth around the existing footings is excavated—making sure not to excavate beneath the bottom of footing elevation—and the soil bearing confirmed by a geotechnical engineer. The concrete donut is then poured and allowed to reach its seven-day strength. Since the upper slab is spreading the load, it is not necessary for the donut to be bonded to the existing concrete footing, although placing a bonding agent can be considered additional security. If the two pieces are placed separately, the new shear plates and reinforcing bars are put in place during the curing period for the donut.

The structural slab requires a substantial thickness to distribute its loads, depending on the size of the footing. This technique may not work if the existing footing is close to the surface of the cellar slab and projections above that slab are not possible because of conflicts with the cellar's use.

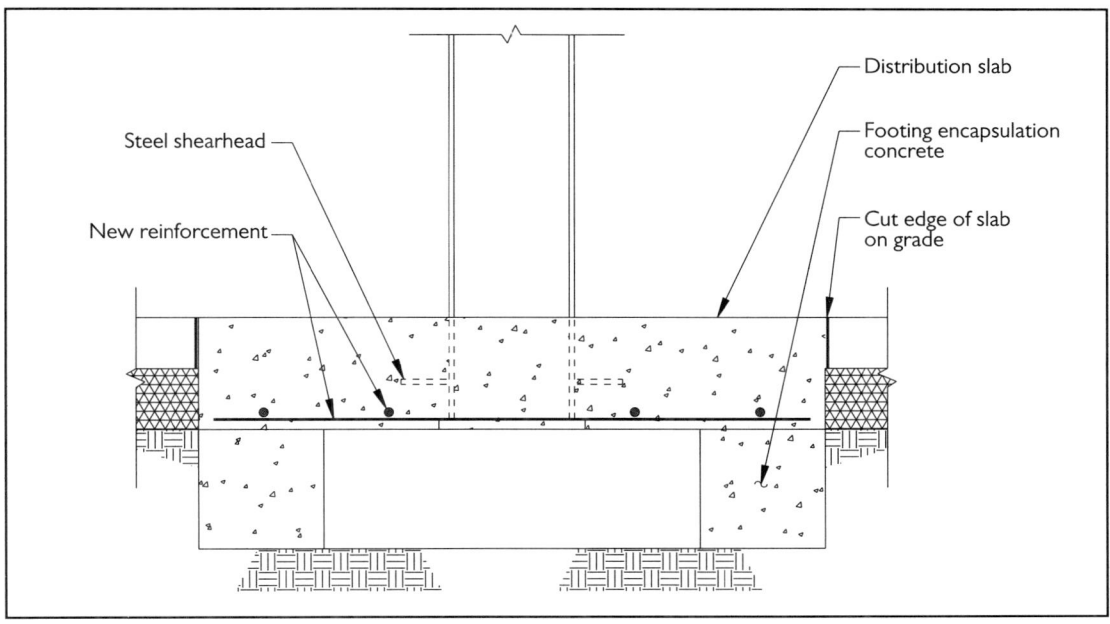

11-1-2. Footing after encapsulation

Case Study 11-2: Injection Grouting

Foundation problems can sometimes take decades to develop, forcing an architect or engineer examining the building to examine the history and current use of the building in addition to the technical problem. In this case, a ten-story apartment house from the 1920s, constructed of masonry bearing walls, interior steel beams, and wood joists, is slowly settling. The building is positioned on a cut into a large hill. The settling is visible in cracks throughout the facade and the uneven surface of the concrete slabs on grade in the cellar. After years of patching, an engineer is brought in to determine the cause of this obviously active movement and propose a fix, if possible.

The engineer proposes a full set of borings and test pits that will allow him to develop a profile of the subsurface conditions. This profile will help to determine the nature of the settlement: is the soil compressing due to inadequate bearing strength or is the soil migrating from beneath the building? In addition,

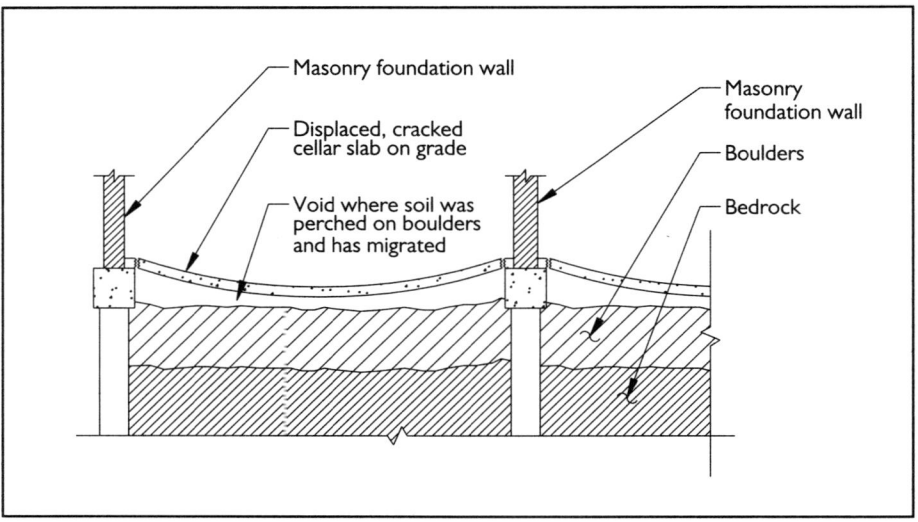

11-2-1. Building sections showing soil layers and soil migration

paper research is performed to find any available information on old streams that may have run through the site. Often, settlement can be caused by soil being washed out from underneath a building by way of buried streams.

A large layer of boulders (possibly excavation debris broken out of the hill prior to construction) is found directly beneath the building. The boulders begin approximately 3 feet (915 mm) below the cellar slab and continue down for approximately 15 feet (4570 mm), to bedrock (figure 11-2-1). In addition, it is discovered that there is an approximately 8-inch (200 mm) deep void between the cellar slab and the earth beneath the most of the slab.

This evidence strongly suggests that there were voids between the boulders and that the soil that was originally beneath the building has migrated into these voids. This occurred very slowly, and is still occurring, causing the building to quietly sink into the ground.

Two separate repairs are required, one to stop the movement of the bearing walls supporting the building, and one to fill the voids below the cellar slab. The structure above can be supported by injection grouting, an often expensive and difficult process. Pipes are driven through the boulder layer and slowly withdrawn while grout is pumped through them into the layer containing the voids. The grout is meant to travel through the voids and thereby consolidate the adjacent soil. If designed and performed properly, this technique is very effective.

Unfortunately, it is impossible to verify proper grout coverage while the building is in place, and removing the building to determine if it is stable is not an available option. Precautions such as monitoring the amount of grout and comparing with theoretical quantities help, but do not provide absolute certainty of the results.

Two solutions are available for the less critical work of filling the void beneath the cellar slab. Either the slab can be removed and replaced with a structural slab attached to the main building structure, or small-scale pressure grouting work can be performed beneath the slab. In this case the grout is easier to monitor through the use of pilot holes. A grid of holes can be drilled in the slab. When grout fills a specific area, the excess grout will exit through these holes. This will provide better, but not absolute, certainty.

Case Study 11-3: New Supported Slab

Often, the owners of large industrial buildings spend years repouring and releveling the ground-floor concrete slab on grade in an effort to maintain proper tolerances for their equipment. In this case, the owner's in-house designers determine that it will be more cost effective to eliminate the problem of the constantly settling slab rather than continue patching.

Borings taken at the site show that the ground floor bears on an unsuitable layer of fill material (figure 11-3-1). While there are methods for stabilizing this layer, such as heavy mechanical compaction or injection grouting, the only way to be sure that the slab will not continue to move is by constructing a new slab as if there were no grade below. If the building foundations are capable of supporting additional load, the new slab can be tied into the existing concrete grade beams. Otherwise, the new slab can be supported on a series of new foundations, either piles or excavated piers extending down to suitable bearing material.

In this case, a large industrial space with ample head room, it is determined that the most economical solution is the introduction of new screw piles in clusters. These clusters are topped with standard concrete pile caps. The caps support grade beams that are laid out in a grid and support the new concrete slab (figure 11-3-2). The only difference between this structural system and a typical floor slab is the use of the earth as a form. Although this earth is not capable of supporting large loads over time, it is more than capable of supporting the temporary dead load of the wet concrete.

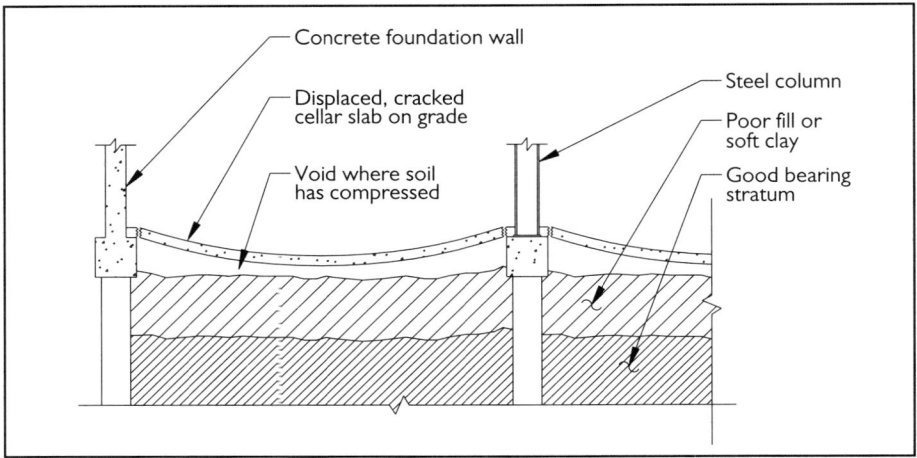

11-3-1. Existing condition with dropped slab on grade

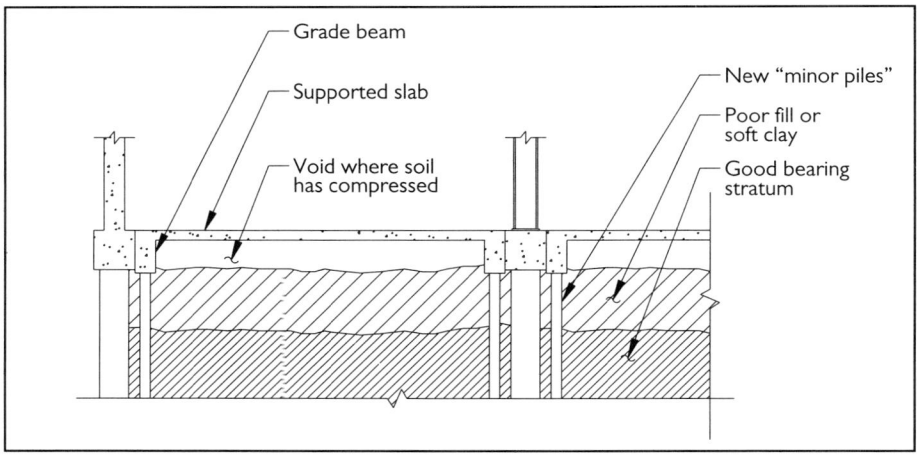

11-3-2. New supported slab

An option that was studied and determined not cost effective was the use of a concrete mat slab supported on evenly spaced piles throughout the space. Although these piles supported less area, requiring a lower pile capacity, the cost of driving a separate pile at each location was prohibitive. In other cases this may be the most economical solution, as the need for pile caps and grade beams is eliminated.

Case Study 11-4: Cantilever Grade Beams

Two stories are being added to a 25-foot (7620 mm) wide, three-story rowhouse. The additional weight would overstress the existing wall footings, so new foundations must be provided to support the additional structure. The difficulty in providing new columns at the side walls is that their footings would extend over the adjacent property line.

The program for the new construction provides for new perimeter columns, spaced at approximately 20 feet on center from front to rear. The columns align with each other across the width of the building. These columns carry down through the existing side wall structure and must be supported by new foundations.

A common solution to the problem of providing property line footings is to use cantilevered grade beams. Grade beams are built running across the width of the building, supported by footings placed within the cellar area as close to

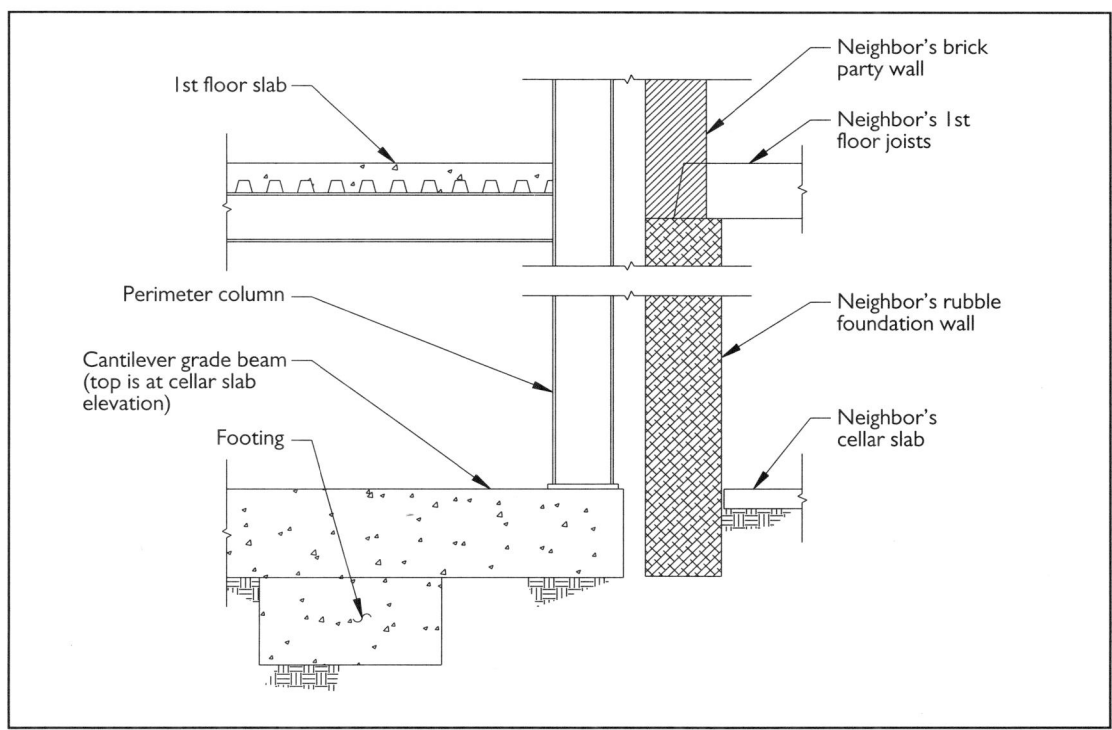

11-4-1. Building section showing cantilever grade beams

the existing perimeter wall as feasible (figure 11-4-1). The cantilever back-arm must be balanced by footings or other loads. In a symmetrical case such as this building, the grade beams cantilever at each end and pick up perimeter columns at either side of the space.

The design of the grade beam is driven by concern for reducing the length of the cantilever and examination of unbalanced load conditions. The designer is using a modern material and design (the grade beam) to solve geometric problems created by the older system (the masonry foundation walls) being modified.

Index

AASHTO, 103
ACI masonry code, 157
AISC publications
    code (1990), 40, 87
    Iron and Steel Beams, 1873–1952, 58
    manual (1937), 87
alterations, *see* renovation
aluminum, 179–80, 184–85
Americans with Disabilities Act, 17
anchors, masonry, 151–52
architects
    education of, 8–9
    engineers, coordination with, 46
    renovation from, 9–10
architectural design, 12–23
    analysis of existing, 12–15
    fireproofing, 19–20
    floor plate thickness, 15–17
    load capacity, 18–19
    material retention, 20–21
    partition thickness, 17
    project scale, 21–22
architectural finishes, 30
attics, openings in, 145–47

Badger, Daniel, 175
balloon framing, 121, 122, 124, 125
barns
    renovation of, 141–44
    roofs of, 128, 129
basic column slenderness, 91

beams
    attaching to masonry, 157–58
    cast iron, 173, 174, 175–76, 181–83
    concrete, 34–35
        hooks for, 98
        reinforcement of, 103, 115–16
        splicing, 111–13
    deflection of, 52
    flitch, 136–37
    grade, 201–2
    LVL, 132–33
    removal of, 30–35
    sistering, 103, 115–16
    steel, reinforcement of, 79–82
        using composite action, 86–88
        using flange addition, 83–86
        web reinforcement, 88–90
bending moment, 37
BOCA code, 66
Bogardus, James, 175
bolts, 76–77, 94
brick
    bearing walls, 152
    foundations, 194
    properties of, 150
    wythes of, 159
buildings
    hazardous condition of, 56
    historical construction standards of, 40–42
    see also materials; specific types of buildings
burned holes, 76–77

caissons, 189, 191
cantilevered grade beams, 201–2
cast iron, 172–76, 181–83
cathedral ceilings, 127
cellar slabs, 193, 199–200
chases, 159, 162–64
clip angles, 83, 94
columns
    basic column slenderness, 91
    jacking of, 44, 52–54, 78
    lateral loading of, 44
    reinforced concrete, reinforcement of, 102–3, 109–11
    steel, reinforcement of, 78–79, 90–93
column strips, slab, 104, 110, 114
concrete, 19
    advantages of, 96
    encasing steel columns, 78–79, 92–93
    testing of, 65
concrete construction, *see* reinforced concrete buildings
concrete floors
    on composite metal decks, 41–42
    design of, historical, 98–100
    draped mesh slab, 99–100, 107
    lateral support of, 43
    one-way slabs
        adding depth to, 105–7
        external reinforcement of, 107–9
        openings in, 14, 15, 30–35
        reinforcement and modification to, 103–5
    two-way slabs, 104–5, 113–15
    weathering of, 29–30
concrete masonry units (C.M.U.), 151
concrete waffle fill, 22
consolidation failures, 190
construction documents
    misleading, 68–71
    original, 57–59
    use of, 55–56
contracts, 27
costs
    alteration v. new construction, 47–48
    unanticipated, 26–27
coursed rubble foundations, 194
Cummings system, 98
curtain walls, 179
    glass, 180–81, 185–86

    loads on, 42
    masonry, 88, 153–56, 170–71

damage, accidental, 26–27, 62–63
dead loads, 18, 19, 81
deflections, 39, 44
diaphragm action, 25
documents, construction, *see* construction documents
double angle connections, 94–95
draped mesh slab construction, 99–100, 107
drawings, construction, *see* construction documents
drilled holes, 76–77

earthquake designs, *see* seismic designs
engineering design, 36–54
    analysis of, 39–40, 48–49
    constructibility of, 45–46
    deflection and jacking, 44–45, 52–54
    lateral loading, 42–44, 50–52
    parameters of, 36–37
    principles of, 37–39
    standards, historical, 40–42
    techniques, historical, 27–28
    unknown structure, 25–27, 46
engineers
    architects, coordination with, 46
    education of, 8–9
    present at probe, 62, 64, 72
    renovation from, 9–10
epoxy bonding agents, 101
erection seats, 28–29
expansion joints, 42, 153, 170–71

facades, iron, 175
failure, testing to, 65–66
field investigation, 59–61
finishes, architectural, 30
fireproofing materials, 19–20
flanges, additions to, 81–82, 83–86
flitch beams, 136–37
floors
    adding, 13
    concrete, *see* concrete floors
    elevation changes to, 19, 22–23
    lateral support of, 25, 43
    masonry arch, 151, 161–62
    plywood tee stiffening of, 144–45
    thickness of, 15–17

foundations, 187–202
    deterioration of, 193–94
    failure of, 189–91
    investigation of, 68, 187–88
    repair and reinforcement of, 191–93
        by encapsulating footing, 195–96
        using cantilevered grade beams, 201–2
        using injection grouting, 197–99
        using new supported slab, 199–200
    types of, 188–89
frames, in masonry walls, 164–67

gable roofs, 125–27
girders, 50–54
glass curtain walls, 180–81, 185–86
glass-fiber reinforced concrete (GFRC), 170
glu-lams, 132
grade beams, 201–2
grout
    columns, 192–93
    injection of, 191–92, 197–99
Guidelines for Structural Assessment of Existing Buildings, 60
gypsum, 19
    partitions of, 17, 162
    plaster, 30

Hennebique system, 98
high-rise buildings
    access in, 45
    column transfer in, 52–54
holes, in steel, 76–77
hooks, concrete beam, 98
horizontal shear, 38–39

injection grouting, 191–92, 197–99
interviews, 56, 61
investigation, *see* research
iron construction
    cast, 172–76, 181–83
    design history of, 27–28
    wrought, 176–77, 183

jacking, 44–45, 52–54
joinery, wood, 129–32
joists, sistering, 134–36, 138–41

Kahn system, 98

laminated veneer lumber (LVL), 132–33
large small projects, 21
lateral loading, 42–44, 50–52
ledger boards, 121
light-gage steel, 177–79
lintels
    chased-in, 159–60, 162–64
    stone, 160, 161
live load reduction, 18–19
live loads, changes in, 18–19, 187
load paths
    modification of, 47–48
    for roofs, 125–29
    in wood framing, 118, 120
loads
    capacity of, 18–19, 81, 187
    for cast iron, 173
    changes in, 13–15
    on columns, 78–79, 91, 93
    full-scale load testing, 65, 66–67, 73–74
    lateral, 42–44, 50–52
LVL (laminated veneer lumber), 132–33

masonry anchors, 151–52
masonry buildings, 150–71
    connections to, 156–58
    design history of, 27, 151
    floors and partitions, 161–62
    GFRC substitution in, 167–70
    probing, 26
    properties of, 150–52
    replacement or removal in, 159–60
    stone lintels, 160, 161
    walls
        bearing, 152–53
        chased-in lintels in, 162–64
        curtain, 88, 153–56, 170–71
        in old drawings, 57
        rigid frames in shear, 164–67
    weathering of, 29
materials
    choice of, 45–46
    construction techniques, historical, 28–29
    design techniques, historical, 27–28
    retention of, 20–21
    variance in, 24–25
    weathering of, 29–30
    see also research; specific materials

mechanical systems, location of, 15, 119–20
members
    forces on, 43
    importance of, 24–25
middle-middle strips, slab, 105, 113
middle strips, slab, 104, 110, 114
minipiles, 189
moment, bending, 37
mortise-and-tenon joints, 130
mullions, 180

National Design Specification for Wood Construction, 120
National Design Specification (NFPA NDS 1991), 66
National Forest Products Association (NFPA) lab, 66
National Lumber Manufacturers Association, 120

overstress, 86

partitions
    masonry, 161–62
    stiffening, 139
    stiffening due to, 119
    thickness of, 17
piers
    foundation, 189
    in masonry curtain walls, 155
piles, 29, 189, 191
platform framing, 121, 123, 125
plywood tee reinforcing, 137–38, 144–45
posts, attaching to masonry, 158
predeflection, 44–45, 52–54
probing, 26, 61–65
    damage potential in, 62–63
    material removal in, 61–62
    safety in, 61–62, 72
    selective demolition, 64–65
    structural material removal in, 63–64
    through finishes, 61
punching (two-way) shear, 114–15

reinforced concrete buildings, 96–116
    beam reinforcement, 103, 115–16
    beam splices, 111–13
    column reinforcement, 102–3, 109–11
    connections in, 100–102
    design history of, 28, 96–99
    detailing of, 43, 97–98
    drawing designations for, 58
    probing, 26
    slab reinforcement and modification, 103–5
        by adding depth, 105–7
        external, 107–9
        two-way modification, 113–15
renovation
    defined, 7–8
    reasons for, 47
renovation design
    influences on, 9–11
    new building design, compared, 7–8, 12
    training for, 8–9
    see also architectural design; engineering design
research, 55–74
    destructive testing, 65–67, 73–74
    documentation of, 56
    field investigation, 59–61
    hazardous conditions, 56
    information sources, 55–56
    limitations of, 25–26
    nondestructive testing, 67–68
    original documents, 57–59, 68–71
    probing, 26, 61–65
ribbands, 121
rising damp, 194
rivet holes, 77
roofs
    additions to, 147–49
    barn, 129, 141–44
    reinforcement of, 145–47
    types of, 125–29
rowhouses, renovations to
    masonry walls, 159, 162–67
    wood joists, 138–41
rubble foundations, 194

secondary stresses, 44
seismic designs
    concrete columns in, 111
    girders in, 50
    lateral load bracing for, 42–43, 49
shear, 37–39
shear tabs, 94
shoring, 85, 159, 163

sidewalk vaults, 175–76, 181–83
single angle clips, 83, 94–95
single plates, 94
sistering
    concrete beams, 103, 115–16
    flitch beams, 136–37
    principles of, 134
    wood joists, 134–36, 138–41
skylights, 145–47
slabs, concrete, *see* concrete floors
sleepers, 22
small large projects, 21–22
soil
    grout columns in, 192–93
    injection grouting of, 191–92, 197–99
    stability of, 189–0
    types of, 188–89
spread footings, 187–88, 189
steel
    allowable bending stress for, 40
    ASTM standards, 75–76, 77
    light-gage, 177–79
    properties of, 75
    testing of, 65, 68
stone lintels, 160, 161
stress
    allowable bending, 40
    internal, 80–81
    secondary, 44
    testing to specified, 65, 66–67
    transference of, 81–82, 85–86
strike plates, 94
structural design, *see* engineering design
structural loading, *see* loads
structural materials, *see* materials
structural steel buildings, 75–95
    analysis of frame, 48–49
    beam reinforcement, 79–82
        using composite action, 86–88
        using flange addition, 83–86
        of web, 88–90
    beam removal in, 30–35
    column reinforcement, 78–79, 90–93
    column transfer in, 52–54
    connection methods, 75–77
    connection reinforcement, 82–83, 94–95
    construction techniques, historical, 28–29

design history of, 27–28
drawing designations for, 58
floors of, 16
probing, 26
weathering of, 29

terra cotta tile, 19
    exterior decoration of, 167–70
    floors, 151, 161–62
    partitions of, 17, 151, 162
testing
    to failure, 65–66
    nondestructive, 67–68
    to specified stress or load level, 65, 66–67, 73–74
tray ceilings, 127
trusses, wood, 129, 130–32

underpinning, 191, 192
U.S. Department of Agriculture Forest Products Laboratory, 120

vertical shear, 37–38

walls
    bearing, 25, 152–53
    removal of, 119
    shear, 164–67
    see also curtain walls; masonry buildings
weathering, 29–30
welding
    to aluminum, 184–85
    to cast iron, 174
    to steel, 75–76, 83
    to wrought iron, 177
wind loads, 42–43, 48–49
wood
    properties of, 118–19
    shear of, 38–39
    testing of, 66, 68
wood-framed buildings, 117–49
    codes for, 120–21
    connectors in, 129–32
    design history of, 27
    framing types, 121–25
    light-gage steel compared, 177–78
    nature of, 118–20
    plywood tee reinforcing, 137–38, 144–45

wood-framed buildings, *continued*
    probing, 26
    roofs in, 125–29
        additions to, 147–49
        barn, 141–44
        openings in, 145–47
    sistering in, 134–37, 138–41
    visual examination of, 60–61
    wood products in, 132–33
wood I-beams, 133
wood panels, 133
wood products, 132–33, 135
wood trusses, 129, 130–32
wrought iron, 176–77, 183

WITHDRAWN